W9-BDK-780

Wildlife and Man in Texas

ENVIRONMENTAL CHANGE

AND CONSERVATION

By ROBIN W. DOUGHTY

Texas A&M University Press
COLLEGE STATION

Copyright © 1983 by Robin W. Doughty
All rights reserved

Library of Congress Cataloging in Publication Data

Doughty, Robin W.
    Wildlife and man in Texas.

    Bibliography: p.
    Includes index.
        1. Wildlife conservation—Texas—History.   2. Hunting
—Texas—History.   3. Fising—Texas—History.
4. Wildlife management—Texas—History.   5. Man—
Influence on Nature—Texas—History.   6. Texas—History.
I. Title.
QL84.22.T4D68   1983   333.95'416'09764   83-45103
ISBN 0-89096-154-9

Manufactured in the United States of America
FIRST EDITION

For Linda, Bridget, and Nicholas

Keith H. Redford
7 April 1986
Gainesville

Wildlife and Man in Texas

Contents

Illustrations

Preface

THERE is a widely accepted opinion that three factors contributed significantly to Anglo-American ingress along the Atlantic seaboard of the United States. First, newcomers arrived with iron tools that fashioned an indelible imprint on the landscape. Second, immigrants believed in individual landownership, and third, these pioneers came in search of a new, improved society that would transform the "howling wilderness" into the image of a garden. Native plants and animals provided the raw materials and foods for the early colonists. By initial reliance on an abundant and varied preexisting biota, Europeans established a secure foothold for the conquest of the continent. They worked hard to reclaim the "wastelands from savagery" and to make them into verisimilitudes of Western Europe.

Certain newcomers made surveys of fauna and took stock of the diverse and fecund wildlife species. A few others, charged by aristocrats and others with transporting back to Europe unusual, interesting, or bizarre animals, made studies of novel creatures. Most settlers, however, simply regarded the new assemblage of animals, birds, reptiles, and fishes as so much meat or so many hides and pelts. Accordingly, they exploited the most useful and most easily secured species, and they destroyed the dangerous and disagreeable ones.

This practice of unregulated hunting shifted westward with settlement. People regarded native wild animals, whether from the eastern hardwoods or later from the western plains, as a free, superabundant resource until they were unable to ignore or easily explain away the large-scale declines of key game species. The realization that settlement simplified, not "improved" and "civilized," nature grew after about 1850 when natural scientists, travellers, writers, and keen-eyed sportsmen recognized a need to change public attitudes toward wild animals and the corresponding ways of treating them. These persons began to push for measures to protect, manage, and eventually rehabilitate preferred mammals and birds.

The size, configuration, physical diversity, and large variety of plants and animals in Texas make it a microcosm of the nation. Herds of mustangs and bison grazed the interior plains, deer browsed brushlands and scrublands, and bears and turkeys frequented woodlands to the east. Elk and bighorn sheep inhabited the western mountains, and the Lone Star State's marsh-filled coastal lowlands were the winter homes for millions of geese, ducks, and other waterbirds. As the "biological crossroads of North America," where tropical and temperate flora and fauna mingle, Texas replicated the United States. Moreover, the human activities connected with the process of settlement and pioneer agriculture became concentrated in time and space in the Lone Star State.

In the half-century after about 1830, settlers and others decimated the larger, important food animals and cleared them from the more densely settled regions. Agriculturalists altered the habitats of many animals by the introduction of foreign plants and animals and by deforestation and reclamation. The journals of Southern planters and of immigrants from England and Germany recorded the process of landscape transformation. They also revealed the range of attitudes, opinions, and values that newcomers held in regard to native fauna. Some persons celebrated the biological exuberance of early Texas; others took the huge numbers of animals for granted and complained about pestiferous species, regarding them as inexhaustible.

Memoirs, diaries, and other literature, much of which was penned barely a century ago, show how people perceived and valued wild animals and how they exploited them. White settlers whittled down the wildlife resource as their ancestors had done on the eastern shores of New England and Virginia, although in a more intensive and accelerated fashion.

Books and journals describe vividly how these Texans hunted wild animals, which species they preferred, and in some cases how the conquest of the land was beggaring the variety and numbers of mammals, birds, and fishes. These works provide a benchmark against which one can measure the rate, degree, and extent of faunal change and habitat transformation. Comparisons suggest a pattern of biological simplification and the process of indelible physical landscape change that still continues in Texas. The Lone Star State exemplifies a large number of experiments with "new" food and ornamental plants and "safe" animals, such as merino sheep, angora goats, camels, honeybees, and carp. Some of these functional organisms had been tested elsewhere in North America; however, some of the animal immigrants were new to the United States.

The importation and release of exotic deer, antelope, and sheep native to Asia, Africa, or Europe occurred about fifty years ago in order to provide sport or attractive embellishments to large ranches. Few experts have cared to predict how the growing numbers of these alien animals will relate to transplants from other states or to native fauna.

In this focus on the Anglo-American colonization process in Texas, I am seeking to articulate and to exemplify how people perceived wild animals and altered animal populations after about 1820. The process of landscape alteration is a product of personal and group attitudes and responses to the North American environment. The settlement of this new land exemplifies a range of attitudes and activities toward animals—from seeing them as simply functional and useful to wishing to preserve endangered and rare organisms because of the aesthetic, interesting, or symbolic qualities they possess.

The introduction to the book demonstrates that knowledge about the geography of Texas was incomplete, and accurate information about its physiognomy, climate, and resources was colored by promotional tracts and by myth or superstition. In general, settlers recognized that Texas consisted of three broad physical regions with a varied, abundant fauna that could serve as a food supply. Some residents traded meat and skins; others killed the animals that could be secured easily or quickly and competed for prized species, bartering them for other foods or household goods.

Chapter one provides details of the techniques that settlers perfected to obtain wildlife for food. Contacts with novel or unfamiliar creatures heightened recreational experiences; chapter two discusses these animals and illustrates which ones were potentially dangerous or irritating in daily life. Chapter three gives evidence of the pleasures and solidarity that hunting and woodcraft generated.

By the end of Mexican rule it was becoming clear to interested persons that agriculturalists and planters had made sizable inroads into populations of game, especially in the most densely settled region of Texas. Incipient warnings about the possible extinction of several key mammals and birds appear in chapter four. Suggestions were made to conserve furbearers, deer, and other useful species, but they fell on deaf ears. Chapter five documents the desire to expand agriculture and the enthusiasm for the importation and diffusion of well-known domesticated plants and animals. The settlers wished to "improve" on nature by substituting preexisting biotic communities with alien food plants and livestock. Consequently, the public finally recognized and decided that it was useful to conserve viable populations of game mammals and birds (for recreational purposes), as chapter six discusses. Large-scale environmental change had diminished the habitats of many species, and Texans turned to lessons from other states where the exploitation of fauna had proceeded earlier but at a slower pace. Chapter seven examines the state's losses and gains in fauna. It reconstructs the history of game laws, which were designed primarily to protect game by slowing down its diminution through regulations on bag limits, closed seasons, and the weapons or methods for hunting.

Federal laws and regulations continue to be the basis for wildlife management in the Lone Star State, where accelerated urban and industrial growth, the spread of agribusiness, and other profound environmental changes present problems for native wildlife. As chapter eight suggests, these problems challenge those who are committed to retaining the interesting and unique fauna and flora that characterize Texas.

I am most grateful to the University of Texas Research Institute for supporting my visits to libraries and archives and for funding clerical and research assistance. Renee Jaussaud deserves special thanks for guiding me into U.S. Fish and Wildlife Service materials in the National Archives, Washington, D.C. I am most grateful to the staff members of the Barker Texas History Center; the Humanities Research Center, particularly May MacNamara; the Smithsonian Institution; and the Texas Parks and Wildlife Department, particularly William Brownlee, who offered expert help and efficient service. I wish to thank Campbell Pennington and Robert Calvert for their support.

L. Tuffly Ellis, Val Lehmann, Terry G. Jordan, Howard Dodgen, and Lawrence E. Gilbert made many helpful comments about the manuscript. Ian Manners, Bharat Bhatt, and Robert Holz also made valuable suggestions. Many students and other friends assisted me and were frequently unstinting in commitments of time and energy; among them are Jacque Cobb, Douglas Barnett, John Cotter, William deBuys, Peggy Frazier, Kirsten Kern, Scott Loy, Jane Manaster, Alexa Mayer, Mike and Judy Morrison, Larry Smith, and Vicki Voight. I owe my greatest thanks to my wife Linda and to Bridget and Nicholas.

Wildlife and Man in Texas

The pine and hardwood forests of East Texas were obstacles to movement and early settlement. Frederick Law Olmsted disliked them.

Introduction

NATIVE American and foreign-born settlers were prepared and even eager to face the uncertainties of the Texas wilderness in order to acquire land and make a fresh start. Some failed to cope with the daily grind. Others pushed into the frontier as sodbusters or stockmen—they cleared the land in order to till the clay and dark, humus-rich soils or they ran their livestock on the open ranges. They discovered a geographically vast, biologically diverse, and unpopulated land.

Early Texas was "a spot of earth almost unknown to the geography of the age," according to Sam Houston, who praised the region's qualities in his inaugural address to the first congress of the Republic of Texas in 1836. British geographer William Bollaert (1807–76), however, gained a good understanding of the character of this "spot of earth" from a stay of more than two years in the early 1840s, and he carried news about the new republic to members of the Royal Geographical Society and to English financiers.[1] Most early settlers were not as well informed. They knew little about the physical geography, natural resources, or regional diversity of Texas. Some read about the new land from emigrants' guides and similar promotional tracts. Others learned from those who had gone before them, and once on the way, they picked up information piecemeal from local sources.

Immigrants discovered that Texas had three basic physiographic divisions. One of them was the so-called Rolling Prairies, a region inland from the Gulf Coast that stretched from the banks of

[1] John J. Linn, *Reminiscences of Fifty Years in Texas*, p. 278; W. Eugene Hollon and Ruth L. Butler, eds., *William Bollaert's Texas*; and William Bollaert, "Notes on the Coast Region of the Texan Territory: Taken During a Visit in 1842," *Journal of the Royal Geographical Society* 13 (1843): 226–44. Bollaert describes the three natural divisions as "level," "undulating," and "mountainous" (226).

the Sabine River to along the Red River in the north and then westward to the Balcones Escarpment, about 98° west longitude. This region was more than gently rolling relief and open grasslands; it comprised a mosaic of soils, vegetation, and fauna where, in general, precipitation decreased from about fifty inches annually in the east to about thirty inches in the west. Tree cover was also most pronounced in East Texas, whereas the openings and prairies occurred more frequently as one travelled westward toward the Balcones Escarpment.[2]

Coniferous forests covered much of the sandstone and clay terraces in East Texas, whose southeast quadrant was filled with long-leaf pines; it was the western extension of a similar parklike woodland in Louisiana that opened up to a wet lowland along the coast. The dissected and heavily leached red clays and sandy soils supported long-leaf pines but proved to be relatively infertile; after settlers had cleared and cropped them, weedy crabgrass frequently invaded their fields.

North and west of the long-leaf pine country was a larger area under pine-oak forest; there short-leaf and loblolly pines as well as oaks and other hardwoods grew on sandier, elevated, and better-drained soils. Dense and impenetrable stands of these pines and broadleaf trees spread into riverine lowlands, which were filled with magnolias, water ash, swamp hickories, and other moisture-tolerant trees. This pine-oak-hickory woodland extended westward across the watersheds of several rivers into Central Texas. All in all, about seventeen million acres of this coniferous-hardwood association existed in this middle region, which included a large variety of trees and shrubs (see Map 1).

These wetter pine-oak lands were suitable for the gray squirrel and eastern race of the wild turkey, and both game animals were limited to timberlands in East Texas. Passenger pigeons were common winter visitors, too, and beavers were populous. Today, furbearers such as raccoons, mink, and gray foxes remain; however, the beaver has never recovered from intensive trapping, and the

[2] For general comments on the physical geography of Texas, see Elmer H. Johnson, "The Natural Regions of Texas," *University of Texas Bulletin* 3113 (1931); Benjamin Carroll Tharp, *The Vegetation of Texas*; and Texas Game, Fish and Oyster Commission, *Principal Game Birds and Mammals of Texas: Their Distribution and Management*, pp. 1–14.

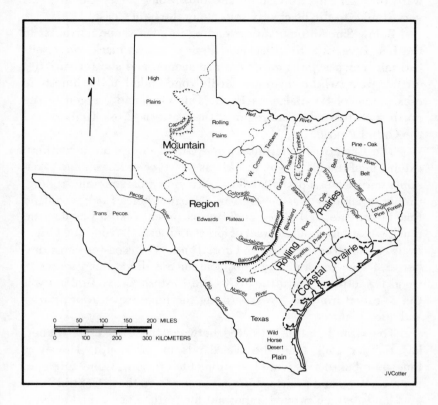

1.   Regions of Texas

passenger pigeon is extinct. The ivory-billed woodpecker, another
bird for which recent authenticated records are lacking, has probably followed the pigeon into oblivion. This largest of all American
woodpeckers—raven-sized and wary—inhabited dense hardwood
stands in the bottomlands of East Texas' Big Thicket.[3]

The western part of this interior, undulating region was more
appropriately named the Rolling Prairies, because a succession of
grasslands extended north from the coastal zone. The first one, the
Fayette Prairie, stretching from present-day Gonzales County east-

[3]Texas Game, Fish and Oyster Commission, *Principal Game Birds and Mammals*, pp. 15–17, 126–27; and Harry C. Oberholser, *The Bird Life of Texas*, ed.
Edgar B. Kincaid, Jr., 1: 527–30.

ward through Fayette County and into Montgomery County, was very similar to the black clay soils along the Gulf Coast.

Below San Antonio and extending in a fan shape northeast to the Red River was the Blackland Prairie, whose black, waxy soils had tall bunch grasses on its eastern section and shorter varieties further west, where this most fertile zone ended at the limestone escarpment of the Balcones Fault. This blackland merged in the north with two other subregions, the Eastern Cross Timbers and the Grand Prairie.

The Eastern Cross Timbers and Grand Prairie are a southern extension of the North Central Plains province of Kansas and Oklahoma and possessed similar flora. Much of this generally rolling, timbered country was covered in a narrow belt of oak woodland that linked the Red River and Brazos River. Like a parallel and much wider but rougher tract of forest and scrub beyond the Grand Prairie, known as the Western Cross Timbers, this easternmost timbered stretch was a physical obstacle for travellers, but a source of wood for settlers. Until the 1870s the Eastern Cross Timbers was the so-called frontier—westward lay the huge expanse of prairies and open plains.

The Grand Prairie, situated between these zones of timber, has thinner soils than the blacklands in the south. However, limestone-based soils were less subject to erosion. Bison, antelope, deer, turkeys, and prairie chickens occurred on these Central Texas grasslands, which proved important for cotton and corn. Few vestiges of the aboriginal flora and fauna are left; the bison, pronghorn, and prairie hen have gone, and removal of wood from the Cross Timbers and riparian environments has reduced the cover for many of the smaller game animals.[4]

A second major region was the Coastal Prairie, a vast arc of lowland characterized by marshes and black clay soils that become progressively sandier and drier southward. This flat grassland, reaching inland fifty to seventy miles in some places, was dominated by grama, dropseed, panic, and other grass species in its northern portions; buffalo grass, curly mesquite, and other plants that were adapted to decreasing rainfall grew from about the San

[4]Texas Game, Fish and Oyster Commission, *Principal Game Birds and Mammals*, pp. 5–7.

Antonio River south to the Rio Grande Valley. Below about 29° north latitude, a more clay-based grassland carried brush or chaparral, and sand-covered prairies next to the bays and lagoons supported scrub and stands of stunted live oaks. These plants helped to stabilize the wind-deposited sand dunes exemplified by Wild Horse Desert, south of Baffin Bay.

This southern, uninhabited, and dry coastal zone, where annual rainfall averages only half of that along the Louisiana border, merges with the much larger South Texas Plain, where mesquite and brush have gradually become widespread by displacing range grasses after livestock severely overgrazed the more palatable species. Experts agree that the suppression of fires, which used to keep down woody vegetation, has also permitted shrubs and bushes to advance northward in this coastal region.[5]

The Edwards Plateau is the southern and eastern terminus of the state's third major geographic region, the so-called mountain zone. This physiographic unit is an extension of the Great Plains of North America, which follow the eastern flanks of the Rocky Mountains. Between twenty and thirty inches of precipitation fall annually on this rough limestone upland, where thin soils supported mid- and short-grasses such as bluestems, grama, and Indian grass, with curly mesquite growing on drier surfaces. Live oak occupied ridges and slopes; juniper or "cedar" existed in rougher terrain such as the canyons, where it was safe from recurrent fires. Cottonwoods, bald cypress, and willows grew along the major streams, and mesquite flourished on sandy, deeper soils.[6]

North of the Edwards Plateau and east of the Caprock Escarpment, which bisects the Texas Panhandle, was the so-called Rolling Plains, where generally short grasses clothed most of the flat-topped hills and cedar brakes existed in rougher areas. Bunch grasses grew in the lower, moister areas; shinnery oak and sagebrush appeared on the looser sands in the north.

The High Plains lay west of the Caprock Escarpment, whose

[5] See Marshall C. Johnston, "Past and Present Grasslands of Southern Texas and Northeastern Mexico," *Ecology* 44 (1963): 456–66; and Jack M. Inglis, "A History of Vegetation on the Rio Grande Plain," *Texas Parks and Wildlife Department Bulletin* 45 (1964): 1–122.

[6] Johnson, "Natural Regions," pp. 129–33; Texas Game, Fish and Oyster Commission, *Game Birds and Mammals*, p. 8.

eastern face in some spots is one thousand feet high. These primarily level lands, or the Llano Estacado, as Spanish travellers named this short-grass, desolate, windy, and droughty area, rise in the northwestern section of Texas to about four thousand feet above sea level. These vast plains were the stronghold of bison, antelope, and mule deer. Turkeys were thick along the water courses, and in spring lesser prairie chickens strutted and boomed their courtship rituals among the short grama and curly mesquite. Both species of birds were to fall before the guns of settlers and sportsmen, who also whittled down populations of the indigenous big game mammals.

The Trans-Pecos is the most remote subregion of this third zone and consists of mountains up to eighty-five hundred feet, separated by basins and high tablelands. Short, sparse-growing grasses originally clothed the stony, shallow soils, where rainfall is highly variable. Higher lands hold oaks, pines, and juniper; desert plants and grasses exist on the harder basin floors, responding to the seasonality and variability of rainfall, which averages from nineteen inches in places on the western edge of the Edwards Plateau along the Pecos River to approximately eight inches around El Paso. Bighorn sheep, black bears, antelope, cougars, and mule deer were the important large mammals.[7]

A remarkably diverse and populous association of native animals in all of these geographic regions provided newcomers with their basic food and clothing. Settlers recalled how as youngsters they had pursued the large herds of mustangs and antelope in West Texas; how they had shot into huge skeins of ducks and geese along the coast; or how they had surprised large numbers of deer in the Central Texas prairie and post-oak belt. Their families and friends instructed them in woodcraft and shot at targets in order to develop marksmanship. These early pioneers drove away wolves, cougars, and other wily critters from around homesteads. They also hunted for sheer pleasure as well as with the idea of bartering whatever meat and skins they secured for other goods. They kept an eye out for Indians on these excursions, frequently providing details of how

[7]Johnson, "Natural Regions," pp. 94–95, 141–48; Texas Game, Fish and Oyster Commission, *Game Birds and Mammals*, pp. 10–13; and W. T. Carter and V. L. Cory, "Soils of the Trans-Pecos Texas and Some of Their Vegetative Relations," *Transactions of the Texas Academy of Science* 15 (1932): 19–32.

these aborigines hunted as well as what prey they captured, used as food, or exchanged.

The early literature is full of such tall tales; however, many of them ring true in respect to the sheer abundance of wild animals, their variety, and the methods of hunting them. Foreign-born travellers and immigrants were amazed by this pristine fecundity and spontaneously acknowledged their surprise and excitement. The legions of larger mammals and birds—deer, antelope, bison, turkey, waterfowl, and prairie chickens, plus herds of feral mustangs and fierce-looking longhorn cattle—drew lengthy comments from authors who were accustomed to the domesticated and heavily transformed countryside of England or to similar landscapes on the European continent, where fauna had been vanquished through centuries of settlement.

The settlers were completely free to exploit this biotic treasure trove in Texas according to their desires and abilities. The wild animal resource, however, had important symbolic value. Settlers saw bison, antelope, deer, and less valuable creatures as signs of nature's bounty—a God-given fertility to be channelled for the benefit of human beings through the establishment of plantations, family farms, and ranches. In one sense these creatures were made into acolytes for the New Order; they indicated the most appropriate localities for settlement and industry, and they offered the promise for a prosperous beginning. Cooperative enterprise set about eradicating and banishing to the wilderness all stock-killing predators, dangerous reptiles, pestiferous crows and hawks, and even crop-thieving blackbirds so that people could be assured that their handiwork was bringing the force of civilization to the New World and an inevitable improvement upon nature.

East Texas and the Rolling Prairies

The first waves of Anglo-American immigrants and travellers entered Texas from the east, and many of them converged on Nacogdoches, the most remote of the three Mexican departments. Passage up the Red River by steamer from New Orleans could be purchased to several places, typically Shreveport or Natchitoches, from which people pressed westward by horse or on foot to the

Sabine, crossed at Gaines Ferry, and traveled on to San Augustine (the old Los Ais mission). Another route into Texas crossed the Red River near Fulton, Arkansas, and was used by yeoman farmers and artisans from the border or upper South, especially from Arkansas and Tennessee. Natchitoches was an important rallying point for wagon trains from Alabama and Mississippi (that is, from the Deep or Lower South) that were starting out for Texas. People from the Upper South passed through those settlements, too, since before 1836 the Mexican authorities had officially disapproved of slavery, thereby inhibiting the influx of Southern planters. Another trail was the Opelousas or Atascosito Road from southwestern Louisiana, which crossed the Trinity River at Liberty (the Spanish military post of Atascosito nearby gave its name to the route) and led to San Felipe, the 1823 headquarters for the Austin Colony. Yeoman farmers and smaller numbers of cotton planters with slaves headed westward for Texas with hopes for a bright future (see Map 2).

Sometimes the rough tracks they followed turned out to be difficult and hazardous. Frequently, immigrants plodding over these trails found the going tedious; they grew dispirited and turned back, or changed their destination and broke off into lands adjacent to the routes to build cabins and plant staple crops.

Many persons of moderate means, such as perceptive William F. Gray (1787–1841), who became an influential figure in Texas politics, were able to take a steamship up the dirty, brick-colored waters of the Red River, backed by swamps. On his first visit in January, 1836, Colonel Gray experienced the loneliness and depression of many others who had despaired after familiar scenes like the bustling quayside of New Orleans lay behind them. Less than one hundred miles upstream, Gray noted that the *Levant* was churning through the waters of "the dreariest region I have ever seen, worse even than the Mississippi."[8] The town of Alexandria, below his disembarcation point at Natchitoches, presented a scene of decay and melancholy. For him and for thousands of others the eight- to ten-day journey to Texas' easternmost municipality, Nacogdoches, proved

    [8] William F. Gray, *From Virginia to Texas, 1835: Diary of Col. Wm. F. Gray*, p. 82; see also Terry G. Jordan, "The Imprint of the Upper and Lower South on Mid-Nineteenth-Century Texas," *Annals of the Association of American Geographers* 57 (1967): 667–90.

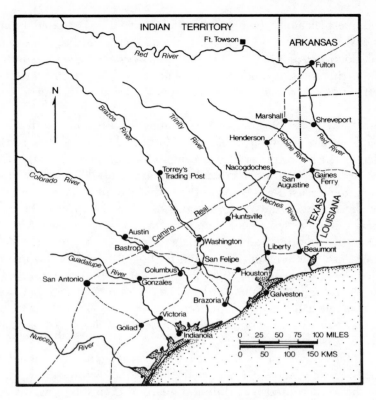

2.   Major early routes in Texas

a trial. Rather than continue, many chose to sell or barter away whatever land rights they owned.

Less fortunate immigrants, traveling on foot or in carts drawn by oxen or mules, encountered especially wet and cold conditions in winter. Frederick Law Olmsted (1822–1902), who toured the South extensively between 1852 and 1857, noted the tired, gaunt faces and plaintive, querulous remarks of emigrant families heading through the piney woods of East Texas in January of 1854. His picture was grim and poignant: under a canopy of gloomy conifers, bullying overseers, accompanied by tight-lipped matrons and "an old granny, hauling on, by the hand, a weak boy—too old to ride and too young to keep up," led slaves and strings of lean animals and livestock along the mirey tracks.[9] Olmsted had a biased opinion against the South, and East Texas was no exception, but the swamps and flood-prone creeks and rivers that intersected the trails indeed made the going frequently hazardous and slow. In fording them, settlers stood to lose household articles, livestock, or, worse, their lives.

Newcomers headed west to establish family farms with a little maize, some vegetables, and a few hogs and oxen, or they started plantations for cotton and sugarcane in the bottomlands of the Trinity, Brazos, and other rivers in lower East Central Texas. Olmsted's diary about East Texas conveys the pathos and physical duress faced by these new Texans entering an unknown wilderness. Many of them did not survive long. Englishwoman Ann Coleman (1810–97) is another who penned a detailed and moving story of early life in Texas; her brother John, a gunsmith, died after only a few months "in a small log cabin on Oyster Creek" near the lower reaches of the Brazos River.[10] Some settlers turned from the rough pathways to eke out a living from unpromising sandy soils or from better lands, which became degraded within a generation by overuse and lack of husbandry.

Many others pressed on, however, because they welcomed opportunities to pioneer, perhaps for the second or third time. These tough folk accepted hardship and guarded themselves against the chicanery of those who tried to take advantage of the settlers' unfamiliarity with the country. They travelled westward to those places that reportedly held the most promise for agriculture.

Twenty-five years before Frederick and John Olmsted recorded details of their four months' travel in Texas, the *empresario* land grants were established, bringing the sound of the axe, hoe, and plow team into the fastness of East and East Central Texas. Beginning with Stephen F. Austin's "Old Three Hundred" families, most of whom came from the Upper South, increasing numbers of land-hungry settlers made their way along the old Spanish Camino Real, which stretched from Nacogdoches to the south and west. After crossing the Trinity River, many people headed south into the

[9] Frederick Law Olmsted, *A Journey Through Texas, Or, A Saddle-Trip on the Southwestern Frontier*, p. 56.

[10] C. Richard King, ed., *Victorian Lady on the Texas Frontier: The Journal of Ann Raney Coleman*, p. x.

Brazos Department, a political unit of pre-Republican Texas located along the central reaches of the Brazos watershed. San Felipe, the capital of this department, had about twenty-five hundred inhabitants in 1835, and was thus larger than the western one, San Antonio de Bexar. Indeed, the latter department reportedly lost residents from 1800 to 1830. San Felipe, Stephen F. Austin's early capital, had only about one thousand fewer inhabitants than the long-established trading center of Nacogdoches, which was the capital of the easternmost Mexican department.

The Austin Colony was located in the interior, attractive, and most fertile region of Texas—that is, in the middle ground between the coastal lowland fringe and the isolated plateau, plains, and desert of the mountain country west of the Colorado River. Both the coastal and mountain areas were commonly perceived as relatively inhospitable and less suitable for settlement. This undulating country was a huge tract of alluvial sandy loams under native prairie grasses, oak mottes, and forestland that commenced in places about fifteen to twenty miles inland from the Gulf and extended approximately three hundred miles northward to the Red River and westward to the Balcones Escarpment. Austin's grant encompassed most of the lower Brazos and Colorado watersheds north to the Nacogdoches–San Antonio Road.

David Barnett Edward (1797–1870), an immigrant Scotsman who published a seminal book, *History of Texas*, in 1836, characterized this middle zone as triangular in shape, with the Sabine River forming a baseline and with the Colorado River (the middle of Austin's second colony) on the apex. As the traveller journeyed westward from Louisiana's pines and swamps, the countryside in Texas slowly opened up. Mirabeau B. Lamar (1798–1859), second elected president of the Texas republic, admired the redlands west of the Sabine as "doubtless productive, but . . . of a thirsty nature." About the same time, abolitionist Benjamin Lundy provided a thumbnail sketch of the same scenery when he passed through Texas in 1832, and again in 1834. "Handsome mill streams" with good land bordered the settlement of Nacogdoches. Hogbacks composed of gravel and red sands and clothed with oaks contrasted with well-watered bottoms filled with dark loams and covered by walnut, pecan, hackberry, cane, and other vegetation. From the Angelina River to the Neches River a few small-sized but increasingly numerous prairies

were evident. The vocabulary of the area included the term *openings*, that is, spots where trees were widely spaced enough to permit a grass understory. In general, the sandy soils and gravels around
Nacogdoches abounded with timber. Between the Neches and the
Trinity larger prairies began to dominate the scenery, and as one
progressed westward, the land appeared to be "of a somewhat better quality," so Lundy judged its soils well suited for corn, cotton,
peaches, horses, and "fat cattle." Game animals proved scarce, but
in the rivers fish and alligators were common. Approaching the Trinity
River, Lundy noted the first signs of mesquite and prickly pear
cactus.[11]

The country beyond the Trinity River drew universal praise.
Lundy was most impressed by the extensive grass-filled prairies
and scenery, which became "charmingly diversified by the alternation of prairies and timbered land, the soil of the latter being in
some places sandy, and generally less fertile than the prairies. The
timber consisted principally of post-oak." Other important writers,
such as David Edward and the English consul in Galveston, William Kennedy (1799–1871), who developed a fund of information
about Texas, admired the openness and fertility of this hospitable
middle ground. "The boundless expanse and profound repose of
these immense plains" west of the Trinity River, according to Edward, "excite emotions of sublimity akin to those which arise from
a contemplation of the ocean."[12]

It was a gently undulating land of river valleys and wide inter-
fluves perfect for settlement. The relief, climate, soils, and natural
resources of these rolling prairies provided the ideal setting for hard-
working immigrants to carve out a "garden" in the watersheds of
the Brazos, Colorado and Guadalupe rivers. Promoters and enthu-
siasts painted a rosy picture, and even Olmsted believed that this
region flowed in milk and honey. Its Eden-like character received
constant attention and attracted settlers. Reportedly, corn and cotton grew immediately; game animals abounded in the woods; shoals

[11] David B. Edward, *The History of Texas*, p. 37; Nancy B. Parker, ed., "Mirabeau B. Lamar's Texas Journal," *Southwestern Historical Quarterly* 84 (1980):218;
Benjamin Lundy, *The Life, Travels and Opinions of Benjamin Lundy, Including
His Journeys to Texas and Mexico*, pp. 118–20; and Terry G. Jordan, "Pioneer Evaluation of Vegetation in Frontier Texas," *Southwestern Historical Quarterly* 76 (1973):
233–54.

[12] Lundy, *Life, Travels and Opinions*, p. 120; Edward, *History of Texas*, p. 37.

of fish sported in the sparkling pure streams and rivers. Riparian woodlands consisting of cedar, oak, and aromatic shrubs contained "numberless clumps of grape vines . . . proving the adaptation of these regions to the production of raisins, wine, and the most delicate fruits of the vine." From the summits of the low hills a settler could contemplate "some of the fairest scenes in nature." From one such eminence between San Felipe and San Antonio, Benjamin Lundy exclaimed, "To the north-west, west and south-west, far as the eye could reach, there rose on the view a country magnificently chequered with alternate prairie and wood-land, like a region thickly settled with farms and plantations. Houses alone were wanting to perfect the resemblance."[13]

This alternation of woodland and open land created a *bocage* effect, which led the viewer to think that the area had been cleared already for settlement. It had not, but settlement was coming. In the mid-1830s the Austin Colony held about nine thousand inhabitants. Port towns such as Brazoria and Harrisburg were exporters of cotton, bringing the Department of Brazos, "Mexican in frame and American in substance," more revenue from cotton, skins, cattle, and other livestock than the two other departments combined.[14] A plantation economy built on cotton, and in places on sugarcane, expanded in both the Brazos and Nacogdoches redlands regions. A dearth of immigrants stymied expansion beyond traditional Hispanic-dominated areas into the more elevated lands to the north and west.

Promotional literature during the Mexican period spread news of *empresario* grants with free, abundant land and thus spurred interest in settlement. Austin's first colony benefitted from the terms of Emperor Augustin de Iturbide's Imperial Colonization Law, which provided for *empresarios* or colonization agents to settle precise numbers of families in approved areas. The law promised farmers a minimum of one labor (177 acres) of land; ranchers received one league (4,428 acres), and immigrants who farmed and raised stock obtained one labor and one league. Upon settlement, families could

[13][A. B. Lawrence], *Texas in 1840, or, The Emigrant's Guide to the New Republic*, p. 83; William Kennedy, *Texas: The Rise, Progress, and Prospects of the Republic of Texas*, p. 16; Lundy, *Life, Travels and Opinions*, p. 42.

[14]Linn, *Reminiscences*, pp. 97–103, citing Juan Almonte's 1834 report; and Donald W. Meinig, *Imperial Texas: An Interpretive Essay in Cultural Geography*, p. 35.

import most tools and goods duty free; they lived without paying taxes for six years and, under certain conditions, were able to become Mexican citizens after half that time. In return for establishing two hundred families, each *empresario* was granted three haciendas (fifteen leagues) and two labors, totaling more than 66,500 acres.

Iturbide's statute was replaced in 1824 by a national law (never really enforced) whereby authorities ordered that no lands were to be granted within ten leagues of the coast or within twenty leagues of an international frontier. The new federal government reserved the right to terminate immigration in the interests of national security and exercised that option from 1830 to 1834 by suspending contracts involving settlers from the United States. The state law of Coahuila and Texas implemented the national law and provided the heads of families with one league of land. It authorized contracts with *empresarios* for precise numbers of families to be settled in specified localities and gave agents six years to complete the terms of their agreements.

The Mexican government paid special attention to Central Texas in order to create a buffer between conservative Hispanic culture and the mixture of French- and English-speaking peoples in the eastern borderland. *Empresarios* wishing to create utopian communities from novel political or social premises, or those with an eye toward personal profit, recruited farmers and other settlers into their grants. Gradually adventurers, fugitives from justice, and people tired of life in the United States formed an increasingly pluralistic group who found sanctuary and new beginnings west of the Sabine River.

The three departments, Bexar (San Antonio), Brazos, and Nacogdoches, fell more or less into the middle or "civilized" zone crossed by the Camino Real, which represented the area of contact between the Hispanic world (San Antonio) and French and Anglo-American culture (Nacogdoches), with a heterogeneous group of traders, adventurers, squatters, and the like. This rolling and, in part, prairie region was the focus of early and sustained land grants represented by Austin's Colony. It also presented a foothold for the permanent establishment of foreigners, particularly Germans, and became the core for the social evolution of the Republic and the State of Texas.

The Coastal Region

South of the Rolling Prairies lay the grass-filled lowlands and marshes of the Gulf Coast, which consisted of shallow saline lagoons and a barrier island chain of sand dunes. People regarded this zone of initial contact from the sea as difficult for settlement, and for strategic reasons Mexican authorities discouraged, but did not prevent, colonization of it. Enroute to taking up land grants in the interior, immigrants and visitors passed into and through the coastal lowland from ports such as Galveston, Brazoria, and Indianola, which acquired reputations as unhealthy cities.

From the early 1830s and increasingly after the Texas Revolution, travellers and would-be residents had the first glimpse of their new homeland from the deck of a heaving vessel after a two- to five-day trip from New Orleans to Galveston or another anchorage. The landscape along the coast appeared just as desolate to these homesick (and frequently seasick) folk as that of the piney woods near the Sabine. The low, dune- and marsh-filled shoreline, which was relieved by occasional cane brakes and riparian woodlands further inland, was unattractive. Ascerbic British diplomat Francis Sheridan characterized his first stopping place, Galveston Island, as "a piece of prairie that had quarrelled with the main land and dissolved partnership."[15] This Texas port and others were hit by epidemics of yellow fever; they were plagued by mosquitos in summer when oppressive heat and "vapors" from decaying vegetation (relieved only by sea breezes) supposedly brought on sickness. In winter, bitterly cold air masses from the interior, carried by biting arctic-born winds, or "northers," tested the endurance of travellers caught out in the exposed Coastal Prairies.

On arrival, some immigrants who were used to well-settled and cultivated places grew despondent enough that they returned to New Orleans and ports further east. Ferdinand Roemer's seventeen-day journey from Houston to New Braunfels in January, 1846, for example, was characterized by exhausting stop-and-go movement on muddy tracks across drab prairies covered by standing water, yellow grasses, and clumps of stark trees.[16] In winter,

[15] Willis W. Pratt, ed., *Galveston Island: Or, A Few Months Off the Coast of Texas: The Journal of Francis C. Sheridan, 1839–1840*, p. 32.
[16] Ferdinand Roemer, *Texas: With Particular Reference to German Immigration and The Physical Appearance of the Country*, pp. 69–91.

the coast was an especially desolate place, and many settlers were discouraged by the physical inconvenience and hardships they endured there. Temperatures could drop as much as twenty degrees in less than an hour as northern air swept across exposed lowlands. Cold and moisture made travel uncomfortable and hazardous, especially to travellers unable to follow the rudimentary tracks or unfamiliar with navigation by compass. In summer it was hot, humid, and, further south, very dry. Indians were a recurrent threat—especially the dreaded Comanches and the Karankawas, a coastal hunting and collecting people with a reputation for cannibalism.

The dune-filled country along the seacoast remained largely unknown, in part because few suitable landing places were found between the mouth of the Sabine and the Rio Grande and because the adjacent lowland, broadening from thirty miles at the Sabine to almost one hundred miles up the Colorado and then narrowing again along the Nueces, was perceived as sterile and unhealthful compared with the fertility of the interior.

Edward and others, however, admired the central coastal area from Galveston Bay south. The prairie lowlands near the Colorado were "rich and truly magnificent," and other riparian areas south to the Nueces were attractive. A descriptive work called *Texas in 1837*, edited by Andrew Muir, suggested that the Coastal Plain from the Colorado to the Nueces was healthier than further north, a remark that helped ease a wealth of disparagement about this first zone by many writers in the 1830s and 1840s.[17] The problem was that these persons deemed the coastal zone unfit for settlement and pointed to outbreaks of cholera (1833 and 1834) and yellow fever (1839) as especially devastating. Decaying organic matter under hot and humid conditions was believed to be the primary source of disease, because plant and animal materials supposedly emitted poisonous vapors called miasmas. Miasmas were thought to cause various ailments, including malaria and dysentery, and a wide array of fevers and chills.

The miasmatic theory of disease was thus closely tied to place. Specific environmental features were considered causes of disease and rendered a place unhealthy, and the coastal zone had an excess

[17] Edward, *History of Texas*, pp. 35–36; Andrew F. Muir, ed., *Texas in 1837, an Anonymous, Contemporary Narrative*, p. 130.

of them. Poorly drained, it possessed extensive tracts of standing water where vegetation decayed. Hot and humid summer weather stimulated vaporous emanations from these swamplands and inhibited air circulation around brush, cane, or wooded places. The concentration of fetid vapors from these wetlands supposedly produced diseases in persons living in the vicinity.

In the 1820s the Austin Colony and Nacogdoches were judged healthful, but by the early 1830s conditions had deteriorated. San Felipe on the Brazos was considered an unhealthful place in 1828 because of stagnant water resulting from floods. Brazoria suffered greatly from cholera, and Mexican official Juan Almonte's report in the mid-1830s declared the coast to be disease-ridden, especially bad for summer chills and fevers.[18]

In 1840, Colonel Edward Stiff reported in his handbook for emigrants that residents along the entire Coastal Plain had contracted agues and that conditions were worsening. Between Goliad and the coast, he wrote, "Where once flowed the wholesome waters of the San Antonio river there are now deposits generating the seeds of disease and death, and where once was the abodes of peace, health, and plenty, squalid poverty, sickness and want now stalk abroad in the land." Further north, in the vicinity of Caney Creek, the gifts of nature were mixed. The fertile soil was infected with miasmatic disease in Stiff's opinion; mosquitos plagued the settlers, and he considered the water unwholesome. Stiff also described Galveston as unhealthy. The area of Texas subject to miasmatic diseases had apparently become more extensive in the decade.[19]

By 1850, however, it was expected that immigrants would learn to become acclimatized to the places where chills and fevers were judged commonplace, especially in ports and in riverbank communities. German immigrant and longtime resident Viktor F. Bracht (1819–86) warned immigrants not to eat or drink to excess, but advised settlers to leave the coastal zone soon after arrival because he judged the whole area unhealthily miasmatic. Cholera and other

[18]J. C. Clopper, "J. C. Clopper's Journal and Book of Memoranda for 1828," *Quarterly of the Texas State Historical Association* 13 (1909): 58, 62–63; Juan N. Almonte, "Statistical Report on Texas," ed. and trans. C. E. Castañeda, *Southwestern Historical Quarterly* 28 (1925): 177–222, especially 200.

[19]Edward Stiff, *The Texas Emigrant: Being a Narration of the Adventures of the Author in Texas*, pp. 29, 40, 149.

diseases contracted by newcomers to be settled by the Mainzer Verein, an association of German noblemen who believed they had purchased land in Texas, caused tragedy and alarm. Hundreds of these foreigners were stranded in squalid conditions on the beaches around Indianola in the winter of 1845–46, and they suffered greatly from contaminated water and insect bites. Bracht, not noted for his understatements, remarked that several hundred Germans had died "due to careless mode of living and to the harmful influence of the climate near the coast,"[20] thereby suggesting that the combined effects of personal indiscipline and environmental constraint took their toll. Although Bracht's characterization of the situation on the coast was biased, conditions were indeed bad, and it is remarkable that, after such an inauspicious start, this colonization effort was ultimately so successful.

The Mountain Region and West Texas

The third zone mentioned in early literature about settlement and travel was the mountain country—"not at present the abode of white men," but the home of wild Indians, feral horses that had multiplied on the ranges, "and almost every description of wild game." Some found in this arcadian retreat a purity and simplicity altered only by the plume of smoke from the new settler's cabin, which spelled the end for the "growl of the prowling wolf, and neighing of the wild horse." Others, wrote Muir, suffered desolation in the mountain country, seeing in its landscapes "the irremediable impress of sterility." They were disappointed to find little that was grand or beautiful in the wild hill and desert scenery west of the Balcones Escarpment. This broken land commenced about 150 to 200 miles from the coast; it was believed to possess valuable minerals, and in some places there were valleys filled with "high waving grass" and "clear crystal water bounding over deep cascades." Pioneer William B. Dewees (1802–78) also argued that this third upland zone was unsurpassed "by those of which poets have sung and novelists have dreamed," but it was hazardous. Comanches swooped down on travellers, made attacks on isolated cabins, ran

[20] Viktor Bracht, *Texas in 1848*, p. 167.

off horses, butchered cattle and settlers, or abducted women and children.[21]

Nevertheless, the woods and prairies of Central Texas east of the Balcones Escarpment, which from a distance had the "appearance of a cultivated park" for DeWees and other early writers, had a starker, forbidding quality once the traveller passed into the mountain zone. There, the hills and plains appeared bleak and inhospitable, but they were homes for enormous herds of wild cattle, bison, and mustangs. This third region was vast, with an emptiness that beckoned stockmen and with numerous fertile valleys that farmers judged to be well suited for irrigation. In travelling through this region some persons discovered a "grand and beautiful" landscape and were impressed by "the multifariousness of nature's witcheries in her most frolicsome mood." Yet most people moved in well-armed parties, and the voyager returned to safer districts in the hills and vales of the middle zone with a sense of relief at having escaped or survived Indian attacks or, more likely, the hazardous conditions caused by drought, tempest, and disorientation in this largely uncharted wilderness. These rolling prairies east of the isolated western region were like the land of the golden mean, where winters were "so mild as to render it unnecessary to take any further care of cattle and other stock than herding and branding the increase during the whole year."[22]

The three regions of Texas, commonly recognized and described by travel and emigrant literature from the 1830s, varied in extent and configuration. It was not always clear where one of them ended and another began. By describing and comparing these regions, authors intended to alert settlers to the choices open to them and to guide them, especially in the 1830s and 1840s, to the middle zone of the Rolling Prairies, which they judged to be best suited for family farms and where husbandry was similar to practices in the woodlands of the humid East and in the temperate areas of Europe. This middle ground was the principal focus for settlement, because one could "improve" on nature there with a minimum of effort. The prairie and oak-motte "parkland"—tending more to grass south of the San Antonio River and to forest east of the Trinity River—

[21] Stiff, *Texas Emigrant*, p. 11; Muir, ed., *Texas in 1837*, p. 121; William B. Dewees, *Letters from an Early Settler of Texas*, p. 130.

[22] Edward, *History of Texas*, p. 40; Dewees, *Letters*, p. 130.

became an outdoor laboratory for testing new crops and applying (and modifying) agricultural techniques from other southern and eastern states and from the Old World, especially the Mediterranean Basin.

As settlements expanded, the growing population of Anglo-American agriculturalists accelerated the process of landscape change. Farmers introduced and established alien plants and animals, and they killed any creature they judged as noxious or harmful to themselves or their livelihoods. Settlers also continued to hunt game mammals and birds, so many species declined or disappeared from the more heavily settled and physically transformed places. As new residents pushed back the wilderness, certain of them began to express both concern and remorse about an environment beggared of desirable biota. These people shifted public attention toward a need to preserve useful animals such as deer, antelope, turkeys, and quail. Approximately fifty years elapsed, however, before reforms aimed at protecting and managing these and other native species became effective. In the intervening decades most activity was directed toward fashioning new agricultural landscapes and improving them, and one image that sustained such zeal was the thought of creating and embellishing an "Italy" in North America's Southwest. Texas was to become this verisimilitude of Italy.

Living off the Land

ANGLO-AMERICAN settlers fed off a plentiful supply of native plants and animals on first arrival in Texas. In remote Red River country, such as along the North Sulphur River, hunting game proved easy because animals were abundant and frequently unused to the presence of human beings. The Indians, however, threatened white settlers. Old-timer Andrew Davis (1827–1906), pioneer and Methodist minister, recalled how his father carried him about half a mile from the cabin at night in order to conceal him from marauding Indians. As a small child, Davis was frightened by nights in the wilderness where "nature had never received a mark from human hand, or the slightest impress of civilization." With Indians around, the children were "like little scared partridges, they hover down as if trying to fill the least possible space," not crying out or speaking above a whisper.[1]

At five years old, however, young Davis could use a gun, and a friendly Indian, one of Chief John Dunn Hunter's braves, taught him woodcraft. Storm Cloud, his mentor, taught him two methods of approaching deer. First, a hunter should watch the movements of the deer's tail because it would shake its tail before raising its head to look about for danger. Then, the hunter must stand perfectly still with both arms placed rigidly by his sides. The deer, after a glance around, would resume feeding, having assumed that the human figure was a tree stump or rock, and the hunter could slowly move within range. The second method was to wave a cloth slowly from a place of concealment; curious animals would investigate and become easy targets. Armed with a light Choctaw rifle, young Da-

[1]R. L. Jones, "Folk Life in Early Texas: The Autobiography of Andrew Davis," *Southwestern Historical Quarterly* 43 (1940): 329; and Andrew Davis, "Hunting in the 1830's," *Texas Game and Fish* 9 (1951): 20–21.

vis would often pass entire days in the woods. He sought out bee
trees for honey and added venison and bear meat to the larder. At
a nearby fort on the Sulphur River soldiers were constantly thinning game; "often buffalo would come and mingle among the cattle
of the fort," and men rode close and shot them. Except for problems
from Indians, Davis's "boyhood life would have been completely
happy on the frontier."[2]

People expressed similar sentiments from other places. Almost
a generation after Davis's youth, Pleasant B. Butler came with his
parents to Texas from Mississippi in order to join his brother Woodward, who had settled on the San Antonio River. Near present-day
Nordheim, his father cleared fourteen acres of brush and planted
corn. The Butler family subsisted on abundant game, especially
turkeys, and Woodward "could go out in the evening when the sun
was a quarter of an hour high and bring in a deer by nightfall."[3]
Later, Pleasant Butler became a ranch hand and made his first journey up the Chisholm Trail to Abilene, Kansas. He found that bison
were so numerous that he had to ride ahead of the herd to prevent
them from cutting into the cattle.

Adults and children hunted a range of animals for sport and in
order to make ends meet, especially when maize, vegetables, hogs,
or cattle were in short supply or becoming established. Dilue Harris (1825–1914) went without bread for three weeks near Stafford's
Point in Fort Bend County in 1834 until her father killed a deer,
"dried it over a fire, and we ate it for bread."[4] However, she spoke
of living well on milk, butter, venison, and small game; both deer
and wild horses fed close to her home in the vicinity of Harrisburg
on Buffalo Bayou, so store-bought staples proved scarcer and more
costly than food provided from the wild.

Similarly, German immigrants in New Braunfels in the late 1840s
charged more for agricultural produce and meat from domestic stock
than for native fare. Venison cost between one cent and one and
one-half cents per pound in New Braunfels—half the price of beef.
In Fredericksburg, the new settlement, bear meat sold for two cents

[2] Jones, "Folk Life in Early Texas," pp. 332–33.
[3] Pleasant B. Butler, "Sixty-Eight Years in Texas," in *The Trail Drivers of Texas*,
ed. J. M. Hunter, 2nd ed., p. 480.
[4] Dilue Harris, "Reminiscences of Mrs. Dilue Harris, I," *Quarterly of the
Texas State Historical Association* 4 (1900): 99.

a pound and beef for four cents; this Hill Country settlement had a reputation as a paradise for bears and turkeys. Viktor Bracht boasted of shooting a gobbler weighing seventeen pounds and exaggeratedly claimed, "I could kill thousands with a good rifle."[5]

The price for wild turkey varied from thirty-five to fifty cents in New Braunfels and fetched as much as seventy-five cents in San Antonio. A tame turkey, however, cost up to one dollar in New Braunfels, and an additional twenty-five cents in the San Antonio market. No tame turkeys were available in Fredericksburg, and wild ones sold for no more than fifty cents apiece. From forty to one hundred birds were brought into town every week from the brush and river bottoms. No signs of diminution were evident from this hunting pressure; in fall months the region swarmed with tasty ducks, deer, bears, turkeys, and squirrels.

Olmsted noted that wheat could not be purchased in New Braunfels in 1854, and corn cost thirty-five cents a bushel. He remarked that the "Germans are not satisfied with corn" and were experimenting with plots of wheat from "Egypt, Algiers, Arabia, and St. Helena." Each house had a "garden-plot" set out for home-grown fruits and vegetables. The relative paucity of food plants contrasted with the wealth of game.[6]

In the East Texas bottomlands of the Nacogdoches area, plantation owners sometimes employed a trusty hand to furnish wild game meat for the house and slave quarters. Olmsted noted an armed scout, who was positioned to shoot at deer or turkeys, at the head of a wagon train of tired immigrants crossing East Texas from the Red River in the winter of 1854. As plantations were established, the practice of augmenting food supplies from wild animals continued. The anonymous author of *A Visit to Texas* spent much of his time in the area between Brazoria and Anahuac in 1831 and noted that at an estate about ten miles from Brazoria an Indian hunter had demonstrated the art of "walking down" deer. The "short, copper-colored, strait-haired man, in a tight buff deer skin dress, mounted on a fiery little horse, and armed with a rifle," was employed to supply the estate with game. He headed toward some deer that

[5] Viktor Bracht, *Texas in 1848*, pp. 43, 146–47, 159.

[6] Frederick Law Olmsted, *A Journey Through Texas, Or, A Saddle-Trip on the Southwestern Frontier*, pp. 170, 179, 182.

were browsing among livestock, then concealed himself by walking beside his horse until he came within range and shot one; this was the customary way of supplying a good portion of the meat.[7]

Many planters lived well by growing most of the produce they needed. Henry Austin's Bolivar Plantation on the Brazos, for example, had a fine table of fish, game, and homegrown plants in 1838. Those on less prosperous plantations and in family cabins sometimes subsisted on pork, corn pone, molasses, and milk—a fare which travellers complained about. Slaves on Jared E. Groce's cotton plantation on the Brazos reportedly subsisted on mustangs, which were large and easy to kill.[8]

In general, settlers depended on native animals, especially deer, for food, for furnishings in their homes, and for clothing. Chair covers, containers, bindings, and clothes were fashioned from buckskin. Kitchen utensils, cups, jugs, jars, knives, and forks were a rarity in frontier kitchens, so animal skins and objects carved from wood or bone filled their functions. A number of authors noted that dwelling construction varied with the availability of suitable building materials. Pine logs were used in southeastern counties; elsewhere oak, gum, and cedar were more common. Some people lived in crude shelters, and Olmsted reported that twelve to twenty men resided in rude huts or caves along the Guadalupe River and that they made a living by splitting shingles. He visited a farming family that was newly arrived from Germany and industriously engaged in erecting a "very convenient long, narrow log cabin, with two rooms, each having a sleeping loft over it, two halls, or rooms open at the ends, and a corn-crib."[9] They cooked outdoors with imported utensils; their furniture had come from Germany, too.

The German habit of carrying household goods into Texas was unusual. Native Texans loved to barter for goods or fashion items from local plant and animal materials. Buckskin dresses, shirts, pants, covers for sleeping on, mattresses or crude palliasses filled with straw, moss, leaves, or feathers from poultry and wild birds supple-

[7] Ibid., p. 56; *A Visit to Texas; Being the Journey of a Traveller Through Those Parts Most Interesting to American Settlers*, p. 45.

[8] Wayne Gard, *Rawhide Texas*, p. 65; Noah Smithwick, *The Evolution of a State: Recollections of Old Texas Days*, p. 19.

[9] William R. Hogan, *The Texas Republic: A Social and Economic History*, pp. 25–26; Olmsted, *A Journey through Texas*, p. 189.

mented cattle horns and hides. Leather and horn objects like buttons, goblets, spoons, containers, wall hangings, pegs (antlers also served), and gunracks were important functional items in daily life. Additionally, settlers blew cow horns to summon hogs or called ferrymen at river crossings with a short blast or two.[10]

Noah Smithwick (1808–99), Austin Colony pioneer, remarked that the unlikely assortment of farmers, woodsmen, and others who comprised the Revolutionary Army in October, 1835, wore "buckskin breeches [which] were the nearest approach to uniform." Some garments were a soft, new yellow; others were black and hard "from long familiarity with rain and grease." One of the finest examples of fashionable buckskin in frontier days was the suit worn by Indian scout Robert Hall, who sported a fringed and beaded suit of trousers, coat, and vest, topped by a coonskin cap. A powder horn, leather canteen, and bowie knife completed his attire so that he cut a dashing figure. His outfit, which reportedly belonged to Lafitte, was presented to Sam Houston, who then gave it to Hall.[11] "General Sam" was noted for an attachment to buckskin. In a state procession as late as 1841, Houston paraded in a buckskin shirt; earlier, Stephen F. Austin had donned buckskin, and Smithwick caught the eye of his future bride when he dressed in "a brand new buckskin suit, consisting of hunting shirt, pantaloons and moccasins, all elaborately fringed."

Apparel made up from other pelts was fashionable. Moses Evans, the "Wild Man of the Woods," wore a vest made from snakeskin to a wedding at Washington-on-the-Brazos, where he lived in the late 1830s. Unfortunately, the garment smelled foully; doubtless the "young cyclones" caused by ladies making liberal use of fans of turkey feathers (not ostrich) helped to make his presence bearable. Black bearskins also proved useful, and many pioneers like Ann Coleman, who lived for a time on a plantation near Brazoria, considered bear meat to be a delicacy. Coleman was not fond of corn bread, but she developed a taste for bear meat, which she judged to be very sweet. After moving onto the estate being opened "through the thickest kind of canebrake, infested with panthers, bears, wild

[10]J. Frank Dobie, *The Longhorns*, p. 217.

[11]David Nevin, *The Texans*, pp. 72–73; Gladys Alexander, "Social Life in Texas, 1821–1836," pp. 78–79.

cats and many other wild animals," she was able to partake of bear meat regularly, as her husband was "an expert bear killer."[12] Furniture in her neatly kept house was all handmade, including chairs with deerskin seats.

It seems, however, that the denizens of that humid coastal woodland took a dislike to Coleman. She was pursued by peccaries and horrified by the calls of panthers, and while carrying her infant she was startled by a live bruin (which seems to have been more interested in her hogs). Strangely, her clothes began to disappear. One day, on the way to draw water from the bayou, Coleman discovered that an alligator had just seized her baby daughter's red flannel coat, which she had spread over a bush to dry. "I put no more there in the future," she remarked laconically. These encounters, and the experience of seeing a horse "which went over his back" into an alligator hole on her two-week trek through the swamps to find a new home in Louisiana, were a hard test for this gritty Cumberland lass, who was more used to bracing sea breezes and the sight of seagulls, moorland sheep, and an occasional fox.[13]

In the same Brazos watershed, Virginian William F. Gray noted that the rude, unfinished, and neglected home of Edwin Waller contrasted with the family's hospitality and excellent supper. Gray, who established residency in Texas in 1837, thought it strange that "people who know how to live better and are able can content themselves to live in such wretched cabins." The frontier was a leveller; that is, it attracted folk who had the resourcefulness to make do with what was at hand, and many were content to do so. Until game became scarce, these settlers partook eagerly of a variety of wild animals and lived cheaply.[14]

Living off wild game was especially commonplace until crops became established or stock became populous enough to guarantee a livelihood. Therefore, the shift from wild animals was gradual, and in times of bad harvest settlers were forced again to depend heavily on wild foods to carry them through. Hunting bear, deer,

[12]Smithwick, *Evolution of a State*, p. 155; Jonnie Lockhart Wallis, *Sixty Years on the Brazos: The Life and Letters of Dr. John Washington Lockhart*, p. 69; C. Richard King, ed, *Victorian Lady on the Texas Frontier: The Journal of Ann Raney Coleman*, p. 109.

[13]King, *Victorian Lady*, pp. 111, 131.

[14]William F. Gray, *From Virginia to Texas, 1835: Diary of Col. Wm. F. Gray*, p. 227.

and other game was a means of recreation as well as an important and at times critical source of supplementing the larder.

Exploration and Travel

Game was staple meat to explorers, travellers, traders, military personnel on patrol or making forays against Indians, and others isolated from agricultural settlements. Often it was tedious fare; some regarded it as "almost a nuisance"; it was the accepted method of surviving in the wilderness, however. Smithwick put it succinctly: "Game, which was the principal source of food supply, was so abundant that we never thought of taking anything along but salt when we went out on duty."[15]

In the first twenty years of the nineteenth century the thinly settled Hispanic lands were the domain of Indian hunters; few Americans or foreigners had seen them, and when they did, the game they glimpsed was impressively varied and abundant. In 1805, on a journey through Texas from the Rio Grande to Goliad, Nacogdoches, and Natchitoches and back again, Bishop Marín de Porras wrote to the viceroy of New Spain: "Bear, wild boar, deer and buffalo are found in such abundance that it is incredible to one who has not seen them. Even more wonderful to see are the great herds and droves of wild horses and mares that are called mustangs here. As well built as the best of Europe and of an incredible agility, they are caught by our Spaniards here with a lasso. They are found close to the roads in herds of four to six thousand head."[16]

The bishop complained of sleeping for six weeks "in the open under a miserable arbour" in his service to the nation. His supply of meat spoiled, so "it was necessary to eat that of the deer and the bear, which are abundant here, and their lard is more tasty than the best oil." His woodcutters managed to blaze a road through the countryside and fashioned rafts for crossing rivers that were "filled with beavers." The Spanish-born bishop, who had jurisdiction over much of northern Mexico, including Texas, believed that Texas was

[15] James T. Johnson, "Hardships of a Cowboy's Life in the Early Days in Texas," in *The Trail Drivers of Texas*, ed. J. M. Hunter, p. 762; and Smithwick, *Evolution of a State*, p. 169.

[16] Nettie Lee Benson, "Bishop Marín de Porras and Texas," *Southwestern Historical Quarterly* 51 (1947): 27; this estimate is likely to have been high.

a fertile land and well suited for settlement. He condemned foreigners on the eastern borderlands, like the "many Englishmen . . .
[who] are frightened like wild animals at the sight of their fellow
creatures. Always immoral, they have illicit relations even with the
heathen Indians." But he acknowledged that hunters based in New
Orleans carried away "an unbelievable number" of waterfowl for
sale in that city. These men also traded beaver pelts and up to twenty
thousand deer hides annually, from "our possessions in that region."[17]

Travel literature, from the time Zebulon Montgomery Pike
(1779–1813) made his pathfinding journey through Texas and published an account of it in 1810, is filled with comments such as "shot
a deer," "killed two turkeys," or "hunted a bear." Pike provided these
sorts of details about game in South Texas. On his return from Mexico along the Old San Antonio Road in June, 1807, he saw numerous large herds of wild horses, which made "immense numbers of
cross-roads" in the landscape between the Nueces and Medina rivers. He was also impressed by the large numbers of deer; he killed
a peccary, which he said incorrectly was "in all parts between Red
River and the Spanish settlements."[18]

Anglo-American prospectors venturing into East Texas lived
comfortably off wildlife. Stephen F. Austin employed two of a
thirteen-man party as hunters on his first visit to Texas in the summer of 1821. Travelling westward from Nacogdoches, they killed
game for food virtually every day, usually in the evenings, over a
two-month period ending in late September. Austin's party knocked
down a minimum of sixteen deer; he noted that they were plentiful
or abundant west of the Brazos and along the lower reaches of the
Guadalupe River on his return eastward from Goliad. Toward the
confluence of the San Antonio and Guadalupe rivers draining into
San Antonio Bay, Austin estimated that he saw in one day 400 deer
and 150 mustangs. Alligators were also conspicuous in the "mirey"
bottomlands. Shortly before he crossed the lower Colorado, Austin
named a creek "Benado," derived from the Spanish word for deer,
after the numerous deer in the vicinity. His journal terminated with
a note that on the blacklands of the lower Brazos, where wild cattle

<hr/>

[17] Ibid., p. 29.
[18] Milo M. Quaife, ed., *The Southwestern Expedition of Zebulon Pike*, pp. 207–209.

and mustangs thrived, a Mr. Lovelace had killed "the fattest Buck I ever saw in my life."[19] Members of Austin's party killed three bison and saw others. They feasted off wild honey from a bee tree and found red grapes along the Colorado River. The biological resources and physical geography appeared most promising in the area taken up later by Austin's land grant.

Later, in the north, especially in the mountain zone, the same practices of living off wild foods flourished. In his book William Kennedy included a copy of the journal and notes made for a survey conducted by the New Arkansas and Texas Land Company. The survey from June through October of 1832 began from the intersection of 32° north latitude and 102° west longitude, and worked westward toward New Mexico. Hunters supplied the survey party with a minimum of fifty-five bison, twelve deer, five antelope, two bears, and several elk and turkeys during the four months of exploration. Members of the survey purchased 191 beaver skins from Comanches and encountered "immense" herds of bison and game "in abundance" on the Plains. After losing three men in a fight with Indians, the party became demoralized and abandoned several horses; finally, under mutinous circumstances it terminated work in Sante Fe, New Mexico, on October 30.[20]

This mountain region remained the last bastion for the large herds of Plains animals, and crossing the arid and featureless prairies was a notable accomplishment in the 1830s. A steady hand, a keen eye, and a dependable weapon were essential; they could easily make the difference between life and death in this strange, often difficult, open terrain.

One of the most remarkable instances in the art of living off animals for survival was accomplished by Aaron B. Lewis on a three-month journey along the Canadian River from Arkansas Territory to Taos, New Mexico, in the fall of 1831. Lewis and two companions were well equipped when they left Fort Towson on the Red River in early September in the company of friendly Cherokee Indians. When Lewis staggered into a cabin on the outskirts of Taos on December 10, however, he had lost his horse, blankets, clothes, and

---

[19][Stephen F. Austin], "Journal of Stephen F. Austin on his First Trip to Texas, 1821," *Quarterly of the Texas State Historical Association* 7 (1904): 306.

[20]William Kennedy, *Texas: The Rise, Progress, and Prospects of the Republic of Texas*, 2nd ed., pp. 175–91.

food. This starving, frost-bitten figure—reeling a few steps at a time in the snow, clad in crude moccasins and tattered remnants of clothing—was suspected of being a Comanche because his hair and body were so black from the smoke of pine fires. He was unable to leave his place of refuge, a hut on the edge of town, for six weeks, and only folk remedies saved his frost-bitten feet and hands.

On his outward journey along the Canadian River, Lewis had drunk antelope's blood to assuage his burning thirst; he had fed off deer, bear, turkey, and further west, black-tailed deer and bison. Fortunately, he was able to carry smoldering sticks from one campsite to another, thereby providing enough heat to avoid death from exposure. By December, on foot, he was dressed only in a "pair of thin linen pantaloons and a shirt, with a pair of deerskin moccasins." Charitably, he gave his moccasins to a companion and walked on new ones fashioned from the rawhide of a bison. He wore rough deer hides next to his skin under his shirt and slept on one of them at night.[21]

Lewis's story is recounted by New Englander Albert Pike (1809–91), who travelled to New Mexico by a more northerly, well-ridden route and returned with Lewis to Arkansas by a southerly trek through North Central Texas in the fall of 1832. Pike, Lewis, and others survived the eastern march by shooting animals. Pike described feeding off prairie dogs, terrapins, and mustangs in addition to more traditional game animals. He noted that, "hawks and prairie dogs do very well, but there is too little meat about a terrapin."[22]

In these kinds of hard circumstances travellers and explorers tasted almost anything. On an excursion to the coast from San Antonio in February, 1854, Frederick and John Olmsted "made a stew for breakfast of such small birds as came within range of the frying pan." Raccoons, opossums, squirrels, and later armadillos (as they spread eastward from the Rio Grande region), were all considered to be tasty fare. Bees were common throughout the woodlands, and their honey was highly esteemed. Locating bee trees was a common method of getting food, and honey was often stored in deerskins. Fish and oysters were usually to be had along the coast, and

[21] David J. Weber, ed., *Albert Pike: Prose Sketches and Poems*, pp. 5–28.
[22] Ibid., p. 53.

The rivers of East Texas, trending generally from northwest to southeast, cut across major routes and impeded progress after winter and spring rains.

Left: The rolling prairie region of Texas drew high praise from Lundy, Kennedy, Muir, and many others. *Right*: Flower-dotted openings in the Rolling Prairies were especially pleasing.

Bollaert was unimpressed by the numerous bays and estuaries along the Gulf Coast. Roemer regarded the coastal prairie as an "endless swamp" in winter.

Many immigrants feared malaria in this humid, dune-filled coastal lowland and soon moved inland.

The incised Edwards Plateau represented the vast reaches of the "mountain" zone west of the Colorado River.

The author of *Texas in 1837* judged the limestone upland of the Edwards Plateau to be sterile and dangerous; Dewees liked its pure springs and cascades and believed it to be Arcadia.

The upper Rio Grande Valley and the deserts and mountains in West Texas were little known. Gregg made them his home. Kendall and Falconer felt isolated and became lost in this arid region.

The truly high peaks above five thousand feet, exemplified by the Chisos Mountains, rise steeply from the desert west of the Pecos River. Vegetation is similar to that of the cool, moist Rocky Mountains zone. Bighorn sheep, elk, and black bear once roamed these uplands.

several shops in Galveston served fried, roasted, or stewed oysters in large quantities and in various sizes.[23]

Furs and Pelts

Skins from bison, deer, bear, cougar, and wolf were important for barter and sale in early Texas. Pelts were the medium of exchange in Green C. DeWitt's colony on the Lavaca River, where Smithwick landed in 1827. Money was so scarce there that animal skins were used as currency, which increased the pressures on game.[24]

Travellers and immigrants frequently purchased animal skins for covers, clothes, or ornaments. Benjamin Lundy, for example, purchased a cougar skin for seventy-five cents in Gonzales, established as the center for the DeWitt grant in 1833. More than a decade later, Ferdinand Roemer's immigrant party bound for New Braunfels, included a German military officer who paid fifty cents for a cougar skin near Columbus. This eight-man group was offered other animal pelts, including wolf skins of different colors that had been stripped from hog-killing canids trapped around Columbus.[25]

The American habit of bartering astounded Roemer, who was offered a horse and a "good cow and a calf" for his black frock coat (the young American coveting it was planning to be married) and also received a good offer for his saddle. Unlike Germans, "a Texan is ready at any moment, even while traveling, to trade or sell anything he wears," complained Roemer, who quickly became acquainted with the rough, direct ways of frontier life.[26]

Trading and bartering involved contacts with persons even less appealing to Roemer, namely native Indians, who passed through settlements or along routeways with buffalo robes, bearskins, and other animal products. Trade relationships with Indians were carried out gingerly and with profound suspicion on the part of many

---

[23] Olmsted, *A Journey through Texas*, p. 229; Hogan, *The Texas Republic*, p. 37.

[24] Smithwick, *Evolution of a State*, p. 18.

[25] Benjamin Lundy, *The Life, Travels and Opinions of Benjamin Lundy, Including His Journeys to Texas and Mexico*, p. 45; Ferdinand Roemer, *Texas: With Particular Reference to German Immigration and the Physical Appearance of the Country*, p. 82.

[26] Roemer, *Texas*, p. 89.

settlers. Other contacts with them were institutionalized by trading-post officials.

An idea of the dimensions of the early fur trade at organized centers comes from Tenoxtitlan, a Mexican fort established in 1830 west of the Brazos on the Bexar (San Antonio)–Nacogdoches Road. Francis Smith, a trader at the short-lived post, noted in March, 1832, that a French Indian trader who had arrived recently with eighty buffalo robes wanted $5.25 apiece for them. Smith expected to add the robes to a supply of beaver pelts he had purchased for $3.00 per pound. He was anticipating the arrival of American hunters with "about 200 beef hides" and wished to know from his contacts in Brazoria what they were worth.

Smith conducted a lively trade near the Brazos crossing. He had just prepared a cartload of "beef hides deer skins buffaloe hides and robes some leopard and beaver" for his oxen to pull to Brazoria. In return he requested a variety of goods, including wine, silk handkerchiefs, bowls, pitchers, plates, brass kettles, and beaver traps for purposes of exchange. Smith explained, "I think that 40 thousand dollars worth of Indian produce can be taken in here" in the coming year, as Indian hunters and trappers had been doing well. Eugene Barker, who discovered this correspondence, judged that Smith's figure was too high.[27] Census reports for the Department of Nacogdoches between 1828 and 1834, however, estimated values of exported furs and skins at more than $42,000, that is, approximately $7,000 per year.

Swiss botanist Jean Louis Berlandier (ante 1805–51) noted that most Texas Indians engaged in trade with the Mexican presidios, selling buffalo hides, bear grease, and dried and smoked meat. About 1830, perhaps as many as 40,000 deer hides, 1,500 bearskins, 1,200 otters, and half as many beaver were carried to Nacogdoches in less than one year. Berlandier noted that he often came upon Indian and white trappers while travelling in Texas in 1828. He reported that they caught beavers along the Brazos, Trinity, and Red rivers, but that beavers occurred most abundantly away from settlements in rivers such as the Rio Grande.[28]

Torrey Trading Post (No. 2), located on a tributary of Tehuacana

[27] Eugene C. Barker, "A Glimpse of the Texas Fur Trade in 1832," *Southwestern Historical Quarterly* 19 (1916):280–81.

[28] Jean L. Berlandier, *The Indians of Texas in 1830*, pp. 47, 108, 120.

Creek some eight miles below Waco and officially authorized as an Indian trading station under a Republic of Texas law of January, 1843, was only one of a line of five trading establishments that the Texas Legislature desired to be constructed between the Indian country and the frontier. Traders were forbidden to sell weapons to Indians in these places, which were designed to demarcate the zone of settled country of the east and south from Indian hunting areas to the north and west. However, Torrey's Post was located one hundred miles below where the law required, and officials accused the traders of selling arms to Indians.[29]

In July, 1846, Ferdinand Roemer (1818–91) visited Torrey's Trading House, setting out from New Braunfels with John Torrey, one of the three brothers who owned it. The post consisted of six or seven unhewn log cabins. The largest contained raw or tanned buffalo hides, frequently painted, and deerskins. Average bison hides sold in Houston for three dollars each, but well-dressed and painted ones fetched as much as ten dollars apiece. These were shipped north for wagon seats; "leather is not made out of the skins since it is too porous and not compact enough."[30]

Roemer observed that bison furnished the bulk of valuable pelts, with lesser quantities supplied by raccoons, cougars, beavers, antelopes, bobcats, and gray wolves. In addition to peltries, live mules, taken by marauding Comanches in northern Mexico, were important items of exchange. Wild or obstinate beasts were broken by Mexican hands, many of whom had lived with Indians, and were sold for an average of forty dollars.

For their skins and pack animals, the Indians received woolen blankets, coarse colored breechcloths, copper wire for ornaments, and an assortment of glass beads and tobacco. Roemer mentioned six residents at the unprotected post; two were Mexican mule breakers ransomed from the Indians; an old trapper, a gunsmith, a pelt finisher, and a government agent for liaison with the Indians comprised the remainder. Members of the post subsisted on dried buffalo meat and tongue, honey, and bread.

Earlier, John W. Lockhart had consumed food cooked by a ransomed Mexican woman who prepared meals in the traditional mode.

[29] C. C. Rister, "Harmful Practices of Indian Traders of the Southwest, 1865–1876," *New Mexico Historical Review* 5 (1931): 231–48.
[30] Roemer, *Texas*, p. 192.

He was impressed by the trinkets, colored calico, and "powder, lead and caps" available in the storehouse and by the bales of bison robes painted by squaws.[31]

Declining Torrey's invitation to accompany him to the Trinity River, Roemer preferred to go with the gunsmith to a Caddo Indian village about sixty miles up the Brazos. On the journey he fulfilled a "long cherished wish" to see wild bison and discovered the countryside covered with countless trails "reminding one of a European grazing ground."

Because of illness, Roemer was forced to lay up at the trading post for ten days on his return, but he dragged himself back to Austin with Torrey, encountering only three places of human habitation on the three-day journey. From there he journeyed back to New Braunfels, where he found buildings that "glittered in the sun" and compatriots he had never expected to see again. The expedition into remote Indian territory tested the nerves and endurance of this German geologist, who passed about eighteen months in Texas. The memory of great numbers of buffalo remained with him.[32]

Ferdinand Roemer provided interesting and useful information about hunting and the trade in animal skins in Texas' mountain region. Four months after his travel to the middle reaches of the Brazos, where Torrey's Post was a remote, isolated facility, Roemer visited Fredericksburg to look at the new settlement and to pursue his interest in paleontology by collecting fossils. He encountered Shawnee Indians who were selling game to newly arrived immigrants and who were camped on the outskirts of this German community on the eastern edge of the mountain region. His story corroborated Bracht's statement about Fredericksburg's rough country as the haunt of black bears. Indians were laden down with bear meat (which he found delicious) and had processed large amounts of bear fat into a clear liquid contained in deer skins. Each brave had about sixty pounds of fat for sale, proof that bears were abundant.

Travellers to and from Fredericksburg, San Saba, and other locations deeper in the unsettled region kept a careful watch for Indians and were suspicious of individuals who approached them. In his march from El Paso eastward across North Central Texas,

[31] Ibid., p. 199; Wallis, *Sixty Years on the Brazos*, pp. 111–13.
[32] Roemer, *Texas*, pp. 206–208, 291; Samuel W. Geiser, *Naturalists of the Frontier* pp. 178–81.

Albert Pike had several encounters with Indians in October and November of 1832. They impressed him with their precise knowledge of topography; they knew where sweet water and good pastures were located. They excelled in hunting. In a Comanche camp he paid with a little tobacco and a knife or two for a substantial repast of cow bison meat prepared in a kettle.[33]

Most warriors were absent from the encampments that Pike's party came upon along the tributaries of the upper Brazos. The northern Comanches were away hunting bison for the winter, so exchanges of tobacco for dried grapes, acorns, and firewood proceeded uneventfully. In December, however, another group of twelve traders heading from Taos to Fort Smith along the Canadian River to the north lost all their animals and had two men killed in a Comanche attack. A wounded man, Ohioan William R. Schenck, and a companion also perished. Pike knew Schenck and had travelled with him. As an obituary of his colleague, he penned a poem that conveyed the terrible isolation, despair, and pain of an untimely and violent death on the prairies:

> O God! it is a fearful thing,
> To be alone in this wide plain,
> To hear the raven's filthy wing,
> And watch the quivering star of our existence wane.
>
> Yes; I am left alone to die—
> Alone! alone!—it is no dream;
> . . . .
> And I must die—and wolves will gnaw
> My corpse, or ere the pulse be still,
> Before my parting gasp I draw. . . .[34]

Suspicion and fear of red men was reciprocated. A recurring opinion in many diaries and in the literature dealing with Indian life in the South Plains holds that Indians resented the arrival of white hunters and traders. A study of the distribution of the buffalo in the Southwest concludes that authorities "were agreed that the plentiful supply of the buffaloes was a necessary concomitant of the

---

[33] Weber, ed., *Albert Pike*, p. 51.

[34] Ibid., pp. 142–43; Josiah Gregg, *The Commerce of the Prairies*, pp. 214–18, relates the same incident, stating that, tormented by hunger and thirst, the ten men divided into two parties. Schenck, spelled also Schenk, was wounded in the thigh and, with two others, was never seen again.

wild life of the savage."[35] Therefore, white men proceeded to extirpate bison.

When the nomadic Indians realized that their principal resource was being destroyed, they protested, and "with no favorable response, the distracted Indians resorted to war." The clearing of the Great Plains was thus perceived as a necessity for white settlement. General Phil Sheridan argued before the Texas Legislature, which threatened to outlaw hide hunters, that "these men have done more in the last two years to settle the vexed Indian question than the entire regular Army has done in the last thirty years. They are destroying the Indians' commissary."[36]

Distrust and avoidance of Anglos came from being victimized by the sharp practices of white traders, whom some called "the jetsam of the turbulent sea of border life." Colonel Richard Irving Dodge (1827–95), a seasoned officer in the Southwest, noted how a Lipan brave at Fort Martin Scott, Texas, bartered five finely dressed wildcat skins for a box of matches. He lit the matches one after another until all were gone.[37]

Dodge loved and respected the Plains environment, where "the magnificence of being" impressed the person who was able to overcome the challenge of its emptiness, isolation, and uncompromising heat, cold, aridity, and tempests. He predicted the exhaustion of all the larger Plains mammals because of unregulated killing, and he blamed professional hunters ("too lazy or shiftless to make a living in civilization") for decimating animal populations. "Like a huge cuttlefish," civilization was passing tentacles of settlement along watercourses. Its sinuous arms throttled the game, drove out Indians, squeezed "the romance, the poetry, the very life and soul out of the 'plains,' and [left] only the bare and monotonous carcass."[38] Aboriginal culture in this third region was doomed by the ingress of an alien, technologically superior culture anchored in the second region—that is, in the less demanding, malleable, bountiful "middle landscape." Anglo-Saxon culture sought to extend and re-create this

[35] C. C. Rister, "The Significance of the Destruction of the Buffalo in the Southwest," *Southwestern Historical Quarterly* 33 (1929): 40.

[36] Ibid., p. 42; Sheridan cited in Mari Sandoz, review of *The Buffalo Hunters*, by Wayne Gard, in *Southwestern Historical Quarterly* 58 (1955): 454.

[37] Rister, "Harmful Practices," p. 232.

[38] Richard I. Dodge, *Hunting Grounds of the Great West*, 2nd ed., pp. 99, 116.

image of a domesticated and subdued environment through aggressive colonization.

Tennessee-born trader Josiah Gregg (1806–50) saw the changes in the land and native culture, too. In May, 1831, he had joined a caravan from Independence, Missouri, bound for Santa Fe; for the next nine years he crisscrossed the deserts and plains of New Mexico, Chihuahua, and West Texas, which combined "so many of the elements of the awful and sublime." One had to learn, according to Gregg, how to brave thunderstorms, mirages ("ravens . . . are not infrequently taken for Indians, as well as for buffalo"), stampedes, hostile and violent red men, and loneliness in uninhabited regions.

Gregg found freedom and excitement in the western Plains. He had a healthy distrust of Indians, however, particularly of Comanches, but he recognized too that traders treated them shamefully. He recounted the incident of a Pawnee chief shot down callously by a Pueblo Indian who was in a caravan of traders. The Pawnees blamed the traders for this tragic incident, and it served to reinforce their dislike of these Santa Fe–based entrepreneurs. In concluding his narrative about a prairie life that enriched and fulfilled him, Gregg expressed his hope to "spread my bed with the mustang and the buffalo, under the broad canopy of heaven—there to seek to maintain undisturbed my confidence in men by fraternizing with the little prairie dogs and wild colts and the still wilder Indians—the *unconquered* Sabaeans of the Great American Deserts."[39] Gregg died of exposure and starvation in 1850 at the age of forty-four, not on the High Plains but in the moist wooded coastal range of northern California while he was endeavoring to reach San Francisco from the area of Humboldt Bay.

Concerns about conflicts with Indians did not ease in the mountain zone, or, more accurately, in West Texas, until after the Civil War. J. T. Hazelwood, an old-time rancher, recalled how his father had moved in 1852 from Mississippi to Northeast Texas, where they found the country full of "vast herds of buffalo and numerous tribes of still wilder Indians." Moving into Palo Pinto County in North Central Texas to set out a ranch in the mid-1850s, Hazelwood was confronted by Indian raids that soldiers stationed at various points in Texas were unable to quell. Young Hazelwood remem-

---

[39] Gregg, *Commerce of the Prairies*, pp. 72, 89, 161, 327–28.

bered when nocturnal thefts of stock were common, and settlers "were compelled to fight for their lives, for the preservation of their herds and for the protection of their families." Soon every colonist ceased to keep mules, because Indians stole them with impunity, and instead used oxen for draft purposes. In 1860, conditions were no better in Stephens County along Sandy Creek, where the Hazelwood family lived in "picket houses, covered with sod and dirt, and the flooring with buffalo hides." They had an abiding fear of Indians.[40]

The situation in the buffer zone of the frontier in the south, near Pleasanton, below San Antonio, was similar. Henry Fest, of French extraction, recalled how his father went away to fight in the Civil War, leaving a wife and eight children to pioneer a ranch two miles east of Pleasanton. Game was easy to get. In addition to obtaining meat, the family dressed hides, tanning them with live oak and mesquite bark extract. Homespun woolen cloth dyed with indigo, coonskin hats, and shoes came from local animals; "coffee" was made from corn, acorns, and sweet potatoes, and honey was substituted for sugar. Fest's simple, rustic, but healthy upbringing was shaken by his recollection of "real savages," lots of them, "who did not stop at stealing or murdering when it suited their purposes to do so."[41] A kind of "home guard" consisted of men too old for military duty, who had the task of warning residents about Indian activities and leading them to places of safety.

Away from the frontier, in the middle region, trading contacts with Indians were frequent and at times brisk; many folk regarded them as risky. Rosa Kleberg noted suspiciously that the Indians "were constantly wishing to exchange skins for pots and other utensils" in the growing settlement of Harrisburg in the early 1830s. This German-born immigrant made up clothes to exchange for moccasins, and her kinfolk around Cat Spring bartered ammunition and household objects for game.[42]

[40] J. T. Hazelwood, "Early Days in Texas," in *The Trail Drivers of Texas*, ed. J. M. Hunter, pp. 555–57.

[41] Henry Fest, "Parents Were Among Early Colonists," in *The Trail Drivers of Texas*, ed. Hunter, p. 421.

[42] Rosa Kleberg, "Some of My Early Experiences in Texas," *Quarterly of the Texas State Historical Association* 1 (1898): 298.

Some traders liked the Indians for the wild animal pelts they offered. John Linn, who owned a store in Victoria in the late 1830s, welcomed a party of Lipans because he admired the quality of their dressed deerskins. In East Texas, Colonel Love from Georgia, a noted trader among the Indians, reported that they carried valuable animal products to merchants in Nacogdoches. Townsfolk, however, were afraid of these "fantastically dressed" braves and others, especially after the Indians' drinking binges.[43]

The problem was that the thefts of stock, ransacked cabins, and unexplained murders were almost inevitably blamed on Indians; therefore, pioneer Noah Smithwick's admiration and respect for the aboriginal natives was unusual. Smithwick associated freely with Comanches about Coleman's Fort and studied their hunting techniques. In that region Indians lived off game; they fashioned vessels from horns, terrapin shells, and deerskins, that is, skins stripped off whole. A preferred food was curdled milk extracted from the stomach of a bison calf or deer fawn whose parents could be stalked by stop-and-go movements fitted to the animal's feeding patterns. Smithwick noted that Indians could catch a turkey out on the open prairie (it was not fooled by stop-and-go movements as were deer) by pursuing it until it was exhausted. This tough outdoorsman was thoroughly impressed by their unparalleled woodcraft.

Indians would taunt old bison bulls by shooting arrows into their shoulder humps and then pulling the barbed points out of the maddened beasts; however, Smithwick concluded that these superb horsemen lived off game without exhausting or wantonly destroying it. He quoted a chief as saying, "When game beats away from us we pull down our lodges and move away leaving no trace to frighten it, and in a little while it comes back." Smithwick placed most of the blame for the decline of bison on the whites, who sparked off hostility between Indian groups when hungry braves had cause to trespass on the hunting grounds of others. He disapproved, too, of the common caricatures of Indians, including the notion that the award of a brave's scalp was determined "according to all the rules of the chase, the man who brought down the game was entitled to

[43] John J. Linn, *Reminiscences of Fifty Years in Texas*, p. 292; William Physick Zuber, *My Eighty Years in Texas*, ed. Janis Boyle Mayfield, p. 35; and Gray, *From Virginia to Texas*, p. 94.

the pelt." Nonetheless, he admitted that when Indians had raided settlements, he had tracked them down.[44]

Sam Houston, like Smithwick, was interested in a future for Texas' Indians. This first president of the Republic of Texas passed most of three years in his late teens with Cherokees, and he grew to admire and respect Indian ways. He became a Cherokee citizen and an Indian agent, and he took an Indian wife (his second marriage) before settling in Texas. However, Smithwick admitted that in talks with General Sam, it seemed that the latter was reconciled to the ultimate demise or expulsion of the Indians, despite the fact that in his second term Houston endeavored to foster better relations with various groups and supported the Torrey Trading Post.

Very few Americans or foreigners, settlers or travellers, had good words for Indians. Most believed they were to be shot down and hunted as vermin, so killing them was a matter for congratulation and approval, not reprobation. Benjamin Lundy's remark at the Aransas Landing in February, 1834, about Karankawa Indians selling a fine deer to a merchant for whiskey, some poor tobacco, and hard biscuit reveals how whites exploited them.[45]

The typical response to an Indian incursion was to track down the offenders. Captain Nicholas Flores's rout of Apaches, who reportedly stole thirty horses in a raid on Bexar in 1723, occurred after he had tracked them for over a month into the Edwards Plateau with a force of thirty soldiers and thirty mission Indians. During his fifty-five-day foray, his men subsisted on bison and deer. More than a century later, an observer setting out for Santa Fe spoke with a party of Texans who had been out four months tracking Comanches. Their hunting shirts were torn and full of grease, they wore their hair long and matted, and, like Aaron Lewis, their faces were as brown as mahogany, so that they appeared to be Indians. Doubtless body and soul had been kept together by living off game.[46]

Settlers or travellers on the frontier lived by their wits. When they heard that an Indian party was nearby, naturally they were on the lookout for places of ambuscade. More commonly, they were

[44] Smithwick, *Evolution of a State*, pp. 122, 188.

[45] Lundy, *Life, Travels and Opinions*, p. 104.

[46] William E. Dunn, "Apache Relations in Texas, 1718–1750," *Southwestern Historical Quarterly* 14 (1911): 207; George Wilkins Kendall, *Across the Great Southwestern Prairies*, 1: 41.

resourceful—opportunists in respect to a quick and easy kill for the meat or hides which could be sold or bartered. Many enjoyed this simple hand-to-mouth living because they knew of no other way and because this existence was not a niggardly one in Texas. As a result of the natural bounty of woodlands and prairies, those who had been reared in the wilderness or who had developed skills in hunting were able to survive and prosper.

CHAPTER 2

Beautiful, Strange, and Menacing Animals

ALTHOUGH they hunted animals for food, clothing, and commerce, settlers and travellers did not fail to appreciate and praise the physical beauty and graceful movements of many species. Some persons grew interested in the habits, distribution, and life histories of wildlife, and they promoted interest in Texas and the Southwest through references to unique or unusual animals.

Large mammals such as bison, mustangs, antelope, and deer satisfied basic material needs; however, many commentators were also fascinated by them. Moreover, these large, prominent creatures became important and necessary elements in landscape images. By its imposing size and sheer numbers, the American bison was the life of the Plains, although it ranged southeastward along the Gulf into western Florida and into Georgia and the Carolinas. The shaggy beast represented the biological wealth of the frontier, and it was to be transformed into monetary gain through opportunities for hunting and barter. The bison was also an obstacle to ranching interests. It competed with livestock for forage and was the fundamental resource for Indians. As such, it was persecuted. It represented, too, the ultimate outdoor experience for foreigners and others who were unfamiliar with, but eager to experience, adventures on the western Plains. Killing bison was exciting sport, and a skin or head was a superb trophy. A buffalo robe was a conversation piece for old men's tales of prowess and danger.

The popular book *Texas in 1840; or, The Emigrant's Guide*, written by A. B. Lawrence but published anonymously, summarized the status and place of these shaggy animals in the popular mind. These "wild oxen" (or "red man's cows," as Edward called them) inhabited the unknown hills and plains of North and West Texas. Vast herds migrated into the Rolling Prairies every winter, following the drainage of the Colorado, Brazos, and other rivers from the interior, to feed on native grasses. The "Arab of the prairies," the Comanche, followed the bison: "Without them, these wandering tribes, with no homes, grain, cattle or property, would scarce be able to procure food or clothing." Popular opinion made the buffalo, as Texans called it, and the Indian inseparable. Dilue Harris recalled that early in the spring of 1836, three or four thousand bison crossed the Brazos and passed in sight of her family's home. The beasts kicked up clouds of dust that made their passing like a sandstorm—"the prairie looked afterwards as if it had been plowed." Harris explained how frightened she had been because it was assumed that Indians were following this herd, the last large one reported in that region adjacent to the upper coast.[1]

In the voluminous literature about the decline of bison, two questions invariably crop up. How many existed, and what was the pattern of their movements? Harris had been excited by the migration of a relatively small herd. Drawing from Bonneville's adventures with bison, William Kennedy reported that numbers were so great in the tightly packed herds that at river crossings the animals would form a living dam, and water backed up by their bodies would pour over their quarters: "The roaring and rushing sounds of one of these vast herds crossing a river may sometimes, on a still night, be heard for many miles," wrote the Englishman.[2]

In 1874, almost two generations later, Billy Dixon (1850–1913), scout and plainsman, provided an enthralling account of buffalo on the move in Texas. This tough, hardened hunter was awed by the elemental power and numbers of the great beasts, whose population was about to be dealt the coup de grace on the southern Plains. Spring migration was late as Dixon and his two skinners camped out near the Canadian River and awaited the return of these large game. One morning at breakfast, Dixon heard that "familiar sound come rolling toward me from the Plains—a sound deep and mov-

[1] [A. B. Lawrence], *Texas in 1840, or, The Emigrant's Guide to the New Republic*, pp. 181–82; Dilue Harris, "Reminiscences of Mrs. Dilue Harris II," *Quarterly of the Texas State Historical Association* 4 (1901): 161.

[2] William Kennedy, *Texas: The Rise, Progress, and Prospects of the Republic of Texas*, pp. 119–20.

ing, not unlike the rumbling of a distant train passing over a bridge. In an instant I knew what was at hand. I had often heard it. I had been listening for it for days, even weeks." The rolling, thunderous noise came from the bulls, who were bellowing a "continuous, a deep, steady roar that seemed to reach the clouds." Their bellows carried more than ten miles over the Plains, where, after a strong gallop, Dixon caught his first glimpse of the migrating herds that year. He saw on the horizon that "as far as the eye could reach, south, east and west of me there was a solid mass of buffalo—thousands upon thousands of them—slowly moving toward the north."[3]

One summer thirty-three years earlier, English barrister Thomas Falconer (1805–82) had set out from just north of Austin for Santa Fe, New Mexico, as a guest in an expedition of more than three hundred men equipped with twenty or more wagons, a military escort with field artillery, and seventy head of cattle as provisions. This ill-fated expedition, proposed by Mirabeau B. Lamar as an incipient means of diverting trade from New Mexico and expanding Texas' jurisdiction over Hispanic settlements there, lost at least twelve members in Indian attacks; others died through disability and disease. The exhausted and disoriented group surrendered to Mexican troops, who eventually conducted the prisoners to Mexico City. Less than a month into the journey, Falconer came upon vast herds of bison "like a black cloud" covering the prairie.[4]

George Wilkins Kendall (1809–67), who participated in the Santa Fe Expedition with Falconer, also reported bison to be numerous and widely distributed. Kendall's narrative of the journey documents the excitement caused by the first appearance of this favorite prey. Within a week, the expedition met up with small groups of bison, or, as Kendall remarked, "the scouting parties, it would seem, of the immense herds we were soon to encounter."[5] He enjoyed the fine-textured, sweet flesh of the first fat cow that the hunters killed but scoffed at an old-timer's story of two or three million head in

[3] Olive K. Dixon, "The Life of Billy Dixon," in J. Frank Dobie, *The Flavor of Texas*, pp. 132–33.

[4] Thomas Falconer, "Notes of a Journey through Texas and New Mexico in the Years 1841 and 1842," *Journal of the Royal Geographical Society* 13 (1843): 199–226; and [Lawrence], *Texas in 1840*, p. 182.

[5] George Wilkins Kendall, *Across the Great Southwestern Prairies* 1: 80.

sight at one time. Then Kendall's incredulity was shaken as he gazed on the enormous herds in ensuing days and weeks. After sober reflection, this journalist concluded that these impressive numbers were indeed declining: "It would seem almost impossible, especially to one who has seen them, numerous as the sand of the seashore, on their immense natural pastures, that the race can ever become extinct; but when he reflects upon the rapid strides civilization is making westward upon the domain of the buffalo, he is brought to feel that the noble race will soon be known only as a thing of the past."[6]

On June 24, 1841, the cry "Buffalo!" went out as the beasts, "spread out over the immense space, and in countless numbers" came into view. Horsemen led by a madcap Irishman named Fitzgerald dashed impetuously into the midst of the massed animals, and the lumbering buffalo scattered, "the larger ones more resembling loads of hay in motion than anything else I can liken them to," chuckled Kendall, who was unable to join in the hurly-burly because of an injury from a fall.

Thomas Falconer, however, participated in the slaughter of twenty-eight bison and the capture of ten or twelve calves that day. Kendall noted that the Englishman, whom he twitted for being dressed badly, in a manner resembling "a New England washing-day dinner," and who had set out on the trek in search of "strange weeds, stones and the picturesque," managed to generate a sedate trot from his lazy mount "after buffalo, with a glass raised to his right eye." But Falconer's double-barrelled gun appears to have inflicted little damage; "he did not essay the killing of any of the huge monsters," opined Kendall, who believed the well-educated Englishman's weapon was loaded only with bird shot.[7]

This vivid and lively story of a bison hunt was one of half a dozen accounts of Kendall's experiences with bison before the expedition was thwarted by Mexican authorities. He enjoyed pursuing the great beasts, and encountered Indians intent upon lancing them. Bison provided the party with much-needed food in later stages; however, they appeared so irregularly that the starving men

[6] Ibid. 1: 83.
[7] Ibid. 1: 88.

consumed anything, including snakes, prairie dogs, tortoises, small birds, their pack animals, and mustangs, before Mexican authorities arrested them.

Other accounts of hunting bison celebrated the teeming primitive life in native America. Commentators were amazed by this "biological storm" in the western Plains, much as they were by the huge flights of passenger pigeons in woodlands to the east. Although it was recognized early in Texas that the mammal's numbers were dwindling, some liked to believe that the animals were able to instinctively flee before the white man's rifle or "melt away like the snows of spring."

The mustang also attracted considerable comment; its habit of associating in large mobile bands made it, like the bison, conspicuous. The individual animals were much admired for their beauty, fluid and swift motion, and wild spirit. J. Frank Dobie's treatment of the mustang exemplifies respect and admiration for the fecundity and nobility of many of these wild horses in the deserts and plains of North America, where the Spanish colonists and explorers had planted, abandoned, or lost them. Dobie had a great deal to say about the methods of securing wild horses and about the treatment they received when broken to the saddle. These free-ranging animals were widely distributed in Texas when Anglo settlement commenced; however, they were finished by the first decade of the present century. Dobie's great admiration and knowledge of the mustangers and mustangs in the Texas trade and range industry is a fine epitaph to a most abundant, wild, but introduced creature of the Plains.[8]

The South Texas Coastal Plain, divided by the Nueces, Frio, and Medina rivers, was an important range for mustangs. It was here that Zebulon Pike met up with them. On June 4, 1807, much troubled by mosquitos and horseflies, Pike's eastbound party saw "great sign of wild horses" adjacent to the Nueces River. Two days later, before arriving at the Medina, Pike noted the "immense numbers of cross-roads" made by mustangs. He had lost two pack animals in fording the Nueces, so when two herds of the wild animals crossed near his path, he doubtless wished to secure a few.

[8] J. Frank Dobie, *The Mustangs*.

Large numbers in several herds also drew admiring comment as Pike progressed further east.[9]

The numbers of wild horses in Texas drew the attention of Bishop Marín de Porras, who traversed Texas two years before Pike, and José M. Sánchez mentioned them a generation later. Sanchez recorded large herds in February, 1828, again near the Nueces and Medina rivers. A few years later in his statistical report, Juan Almonte listed wild horses as so abundant in the Department of Bexar that they were inexpensive to purchase and travelled close to the environs of San Antonio and Goliad at certain times of the year. Later, the size of the herds between the Nueces and the Río Grande astonished John Crittenden Duval (1816–91), who, in pursuit of Indians, met a mustang drove "so large that it took us fully an hour to pass it," even though the herd was galloping in the opposite direction. The hooves of these wild horses resounded "like the roar of the surf on a rocky coast."[10]

Spanish and English-language records demonstrate just how abundant mustangs were, especially along watercourses on the South Texas plain and on the oak-motte prairies of the coast. Numbers were high—too high for the settlers who regarded them as vermin because they enticed tame horses away, trampled the range, competed with stock for forage, and muddied and fouled water holes. Ranchers and farmers were glad to see the wild horses run off their lands or rounded up, and many shot them. Mustangs had other qualities, however, which, if they did not redeem them in the eyes of ranchers, added an aesthetic dimension to a life characterized as hard, tedious, and unstinting in physical demands. Andrew Muir was "compelled to stand in amazement and contemplate this noble animal as he bounds over the earth with the conscious pride of freedom." Such larded anthropomorphism was not unusual, as certain horses aroused admiration because of peculiar characteristics

[9] Milo M. Quaife, ed., *The Southwestern Expedition of Zebulon Pike*, pp. 207–208, 218–19.

[10] José M. Sánchez, "A Trip to Texas in 1828," trans. Carlos E. Castañeda, *Southwestern Historical Quarterly* 29 (1926): 253, 256; and Nettie Lee Benson, "Bishop Marín de Porras and Texas," *Southwestern Historical Quarterly* 51(1947):27; Juan N. Almonte, "Statistical Report on Texas," ed. and trans. C. E. Castañeda, *Southwestern Historical Quarterly*, 28(1945): 189, 191; and John C. Duval, *Early Times in Texas*, p. 27.

or abilities. Muir's book noted that one stallion, "remarkable above the rest for his perfect symmetry and great beauty," roamed the prairies around Houston and, as far as he knew, eluded all attempts at capture simply by outdistancing pursuers.[11]

Lawrence's *Texas in 1840, or, The Emigrant's Guide* paid careful attention to the horse, a combination of usefulness and beauty. Lawrence cited a bucolic, seemingly ethereal, encounter with a sorrel with a black mane and tail. The wild horse was first glimpsed speeding over a sunlit prairie decked with sunflowers. It stopped as if to encourage pursuit, then was off again with "arrowy fleetness." The stallion circled the observers, who "longed—hopelessly, vexatiously, longed to possess him," then tossed his flowing mane and galloped away. The physical beauty of the wild horse, its habitation in the air-filled open spaces, and its untrammeled roving existence recalled a primitive arcadian situation. The observers described in *Texas in 1840* "might have shot him . . . but had we been starving, we would scarcely have done it." Why not? Because the mustang was free, and "we loved him for the very possession of that liberty."[12]

William Bollaert, however, had serious reservations about the Texas mustang; it was "a sort of mongrel," he believed, which Comanches or Apaches purloined from the northern Mexico frontier and feasted on. These poorly bred animals, preyed upon by Indians who failed to care for them properly, compared indifferently in blood, looks, and numbers with the wild horses of the Pampas. Bollaert may have seen some of the latter horses in South America or may have had a good knowledge of them, and he judged that they were descended from "better and purer stock, the best sort of Spanish horses from the Barbary or Jennet."[13]

The wildness of mustangs provided a challenge. Many ranch hands and travellers dashed off in pursuit of what appeared from a distance to be fine specimens; however, in doing so a hand as likely as not "killed a fifty-dollar horse trying to rope a twenty-dollar mus-

[11] Andrew F. Muir, ed., *Texas in 1837, an Anonymous, Contemporary Narrative*, p. 125.

[12] [Lawrence], *Texas in 1840*, p. 134; Kennedy, *Texas*, pp. 121–23, provides the same account.

[13] W. Eugene Hollon and Ruth L. Butler, eds., *William Bollaert's Texas*, pp. 255–57.

tang." Some of the animals, especially legendary white stallions heading their *manada* of mares, achieved fame because they were too wily and defiant to be caught by those who coveted them. However, in reality professional horse catchers took a constant toll of wild mustangs, and good animals became increasingly rare as the ropers picked the herds over. What appeared to be a good steed against a backdrop of rolling, sun-dappled prairie was "likely to appear gimlet hammed and narrow chested" once it had been roped.[14]

The prejudice against horse flesh for food existed in Texas, though not among the Indians. Yet Smithwick reported that it was mainly mustangs that were shot for meat by the two professional hunters on Jared E. Groce's cotton plantation on the lower Brazos. Smithwick himself was sickened by the thought of eating mustang meat, even when food once ran out along the Mexican border near Laredo; but after a two-day fast, he was not so squeamish. Mustangs were something people fell back on. George Kendall evinced a real liking for horse flesh. In spite of his eulogy about wild horses, including admiration for a bright bay stallion that gamboled near the riders of the Sante Fe Expedition and tossed its long mane like a "ringleted schoolgirl," Kendall was fond of delicately flavored and tender three-year-old mustang meat, "really better than either buffalo or common beef." Not many others agreed with him; more people tended to side with Kennedy, who spoke disparagingly of horse meat, "eaten by the wild Indians of the Mexican frontier," and only in times of scarcity.[15]

The useful and aesthetically valuable characteristics of wild horses were cited to disprove the idea of biological degeneracy in the New World. French natural historian George-Louis Leclerc, Comte de Buffon (1707–88), had argued in the late eighteenth century that because civilization had been so recently implanted into North America, the native fauna had not benefitted from the "hand of man" and therefore remained unimproved and savage. Curiously, in 1908, Judge Oscar Waldo Williams (1853–1946) used the past numerical strength of the mustang in Texas to refute any lin-

[14]J. Franke Dobie, *A Vaquero of the Brush Country*, p. 225. Kendall, *Southwestern Prairies* 1: 94–95, also pays attention to the myth of the "White Steed of the Prairies."

[15]Smithwick, *Evolution of a State*, pp. 18–19, 42–43; Kendall, *Southwestern Prairies* 1: 157–58; Kennedy, *Texas*, p. 120.

gering beliefs in degeneracy. The transplant of horses to the United States had been an outstanding success, and for 250 years wild horses had multiplied and filled the Plains. The United States, he argued, was supplying cavalry horses to European nations. Texas stock made excellent mounts for polo, and the initial (although ill-fated) expedition into Texas territory by American Philip Nolan was made ostensibly to make a fortune from catching wild horses for the Louisiana market. Williams believed, therefore, that the abundance and quality of Texas horses were clear proof against railing and slighting judgments (Bollaert's, for instance) about the impoverished state of wild animals in the New World.

Williams admitted sadly, however, that "the wild horse has almost as completely disappeared in Texas as the buffalo." He recalled that in the 1870s, a band of mustangs in Floyd County, above Lubbock, had struck him with its beauty, lines, grace, speed, and bearing—qualities that were absent from captive animals, which quickly lost their spirit under harness. Judge Williams had witnessed the elimination of wild horses from the Pecos region. Most of them, he believed, had been shot or were captured in the early 1890s by a New Mexico mustanger, so by 1908 only a small band of about fifteen inferior-looking horses ran wild near the Pecos River. This sealed the fate of a most successful transplant in Texas.[16]

Unique to North America, the pronghorn antelope received applause and respect in early literature about the Plains and the Southwest. Dodge delighted in the antelope's upright carriage and its light, deft movements; however, the animal's insatiable curiosity, he felt, caused many to be shot and killed.[17]Pronghorns had the vulnerable habit of investigating wagons and other objects that looked out of place in their prairie habitat. Marksmen capitalized on this curiosity by waving a bright cloth from a semiconcealed position and luring these fleet-footed, naturally timid Plains denizens within rifle range.

The pronghorn antelope was well distributed in the upper and

[16]Oscar W. Williams, *Historic Review of Animal Life in Pecos County*, pp. 8, 11–14; Lehmann believes that some mustangs persisted on the King Ranch until "the early 1900s."

[17]R. I. Dodge, *The Hunting Grounds of the Great West*, 2nd ed., pp. 195–97; Kendall, *Across the Great Southwestern Prairies* 1: 100–101, among others, referred to this weakness.

lower plains of Texas, occupying an area estimated at some seventy thousand square miles and ranging eastward to about the ninety-seventh meridian.[18] Prior to 1880 many persons reported it as common in the mountain zone, and it fed in hardpan flats in South Texas on grasses, forbs, and shrubs. It was a common inhabitant of open, wide, unobstructed plains and prairies, and, as Bolleart remarked, the "graceful" large-eyed antelope frequented areas where the "powerful" bison ranged.

Curiously, however, many authors had little to say about this important native species. Kennedy described bison, mustangs, and deer as key game animals, but not antelope. Edward makes no mention of it, and Lawrence's *Texas in 1840* merely separated antelope from "wild goats." William Bollaert's first encounter with a pronghorn antelope as he entered the remote area of the Kennedy Grant in South Texas was unremarkable.

One reason why the antelope drew relatively little comment was that it was unknown to many writers who had first-hand knowledge of other game. In 1848, Viktor Bracht's summary assessment of Texas game species noted that "flocks" of pronghorn were to be found on the upper reaches of Cibolo and Salado creeks and "on the slopes of the Guadalupe Mountains." However, they were very shy and difficult to take; thus, "so far only two or three have been killed." He implied that because their meat differed little from venison, it was preferable to hunt deer, which were well distributed and at times "so numerous that one or two thousand may be counted on a ride of twenty miles through the wilderness."[19]

Persons like George Kendall, who made surveys or long-distance journeys into unexplored regions, had most to say about pronghorns. Along the Bosque, on July 5, 1841, twelve or fourteen days into the expedition to Santa Fe, Kendall recalled seeing the first antelope, or "mountain goat," whose flesh he judged to be superior to venison and cabrito. The remarkable speed of the pronghorn astounded him: an animal whose foreleg had been shattered by a

---

[18] Helmut K. Buechner, "Life History, Ecology, and Range Use of the Pronghorn Antelope in Trans-Pecos Texas," *American Midland Naturalist* 43 (1950): 257–354; Paul V. Jones, "Antelope Management," *Texas Game and Fish* 7 (1949): 4–5, 18–20, 24–25, 28–29; and Tommy L. Hailey, "A Handbook for Pronghorn Antelope Management in Texas," Texas Parks and Wildlife Department, F. A. Report Series 20.

[19] Bracht, *Texas in 1848*, p. 42.

rifle bullet managed to outdistance a rider on a good horse after a considerable chase. John Russell Bartlett (1805–86), the explorer, historian, and ethnologist whom President Zachary Taylor appointed U.S. Commissioner of the United States–Mexican Boundary survey, reported antelope frequently. Bartlett travelled in Texas in the early 1850s, and on a journey from Ringgold Barracks (Rio Grande City) to Corpus Christi he espied "thousands of deer and antelope" on the short-grass, dead-level plain. On New Year's Day, 1853, in the course of a day's ride outside Corpus Christi, Bartlett was impressed by the numbers of animals; "the deer and antelope were usually grazing in herds from ten to fifty," and some of the pronghorns were pure white.[20] These accounts suggest that antelope were common in parts of South Texas. They also proved numerous (though apparently in declining numbers) in the lower Panhandle, where they were recorded by Captain Randolph Barnes Marcy (1812–87), who was exploring the Red River drainage when Bartlett was in Texas.[21]

Fifty years later, pronghorns had virtually disappeared. In his "Biological Survey," published in 1905, federal mammalogist Vernon Bailey (1864–1942) counted thirty-two pronghorns in a ninety-five-mile railroad journey from Canyon, Texas, to Portales, New Mexico. In South Texas, a few remained west of Alice, and small bands roamed near Cotulla and Rocksprings. But antelope had disappeared from the vicinities of Alpine and Marfa and from the outwash plain of the Davis Mountains.[22] Reduced to low numbers in scattered bands, the pronghorn antelope required intensive (and expensive) efforts to save it from extinction in Texas.

The white-tailed deer proved to be another interesting and pleasing animal in Texas and was a preferred game species. This widely distributed cervid attracted interest beyond utilitarian needs in two ways. First, the sight of deer browsing along a line of brush or bounding away over the prairies with "flags" held high pleased

[20] Kendall, Southwestern Prairies 1: 100; John Russell Bartlett, Personal Narrative of Explorations and Incidents in Texas, New Mexico, California, Sonora and Chihuahua 2: 521–26.

[21] Randolph B. Marcy, Exploration of the Red River of Louisiana in the Year 1852, p. 62, Appendix F, and Randolph B. Marcy, Thirty Years of Army Life on the Border, p. 174.

[22] Vernon Bailey, "Biological Survey of Texas," North American Fauna 25 (1905): 67–68.

travellers and settlers. Deer were important, integral elements in all three regions in the Lone Star State. The pattern of distribution and high numbers proved that forage, water, and other requirements were there for the taking, and they exemplified the natural bounty of Texas, where every type of domestic animal could prosper and flourish with little expense. Furthermore, deer "composed" a scene; they were mobile, vibrant elements in picturesque landscapes. The presence of deer against a backdrop of flowers, lush greenery, checkered light, and the changing hues of the seasons made them appropriate subjects through which Texas could be promoted.

The anonymous writer of *A Visit to Texas* journeyed between Brazoria and Anahuac in March, 1831, and celebrated the "indescribable beauty of a Texas Prairie" in spring by describing the colors, variety, profusion, and delicacy of wild flowers as well as the activities of deer and their fawns. In the same decade Andrew Muir expressed wonderment at the wooded Brazos Valley, "alive with deer," which "start up . . . in droves." Nature's prodigality was tempered by a heavy toll from predators, which especially singled out spotted fawns "bouncing through the grass after their dams." Nevertheless, the hunter rejoiced in the sport that such natural fecundity provided.[23]

In regard to numbers, deer ranked with bison, mustangs, and wild cattle. Mary Austin Holley (1784–1846) argued that "deer are still more numerous than the buffalo, being found in every part of Texas in great abundance." A tract put out by the Galveston Bay and Land Company in 1835 stated that these creatures, along with wild horses and bison, "amidst luxuriant natural pastures have multiplied to an extent almost incredible." Although widely distributed, Kennedy believed that deer excelled numerically in the coastal region, where killing them as a staple food was akin to slaughtering domestic sheep from a flock. He and other authors noted that travellers had deer constantly in sight, espying them "grazing in flocks on the flowery prairies, heightening the resemblance of those wooded meadows to the parks of the British aristocracy."[24]

[23] *A Visit to Texas; Being the Journal of a Traweller Through Those Parts Most Interesting to American Settlers*, pp. 186–87; Muir, ed., *Texas in 1837*, p. 75.

[24] Mary Austin Holley, *Texas*, p. 99; Galveston Bay and Land Co., *An Address to Emigrants*, p. 4; Kennedy, *Texas*, p. 123.

The park analogy was extended by other pioneers such as William Dewees, who drew attention to the "remarkable feature" of Texas that much of the timber was situated on watercourses separated by prairies bearing at a distance "the appearance of a cultivated park."[25] Pleasing and tame animals like deer fitted in well with this image of a "garden" where nature's bounties were tended and tastefully displayed. The garden metaphor was contrasted with the image of a wilderness in which dangerous beasts, "red in tooth and claw," abounded and where nature was in chaos and intractable to human endeavors.

This idea of deer as "nice" animals, suitable for a park or landscape garden, represents the second way in which people valued them for nonmaterial purposes. The fact that deer browsed on shrubs and bushes instead of feeding on valuable grasses (except on new growth), as did the mustang, bison, and prairie dog, doubtless made agriculturalists feel more sympathy for them. The appearance and activities of the graceful doe, noble buck, or delicate fawn gave pleasure to observers and caused many authors to single out anthropomorphic qualities in deer, much as they did in their comments about mustangs. Moreover, promoters of Texas referred to the practice of keeping deer as pets about settlements and plantations to persuade readers that Texans were gentle and compassionate. Deer touched off this sentimental response to mammals and birds as "little people."

Lawrence mentions in his *Texas in 1840, or, the Emigrant's Guide* that at breakfast at a planter's home near Washington-on-the-Brazos, on January 4, 1840, he was "gratified and surprised" to see a lovely doe, with a bell on her neck, enter the house and receive corn bread before returning to the outdoors. "The landlady," whom this Presbyterian minister complimented for her hospitality and whose well-to-do husband was generous to new settlers, "remarked that it thus came every morning and disappeared till the morning following."[26]

Such St. Francis–like qualities could be expected from the better-educated middle-class immigrants; this humaneness was also found among German immigrants whom Frederick Olmsted ad-

---

[25] William B. Dewees, *Letters from an Early Settler of Texas*, p. 130.
[26] [Lawrence], *Texas in 1840*, p. 35.

mired. Olmsted noted in 1854 that certain residents of New Braunfels kept a pet doe, complete with collar and bell, which was given
the freedom of the settlement. This beautiful deer proved so docile
that it licked his hand. It wandered among the houses of this rustic,
well-kept, industrious community, whose members were by and
large unfamiliar with firearms. "In what Texas town, through which
we have passed before, could this have occurred," exclaimed Olmsted
rhetorically.[27]

Such attachment to animals was not unusual. Many ranch hands,
cowboys, and hunters were known after their animals and gave
nicknames to the horses, dogs, or stock they possessed; many a
hardened outdoorsman became greatly attached to his faithful animals. Charles A. Siringo (1855–1928), born on the Matagorda Peninsula, led a hard itinerant existence; he was a cowpuncher on the
Chisholm Trail from a tender age. However, in writing of his experiences, Siringo confessed unashamedly to a tearful farewell as an
adolescent to old Browny, the family cow, which "would let me go
up to her on the prairie calf fashion and get my milk."

After a stint in New Orleans, Siringo returned to Texas to drive
longhorns to Kansas and became greatly attached to his cow pony
Whisky Peet. Leaving tired Whisky Peet at his mother's cabin on
Cash Creek (Matagorda County) for another trail drive in the late
1870s "was almost as severe on me as having sixteen jaw teeth pulled,"
Siringo admitted. The intelligent pony who had borne him so faith-
fully on previous drives died before Siringo returned, and he never
saw the animal again.[28]

The practice of keeping young animals was common. Bear cubs
were carried back to cabins and settlements, antelope fawns sometimes were raised in West Texas, and bison calves would follow
horsemen like dogs once their mothers had been killed or driven
away. Major Edgar A. Mearns (1856–1915), surgeon and biologist
for the U.S. Boundary Survey, which operated from El Paso to
California from 1892 to 1894, knew ranch hands who could lasso
peccaries from horseback and who sometimes would take care of
piglets and raise them. In Arizona he met a ranch woman who was
much attached to a peccary given to her by a local Indian. From a

[27] Frederick Law Olmsted, *A Journey through Texas, Or, A Saddle-Trip on the Southwestern Frontier*, p. 146.
[28] Charles A. Siringo, *A Texas Cowboy*, pp. 19, 119.

Mexican lad Mearns purchased one that "followed us about in the camps." If not maltreated, peccaries caught young "became gentle and affectionate" and made excellent pets, reported Mearns, who also found mule deer taken captive in Arizona to be equally docile.[29]

Female deer appeared particularly friendly and attractive. Several persons had ulterior motives in raising animals they had discovered in the wild. William Bollaert, in a piece entitled "On the Different Sorts of Hunting and Species of Game in Texas," noted that sending a pet doe out into the woods "entices the bucks to the house," with obvious results. Sometimes such chicanery was unnecessary. John Duvall was impressed with the fearlessness of great numbers of deer between Copano and Goliad, and he had no difficulty in getting close and obtaining fresh venison on his travels through that coastal lowland.[30] Other species such as bear cubs could be raised and taught to perform tricks.

Social animals associating in herds—bison, mustangs, antelope, and deer—impressed residents and visitors by their numbers; moreover, residents perceived them as integral and important elements in the biogeography of the state. In the remote mountain country of the west and north, the traveller expected to meet up with herds of bison, antelope, and mustangs (as well as with Indians) and came back impressed and eager to communicate these experiences. In the middle ground of the Rolling Prairies, deer and mustangs abounded; so, too, did wild cattle, which people hunted and rounded up, especially after the Civil War, for the great trail drives to northern markets. These animals were living witness to the natural wealth of the region under a benign climate. They were proof that here was the best of all possible worlds. The coastal lowlands was again the place to observe scampering deer and galloping mustangs.

Other gregarious animals occurred, too, especially such birds as turkeys, prairie chickens, and waterfowl, which assembled in flocks in the same coastal zone. In fact, Bollaert claimed that coastal

[29] Edgar A. Mearns, *Mammals of the Mexican Boundary of the United States*, pp. 168, 200. Mention of a bear cub as a gift comes from Llerena Friend, ed., *M. K. Kellogg's Texas Journal, 1872*, p. 91.

[30] Hollon and Butler, eds., *Bollaert's Texas*, pp. 252–53; Duval, *Early Times in Texas*, pp. 26–27.

Texas was the "great nation of geese,"[31] with its millions of wintering Canadian, snow, and white-fronted geese, twenty-five or so duck species, and innumerable cranes, pelicans, herons, gulls, shorebirds, and other aquatic fowl. Some of these water birds seemed strange because of their size, habits, or appearances, and promotional literature tended to comment on the numbers, colors, and vocalizations made by different species, which were, after all, prodigies of this new land.

Almost everyone who sailed along the coastline from New Orleans to Galveston made some mention of the pelicans that inhabited Pelican Island near the entry to Galveston Bay. In season, this sandy island contained the nests of thousands of large brown birds, a family which European immigrants and travellers would have encountered rarely but recognized easily. Sheridan made sarcastic comments about the primitive and drab character of the environs around Galveston, which he described as a small place "of a similar hideousness and called Pelican I. by reason of its being colonized by nobody but the Pelicans.[32] Others, less haughty, spoke about Pelican Island with excitement and admiration. Pelicans were large, strange-looking birds and were obviously portents of other curious, exciting wild animals the visitors were about to encounter—such as alligators, which drew much interest but no regard.

David Edward's geographical description of Texas included pelicans in a list of interesting fowl "which the mildness of the weather and the quantity of marine food bring together in Texas." He admitted that naming all the species would be difficult, but particularly mentions Pelican Island and the "immense flocks" of water birds inhabiting Galveston Bay, which was kept "literally alive with their noise and motion" as they laid great quantities of eggs on the shores. In April, 1836, William Gray visited the same harborage and collected beautiful beach shells for his children. Gray saw numbers of "cranes, curlews, gulls and pelicans," noting that pelicans "at a distance resembled companies of soldiers, white and grey; the two colors flock together." Gray used a similar military epithet in describing a scene a month earlier at Washington-on-the-Brazos: "the wind is from the South, and the wild geese are mustering for

[31] Hollon and Butler, eds., *Bollaert's Texas*, p. 317.

[32] Willis W. Pratt, ed., *Galveston Island: Or, A Few Months Off the Coast of Texas, The Journal of Francis C. Sheridan, 1839–1840.* p. 32.

the North. Large flocks are seen flying over, but in a very militia-like style. They have not yet got drilled into a regular echellon [sic] form of march."³³ Interestingly, Gray was anxiously awaiting news about the Alamo as he witnessed the departure of these waterfowl on spring migration.

John James Audubon (1785–1851), accompanied by his son John Woodhouse, visited Galveston a year later to observe and collect birds. He procured five specimens of the strangely shaped, un-usually colored roseate spoonbill. He noted that shorebirds and gulls were breeding commonly and then experienced a gale on April 25, 1837, which grounded thousands of birds arriving from across the Gulf of Mexico. The next morning, he wrote that birds, "arrested by the storm in their migration northward, are seen hovering around our vessels and hiding in the grass, and some are struggling in the water, completely exhausted." Spring rains and contrary winds con-tinued to cause great destruction to small land birds buffeted over the sea. Audubon appeared to be uninterested in the pelicans but reported that colonies of herons (and probably the pelicans, too) were being preyed upon by snakes, "whence the old name for Gal-veston Island of 'Snake Island.'"³⁴

The author of A Visit to Texas recognized two species of peli-cans about Point Bolivar in April, 1831; both appeared to be imper-vious to shot as they flew in chevrons near his grounded vessel. In addition to novel pelicans, the author came upon a large egret col-ony, a "bank of snow" in the green bushes near the point. These strange birds were "useless to eat" but possessed bodies the size of a small duck "mounted on legs measuring a foot and a half below the knee." The cacophony of squeaks, grunts, and general clatter startled him; he was astonished, too, at the abundance of other aquatic birds around Galveston Bay, especially the geese, "whose noise may be heard several miles."³⁵

Other large, unusual-looking birds inhabited the coast. Wil-liam Bollaert reported "man-of-war birds"—that is, the frigate bird, a speedy, predatory sea bird found in the tropics—that forced gulls

³³ David B. Edward, The History of Texas, p. 61; William F. Gray, From Vir-ginia to Texas, 1835: Diary of Col. Wm. F. Gray, pp. 156, 130.
³⁴ Samuel Wood Geiser, Naturalists of the Frontier, 2nd ed. rev., pp. 79–94, quotation p. 87, 88.
³⁵ A Visit to Texas, pp. 92, 151–52, 168–71.

and terns to disgorge fish they had captured by flying in pursuit of them. Bollaert's frigate birds associated with "myriads" of pelicans that were splashing headfirst into fish-laden waters around St. Joseph's Island.[36]

Conspicuous predaceous birds, like hawks and vultures, patrolled the grasslands next to the seashore. One of them was the "prairie" or marsh hawk, which "sailed in sport and joy" above the Coastal Prairie, whose level surface dulled the senses because "there is so little to give them exercise." This magnificent brown and white bird fitted into the picturesque scene perfectly. Lulling the observer's mind, the hawk swung lightly, easily, seemingly carelessly across the "vast sheet of velvet" in an hypnotic motion that resembled "the swell and depression of a gentle wave." Its flight changed instantly, however, into a darting, arrowlike swiftness whenever the predator spied a small mammal or a bird.[37] The glimpse of a young prairie chicken, for example, crossing an open area in the tall grass prairie would cause the marsh hawk to dash after it.

These abundant and tasty prairie chickens, largely ground-dwelling birds, delighted settlers and travellers between the Sabine and the Nueces rivers. Periodic flights of prairie hens occurred "in such numbers that they would obscure the sun," declared an authority on old times. He said, "I remember having stood on my father's gallery and shot at prairie chickens in the tops of the old post oak trees that stood in the yard. They didn't quite fall into the frying pan, but they dropped so close . . . that the cook had only to dress and clean them to put them there."[38] These hordes of prairie chickens, a race of the greater prairie chicken from the interior Plains, once endemic to Texas' coastal zone have been enormously reduced in numbers through decades of exploitation and the encroachment of human activities on their habitat.

Further inland, in the rolling country between San Antonio and Austin, Frederick Olmsted once caught sight of several large white objects that he initially took to be either sheep or cattle. "Llamas—or alpacas," he exclaimed; then, "Ostriches." But as the huge birds raised their black-edged wings, stretched their necks, and lumbered into the sky, Olmsted recognized them as "a species of

[36] Hollon and Butler, eds., *Bollaert's Texas*, pp. 378–79.
[37] [Lawrence], *Texas in 1840*, p. 194; *A Visit to Texas*, pp. 18–19.
[38] John T. Allen, *Early Pioneer Days in Texas*, p. 34.

crane, very much magnified by a refraction of the atmosphere." Later, near Salado Creek, he passed a second flock of the unusual whooping cranes, which proved extremely wary and would not come in range of his Sharps rifle.[39]

These birds and others were strange; however, they were attractive, too, because, as leading ornithologist and Audubonist Frank M. Chapman said, "Everyone is born with a bird in his heart." People found their appearance and behavior interesting and drew inspiration especially from the melodies of songsters around settlements and cultivated places. William Kennedy remarked that songbirds appeared to seek out the companionship of settlers; they "seldom enliven the deep solitudes of the forests" but followed the "march of population." Certainly, George Kendall believed that this was the case as he was awakened one morning in the wilderness of West Texas by the "warbling of innumerable singing-birds," recognizing among them the notes of the robin, meadowlark, and bluebird. Men in the Santa Fe–bound party, which had become thoroughly disoriented by late August, 1841, believed with Kendall that singing birds indicated the proximity of settlements. They soon discovered, however, that the serenade was a set of "fallacious promises" and served to kindle memories of home.[40]

Similar homesickness had been experienced a decade earlier by Albert Pike in traversing the Santa Fe Trail. In 1832, hearing a March robin singing in the Valley of the Tesuque near Santa Fe, Pike was filled with longing for his New England birthplace:

>Hush! Where art thou clinging,
>And what art thou singing,
>Bird of my own native land?
>· · · · · · · · · · · · · · · · · ·
>
>Hush! Hush!—Look around thee!
>Lo! bleak mountains bound thee,
>All barren and gloomy and red;
>· · · · · · · · · · · · · · · · · · ·
>
>And here thou, like me, art alone.
> Go back

[39] Olmsted, *A Journey through Texas*, pp. 135, 224.
[40] Kennedy, *Texas*, p. 126; Kendall, *Southwestern Prairies* 1: 216.

On thy track;
It were wiser and better for thee and me
· ·

Let us go—let us go—and revisit our home,
Where the oak leaves are green and the sea-waters foam.[41]

Pike likened New Mexico to Siberia, so the familiar robin in the arid landscape of "desolate pine" was as out of place as his human listener.

Smaller songbirds were most abundant in the "settled" Rolling Prairie zone of Texas, and certain authorities figured that robins, wrens, hummingbirds, and buntings, those beautiful creatures that caused observers to look "from nature's beautiful works, to nature's God," were increasing in numbers and expanding their ranges as land was put under cultivation.[42] These "garden" birds and others from the "wilderness," such as hawks, eagles, vultures, owls, and the much-admired woodpeckers, enlivened Texan landscapes with their colors, activities, calls, and melodies. Most of them could be found in areas bordering Texas; indeed, some species in Texas appeared to compare unfavorably in size with similar birds in other states. However, several birds had a remarkable aesthetic appeal. The feisty mockingbird, considered the nightingale of Texas because of its ebullient song and its habit of nocturnal vocalization, drew praise. It impressed Muir as such a splendid mimic that other species listened in "apparent despair or move[d] off to hide their chagrin" as the mocker taught them their song. He was captivated by the bird's "buffoonery, versatility, and I might add, coquetry."[43]

The "bird of paradise" (scissor-tailed flycatcher), found in the mesquite and semiopen country, was regarded highly for its subtle coloration, pleasing song, and long, flexible forked tail, which Olmsted likened to a "pair of paper shears half opened." This bird and others (such as screaming green paroquets—"gay, clamorous, and pilfering," grumbled Kennedy) added vigor and variety to the

[41] David J. Weber, ed., *Albert Pike: Prose Sketches and Poems*, pp. 83–85.
[42] Edward, *The History of Texas*, p. 75. Ferdinand Roemer, *Texas: With Particular Reference to German Immigration and the Physical Appearance of the Country*, pp. 140–41, argued that the German forests harbored few birds compared to the uncultivated places in Texas.
[43] Muir, ed., *Texas in 1837*, p. 126.

bird life of Texas, making its list of avifauna a long and interesting one. "Valorous" kingbirds, "pleasing" swallows, "homely" wrens and chickadees, and many other insectivorous species reassured settlers that nature was both bountiful and helpful in this new land.

Beautiful or strange mammals and birds had equivalents in the orders of reptiles and fish. The horned frog, actually a type of lizard, was very odd. Some called it the link between frogs and lizards, appearing "so much like either that it is hard to say of which he most partakes." The horned frog was fierce-looking, but quite harmless and useful as an insect-devourer. However, "if he were as big as an elephant, he would be the most monstrous of creatures." People collected them as curious pets. A Galveston sailor offered some horned frogs he kept in the crown of his hat to William Kennedy for ten dollars apiece. Olmsted mailed one or two "horny toads" back to New England as keepsakes. But John Duval took no chances with the first horned frog he encountered. He had heard of dangerous tarantulas and centipedes, so assuming that the frog was one or the other, he "picked up a stick about ten feet long" and slew the supposed dragon "as flat as a pan-cake!"[44]

Often derisive Francis Sheridan had a soft spot for horned frogs, which he characterized as "having the head of a frog, the back and belly of an alligator, and the tail of a turtle." He took an unusual interest in the diminutive creatures and kept several in a large cigar box strewn with "rocks, varied with little lumps of mud." He fed them on three large flies a day, with a few mosquitos as a luxury. Expressing a desire to add "tone" to their stomachs, he added cockroaches "twice a week and every other Sunday." Never failing to add a barb about Texas, he volunteered that he could supply "the best and freshest [cockroaches] in the Market!" How long this foreign diplomat sequestered these pets is not certain; however, he assured his readers that, ensconced in the ingenious cave he had fashioned for them, complete with a "whity brown paper" covering and pierced by arrow slits in the best Gothic design, the heart of a horned frog could have desired no more.[45]

Among fishes, the alligator gar, "in form half fish, and half alli-

[44] Duval, *Early Times in Texas*, p. 89.
[45] Pratt, ed., *Galveston Island*, pp. 103–104.

Like that of the passenger pigeon, the bison's demise was relatively sudden. Commercial hunters took such a heavy toll in North Texas that after 1880, except for stragglers, only captive animals remained.

Alligators were given no quarter; protective laws, however, have enabled their numbers to rebuild dramatically in recent years.

Like all stock killers, the coyote was attacked. This animal enters water before he "bays." (*Courtesy Dobie Collection, Humanities Research Center, University of Texas*)

A successful turkey hunt. Similar successes virtually eliminated the wild turkey from East Texas. (*Courtesy Humanities Research Center, University of Texas*)

Left: The endangered whooping crane was never easy to hunt. Unlike the sandhill crane, this species was wily and hard to stalk. *Right*: Golden eagles were shot to reduce predation on pronghorn antelope fawns in West Texas. This one was taken near Van Horn in 1937. (*Courtesy Smithers Collection, Humanities Research Center, University of Texas*)

Despite the reputation of the adults for meanness, peccary piglets were attractive pets. This shepherd dog from Shumala, Texas, was more attracted to this wild piglet than to her own puppies. (*Courtesy Smithers Collection, Humanities Research Center, University of Texas*)

Antelope traps near Marfa, Texas, in 1940. An airplane herded wild antelope into the catching area, then individuals were placed in wooden crates for shipment to new ranges. (*Courtesy Smithers Collection, Humanities Research Center, University of Texas*)

Game warden Ray Williams, who worked hard to bring back antelope in West Texas, bottle-feeds a fawn he has collected near Van Horn in 1937. Nanny goats nursed the fawns until they were returned to the wild.

gator," drew much attention because of its large size and menacing appearance, but it proved largely inedible. William Kennedy termed this fish worthless, but because of its voracity, it was truly a "river-shark" preying on unsuspecting and more edible species. A suggestion made by Lawrence's *Texas in 1840* was to skin the gar and nail it to the mold board of a plow to provide a resilient "hide" or wrapping for the wood. People shot them for target practice as they basked near the surface of rivers. A story from the Sabine (related by Sheridan) suggested that the formidable brute was not averse to making unexpected attacks on persons. A fisherman paddling a canoe attracted a gar, which sprang for his arm when he lowered it near the water; however, the daring fish feasted only upon the torn sleeve of the fisherman's shirt.[46] Sheridan was not prepared to accept this story wholly, but he noted that if such an act had occurred, the gar showed more "gallantry" than its namesake, the alligator, which persons judged, in general, to be pusillanimous.

The alligator inhabited the lower reaches of all the major drainage systems from the Red River to the Rio Grande, reportedly occurring north to the San Gabriel, near Marlin on the Brazos River, and into Kinney County along the Rio Grande. A score of writers noted, mostly with disdain, this reptile's appearance, great size (up to thirty feet, exaggerated Mary Austin Holley), menacing shape, and death-dealing activities. Smithwick summed up the general dislike for alligators by characterizing them as gaunt and grim animals, "certainly the most hideous creatures God ever made," whose horrible bellowing (and carnivorous ways) were amplified by the solitude of the wilderness. Prince Carl of Solms-Braunfels, commissioner general of the German colony in Texas, recorded alligators from the "clearest waters of the West" and some reptiles from Comal Creek measuring fourteen feet. A sixteen-foot alligator was shot near the confluence of the Trinity River and Galveston Bay in 1831; large specimens were not unusual.[47]

Alligators preyed on colonists' dogs and livestock but were reportedly not averse to attacking unsuspecting persons. Such attacks seem to have been uncommon, however. Generally, the alligator

[46][Lawrence], *Texas in 1840*, p. 197; Pratt, ed., *Galveston Island*, p. 124.
[47]Smithwick, *Evolution of a State*, p. 16; Prince Carl of Solms-Braunfels, *Texas, 1844–1845*, p. 30; *A Visit to Texas*, p. 122.

was regarded as lazy and harmless, although immigrants were warned constantly to keep a careful watch for them at fords and river crossings and to guard against falling into partially concealed "gator" holes in Southeast Texas. Bollaert, on a visit to the Kennedy grant on the upper reaches of the Nueces River in June, 1844, mentioned that an alligator went after Fanny Baker, his horse, near the Laredo-Goliad Road. Later, alligators were "jumping about" in the Nueces not far from San Patricio.[48]

Because of alligators' menacing lines and uncouth habits, people had no compunction about shooting them. Gator killing was, for some, a genial sport and was frequently practiced along the Mississippi drainage, where passengers on paddle steamers relieved their tedium by blazing away at larger individuals on the banks of the Red River and other tributaries.[49]

These nimrods didn't get too near the animals, which could prove extremely dangerous when wounded. Only the real woodsman knew that "an alligator is not dead when he is dead," meaning that its grip on life appeared similar to the proverbial cat's. One person claimed to have seen a beast "walk around with three boys on his back a half hour after his brains had been blown out." To get a dead gator to lie still and be skinned, the admonition went, one should take a sharp hatchet and chop its backbone in two, then run a long bulrush over the marrow of its backbone from neck to tail so that the tail will not slap you and the legs will behave.[50]

Snakes, although evil-looking and in some instances venomous, had a reputation, similar to that of alligator, of being relatively harmless; certain species were known to assist farmers by making inroads into rodent populations. Olmsted's remarks typified the attitudes of fellow travellers—that snakes were so commonly seen "as hardly to excite an exclamation." Settlers seemed to take them for granted; fatal accidents were rare. One had to be careful, though, especially when sleeping outdoors. Olmsted recalled the oft-repeated tale of a rattlesnake creeping under the blankets of a slumbering person to benefit from body warmth. However, his source had no

[48] Smithwick, *Evolution of a State*, pp. 16–17, 76; Hollon and Butler, eds., *Bollaert's Texas*, pp. 371, 375.

[49] Sam H. Nunnely, "Associated with Frank James," in *The Trail Drivers of Texas*, ed. J. M. Hunter, pp. 763–64.

[50] Forest W. McNair, *Forest McNair of Texas*, p. 32.

first-hand experience of such a happening. "nor had he ever heard of a man's having been bitten on these occasions."[51]

Kendall, who had close encounters with rattlers several times and saw large numbers of them on the route to Santa Fe, insisted that they would never bite unless provoked, except in August, "when they are said to be blind, and will snap at anything and everything they may hear about them." Yet he took the story of rattlesnakes in bedding very seriously, noting that "very frequently, on the great prairies, a man wakes up in the morning and finds that he has had a rattlesnake for a sleeping partner." But apparently the reptiles would slither away quickly and avoided disturbing people. Lore dictated that an effective deterrent to rattlesnake "companionship" was a horsehair lariat placed around a sleeping person; a snake would never cross this lasso.[52]

Settlers, notably Poles and Germans, feared snakes and killed them around homes; their practice of burning prairie grasses annually to stimulate regeneration also reduced rodents and the reptiles that preyed on them. As with ugly alligators, persons enjoyed killing creatures they considered vermin. William H. C. Whiting noted in his *Journal*, in an entry dated May 12, 1849, that on the divide between the Pecos River and Devil's River the monotony of travel was lightened by shooting rattlesnakes, "great numbers of which were met and slain." Bartlett's party killed hundreds, too, in the exploration of Texas' boundary. Settlers in the Castroville area even hunted rattlesnakes "as game" and consumed them. Antidotes for a rattlesnake bite, according to Solms-Braunfels, consisted of enlarging the wound and applying "cropped tops of corn to draw out the poison," then adding later "a solution of volatile alkali, so that, with precautions, a bite was not fatal.[53]

Water moccasins were another, more profound disturbance to Texas' Eden, and even hogs reportedly refused to devour them. These poisonous serpents lacked "one spark of generosity," declared Edward, while others had much gentler dispositions and also proved

[51] Olmsted, *A Journey through Texas*, pp. 308–10.

[52] Kendall, *Southwestern Prairies* 1: 98–99.

[53] Arthur Ikin, *Texas: Its History, Topography, Agriculture, Commerce, and General Statistics*, p. 37; P. St. George Cooke, William H. C. Whiting, and Francis X. Aubry, *Exploring Southwestern Trails*, ed. Ralph P. Bieber and Averam B. Bender), p. 342; Solms-Braunfels, *Texas*, pp. 30–31.

colorful. One remarkable instance of a snake "charming" its quarry came from a resident in East Texas, where reptiles abounded; the rattlesnake in question was coiled open-mouthed at the base of a tree from which a small bird slowly descended "in convulsions of fright," to be seized and swallowed slowly by the snake.[54]

Prejudices against serpents extended, with much more reason, to another phylum of diminutive animals, the arthropods, such as spiders, scorpions, and insects. These were disliked not for their menacing appearances, although Texas-sized tarantulas and scorpions looked terrible enough, but rather for the irritation and pain that these insects especially caused man and beast along streams and rivers and in the prairie lands of the rolling plains and coastal regions. Without knowledge of the microscopic agents of communicable disease, people usually underestimated the role of insects as vectors in spreading diseases. People disliked mosquitos, for example, because their bites caused such torment, not because they carried malaria, which was believed to be caused literally by vapors emanating from swamps and wet places.

Likewise, many ticks, flies, and bugs were seasonal irritants in different localities. Texas, many observers opined, had more than its fair share of creeping, crawling, and winged animalcules, and most of them were thoroughly unpleasant. One could seek to neutralize the pain of stings and bites by the liberal use of calomel, or, even better, one should abandon coastal lowlands in summer and dwell in the hillier, better ventilated uplands where insects were reportedly less abundant. Bollaert complained bitterly about mosquitos feasting on everyone and everything in Galveston in the summer of 1842. They even harrassed him while he bathed in deeper water away from the shore.

Galveston, indeed, was a difficult place to live in during the summer. Except for some respite thanks to mosquito "bars," or gauze curtains, and strong sea breezes, insects plagued the city. Viktor Bracht reported in July, 1847, that mosquito bites disfigured the faces and bloodied the feet and knees of German immigrants newly arrived in the port. He was forced to suspend writing letters on account of these insects; however, in a missive from Galveston dated

[54] Edward, *The History of Texas*, p. 60; and Olmsted, *A Journey through Texas*, pp. 309–10.

July 23, 1847, this pioneer of the New Braunfels colony, a much finer locale with respect to fewer insects, stated, "Heat and mosquitoes, even stinging flies, torment people here beyond measure." He judged that inland ("in the West") there were no mosquitos and that even some places on the lower coast were free of them. But along the upper coast, insects, including "green stinging flies and horse flies," annoyed man and beast in the warmer months.[55]

Bollaert, for the most part, agreed with Bracht's opinion. Headed toward Kennedy's grant in May, Bollaert was "persecuted by mosquitos" near Sealy, but a few days later he mentioned that they were gone from "the muddy part of the country and the *miasma* of the lowlands" (from Columbus westward), except near water. Away from Galveston, his complaints were about ticks and chiggers, "an almost imperceptible bug, that attacks the traveller, covering him with pustules" and making him itch terribly. He was able to bathe in Cibolo Creek "to ward off the poisonous matter of the bugs [chiggers]. My body was in one mass of inflamed pustules." Mosquotos also occurred in San Antonio, although the Englishman mentioned them as "unusual." They annoyed folk because mosquito bars were not used "so far west;" he reported more of them in his travels between the Frio and Nueces rivers (between present-day Pearsal and Uvalde).[56]

In terms of annoyance, therefore, the mosquito ranked high. Prince Solms-Braunfels, who passed eleven months in Texas from July, 1844, lectured compatriots about this "most unbearable of all insects," (which were worse than the snakes). Prince Carl noted, however, that mosquitos were happily absent from the Rolling Prairie country. In addition to "cedar gnats" (whose touch was "fire") and tarantulas (weighing up to "a quarter of a pound each!"), the "musketoe" was also Gideon Lincecum's (1793–1874) chief small adversary, mainly because a person could be enveloped quickly by clouds of mosquitos so thick that "when you withdraw your arm suddenly . . . you may see the hole where it came from"; bites from

[55] Hollon and Butler, eds., *Bollaert's Texas*, p. 124; and Viktor Bracht, *Texas in 1848*, pp. 49, 192–93. Olmsted, *A Journey through Texas*, p. 129, defined "West Texas" as the region west of the Colorado River.

[56] Hollon and Butler, eds., *Bollaert's Texas*, pp. 221, 339, 342, 345–46, 351–357; Kendall, *Southwestern Prairies* 1: 91, complained about the burning itch of "seed ticks."

such hordes were scarcely bearable. Centipedes, ants, scorpions, ticks, hornets, and tarantulas were the devilish creatures whose stings or bites most authorites claimed to be vexatious, even life-threatening. Edward added the housefly to this list and came close to a nonmiasmatic explanation for disease by suggesting that from large populations of flies in early months of the year "we may with certainty calculate that ratio of sickness to be found in the ensuing fall; as putrified substance, impure air, and a warm sun, are at once breeder, feeder and supporter of this troublesome insect." The housefly was the most "prominent" insect for him.[57]

On the distant plains where travellers celebrated so many aspects of the awful and sublime, poor Josiah Gregg experienced the visitation of a small, corporeal creature, literally "awful"—the buffalo gnat. This small black insect attacked exposed parts of the body, luxuriating in places "which one is most careful to guard against intrusion." Bodily parts exposed to the gnat took on the appearance of a "pustulated varioloid," whose name conveys an uncertain form but a grotesque nature.[58]

In addition to cold-blooded reptiles and arthropods which people judged to be harmful, certain warm-blooded mammals proved menacing and troublesome. Wolves; big cats such as cougars, bobcats, and jaguars; feral hogs; and peccaries tended to receive short shrift because they preyed on livestock or at times reportedly threatened settlers and travellers in Texas.

Discussion about the taxonomy and classification of doglike carnivores remains; three species, the timber or gray wolf, the coyote, and the red wolf, occur, with hybridization between the two latter species having led to genetic swamping of the red wolf. However, early writers like William Bollaert identified only two species of wolf: a large black wolf and the prairie wolf. "They are hunted and shot. They destroy young cattle," he noted pithily. Curiously, his mentor, William Kennedy, had little to say about wolves, except that they could be troublesome around the more remote settlements. Others added that these large canids—a large, variously

---

[57] Solms-Braunfels, *Texas*, p. 31; Gideon Lincecum, "Journal of Lincecum's Travels in Texas, 1835," *Southwestern Historical Quarterly* 53 (1949): 194; Edward, *The History of Texas*, p. 88.

[58] Josiah Gregg, *The Commerce of the Prairies*, ed. Milo Milton Quaife, pp. 191–92.

colored one and a smaller, less fierce "prairie" species—devoured pigs and sheep and "by their numbers are still very annoying to inhabitants."[59]

The lobo or "loafer" (*Canis lupus*) was the size of a Newfoundland dog; Smithwick mentioned it as three feet high and six or seven feet long. These animals with shaggy, lionlike manes roamed the brushy area north of Austin in the early 1850s and could drag down a grown milch cow.[60] When cattle operations were established in the southern plains and bison were decimated, the large lobo wolf assumed the image of a yellow-eyed, cold-blooded killer, and it paid the penalty. One author in the mid-1850s noted that ranchers set out poisoned carcasses for wolves, used dogs to track them down, dug into dens, and shot individuals on sight. Frank Dobie declared that one test of a ranch hand's ability was to run down a lobo; however, not many could accomplish this without breaking down their horses. A better way was "to stake out the head of a slaughtered beef, and then with two dry hides, which would stay in any kind of propped position, make, a little off to one side, a tent-shaped blind for concealing a man with a gun."[61]

The coyote, or "prairie wolf," preyed mostly on smaller animals such as sheep, goats, and hogs and was not averse to raiding farms for poultry. Judge Oscar Williams mentioned that hogs turned loose in the Pecos County to forage on mesquite beans and chufas, an edible root, lost piglets to coyotes and bobcats, even near farmsteads. Shepherds in Pecos County poisoned these smaller canids, but their overall numbers remained unchanged. He doubted whether the idea of introducing mange disease would work well.[62]

In the wooded bottoms and coastal prairies was the "black wolf" (red wolf), larger than the coyote and adapted for preying on animals in the brush and forest of East Texas. Old-timers recalled how wolves would kill dogs unless the domesticated canines were tied up for the night.

Vernon Bailey's 1905 report to the U.S. Biological Survey, which

[59] Hollon and Butler, eds., *Bollaert's Texas*, p. 255; Edward, *The History of Texas*, p. 74; [Lawrence], *Texas in 1840*, p. 191.

[60] Smithwick, *Evolution of a State*, pp. 289, 291.

[61] John C. Reid, *Reid's Tramp*, p. 58; Dobie, *The Flavor of Texas*, p. 120; and J. Frank Dobie, *The Longhorns*, p. 234.

[62] Williams, *Animal Life in Pecos County*, p. 39.

promoted research into the economic relationships of mammals and birds to agriculture and assisted in the conservation of useful and beneficial wild animals after 1900, complained that canids were not scarce enough. The big lobo "is still common over most of the plains and mountain country of western Texas, mainly west of the one hundredth meridian," noted this government researcher. Ranchers reported them as abundant in the Davis and Guadalupe mountains, the Staked Plains, and east of the Pecos River, despite bounties of as much as fifty dollars per animal and the activities of professional wolf hunters. Some unscrupulous persons took advantage of monetary rewards by saving females with pups or by importing and releasing animals. The wolf known as Big Foot, whose track was recognized by an enlarged right paw, prowled unscathed in the Monahans area for many years about 1902, refusing to consume poisoned baits and eluding all trackers, who were eager to make seventy-five dollars on its head.

Twenty years later, largely through a campaign of trapping and poisonings by government personnel that was initiated in 1915, the larger grey wolf had been cleared from much of the Pecos River valley, and it was disappearing quickly from the larger cattle ranches. On the southern Edwards Plateau both the smaller red wolf and the coyote proved more difficult to exterminate, and sheep and goat raisers backed a coordinated program for extermination, claiming that flock losses averaged some 10 percent annually.

The "black wolf," as the red wolf was called, was beginning to fade away in the early 1900s, and a bounty of ten or twenty dollars per animal because of its depradations on colts, sheep, and goats appeared effective. However, Bailey noted that the coyote was holding its own "in spite of the enmity of man, in spite of traps, poison, gun, and dogs." This sheep killer was known to supplement its diet with rodents and jackrabbits in the desert country of the Pecos Valley and the brushlands of the Rio Grande Valley as well as throughout the mid-sections of the Hill Country. This varied diet did not save it from prolonged efforts of trapping and poisoning.[63]

The doglike carnivores had unenviable reputations as killers of stock, but generally humans had little to fear from them. Cowhands even crawled into dens along the Caprock and elsewhere on the

[63] Bailey, "Biological Survey of Texas."

plains to shoot female wolves and pups. One threat to a human occurred, however, when William J. Wilson, on a cattle drive to New Mexico in 1867 with Oliver Loving, managed to escape from an Indian attack along the Pecos by floating down and across the river under cover of darkness after Loving had been mortally wounded. After a three-day march he was finally picked up by Charles Goodnight and the trail hands. Wilson remembered that, on his third night in the cactus-filled country, several wolves had trailed him, awaiting his final collapse. Awakening from short cat-naps, "I would take up that stick [part of a tepee pole he had found], knock the wolves away, get started again and the wolves would fol-low behind," said Wilson, who was forced to trudge barefooted through the desert scrub. The carnivores left him at daylight after he found a shallow cave, where the trail hands discovered him. The tough Wilson had no doubt that the wolves intended to consume him.[64]

There was a common belief that if wolves did not openly attack people, they would challenge them for food, and anyone incapaci-tated was exposed dangerously to these camp scavengers. One case of such danger supposedly occurred between Lockhart and Austin, where James W. Nichols noted that "fifty to five hundred" famished canids were attracted by bison meat in his camp. Nichols's group killed twenty or thirty wolves and wounded many more as the beasts entered the campfire's circle of light in order to snatch meat from the nearby wagon; the wolves finally retreated. Next morning, Nichols claimed that he and his companions finished off the maimed animals before striking camp and continuing to Austin.[65]

Plains cattlemen, who were joined by sheep and goat raisers, waged a fierce and lasting war of attrition against wolves and coy-otes. From the 1870s both types of animal were the target of local poisoning, trapping, and hunting pressures, especially in West Texas, where a big lobo would unhesitatingly attack a yearling and even grown cows. As late as 1908, the larger, more destructive lobo wolf was still encountered in the Pecos country. Williams judged that these wolves had moved in with the arrival of cattle because bison

[64] W. J. Wilson, "W. J. Wilson's Narrative," in *The Trail Drivers of Texas*, ed. J. M. Hunter, p. 912.

[65] Catherine W. McDowell, ed., *Now You Hear My Horn: The Journal of James Wilson Nichols, 1820–1887*, pp. 44–46.

had never been abundant. One pack in Pecos County, ranging about thirty miles above Sheffield, reportedly subsisted off cattle introduced in the mid-1880s. Poisoning was effective, but old lobos grew wary of baits, so certain animals had sizable bounties placed on them, as they were so destructive to calves. Commissioner's court records for Borden County at the headwaters of the Colorado River show bounties in 1891 of 3½ cents for prairie dogs, 8⅓ cents for jackrabbits, $1.00 for bobcats, $2.50 for "coyote wolves," and $5.00 for lobos.[66] "Wolfers" could make good money controlling these canines, and authors have considered them to have been the most effective destroyers of these wily predators.

Texas had the bragging rights to be "first" in the kinds of wild cats (six species) existing within its borders. Naturally, the distinction was a dubious one for early settlers, and, as was the case with wolves, the ranchers and farmers made efforts to destroy and eliminate the felines, especially cougars. William Bollaert summed up common beliefs about the cougar, or, as people called it, the panther: "Panther: or American lion is generally met with in the river "bottoms" or in the cane breaks [sic] and peach thickets on the margins of rivers. He is hunted with dogs and brought down with the rifle. The skin is valuable."[67]

Panthers could be unpredictable, and a wounded animal made a formidable enemy. E. L. Deaton was attacked by a cougar: "It was then he lunged at me, but another shot hit him in the neck. Yet, again he came." The lion may or may not have been stalking him, although such purple prose heightens the encounter. Cougars, or mountain lions, are shy by nature and nocturnal in movements; therefore, the cat's nightly screamings or an unusual restlessness among draft animals or stock were frequently the only signs of the big cat's presence. To stumble across a large animal weighing up to 180 pounds, as did the youngster August Santleben one foggy morning as he was searching for his oxen, was an extremely frightening experience. The boy was startled suddenly to find in his path a panther devouring a calf. Santleben backed away slowly, "but a spell of fascination crept over me which kept my eyes fixed on him."

[66] J. A. Rickard, "Hazards of Ranching on the South Plains," Southwestern Historical Quarterly 32 (1934): 318; Williams, Animal Life in Pecos County, pp. 47–48.

[67] Hollon and Butler, eds., Bollaert's Texas, p. 254.

Turning from the sight, the boy ran for home but stepped on a rattlesnake in his panic. He leaped into the air to escape being bitten. "The accident caused my fear of the panther to subside and reduced my gait to a walk."[68]

One didn't fool with the larger, more powerful predatory cat, the jaguar. Restricted to dense brush and timberlands of the Rio Grande Valley and coastal Texas, *el tigre*, as the Mexicans called it, was relatively rare in the Lone Star State. Shy and retiring, like the cougar, the jaguar was a dangerous killer. However, in 1945, William B. Davis, an authority on Texas mammals, could authenticate only two records of jaguars being killed in Texas after 1900—one being killed near Benida in 1946. Before then, Bollaert (about 1843) stated cryptically: "Leopard (spotted) the *Jagua*: Its habits and manner of taking same as the panther. Skin is valuable." Bracht was more explicit: "The cat family is represented in Texas by the beautifully spotted American tiger, or jaguar. It is found only in the western part of the country, especially between the Medina and the Rio Grande. This animal is very destructive to domestic hogs and red deer, and when harrassed would probably attack man. It is very rarely found, and its fur is very valuable."[69]

In his *Campaign Sketches of the War with Mexico*, Captain W. S. Henry recalled that a colleague hunting coons on the Bernard River found that his dogs had treed a large animal in a huge live oak. He climbed the tree and found "an immense spotted tiger," so swinging himself under a limb, he allowed the jaguar to walk over him and down the tree; it moved "through a crowd of nine dogs, as fierce as there were in Texas who never growled at him."[70] The officer was fortunate to extricate himself from his tight spot.

In 1880, Cope noted that the jaguar still persisted. It was "not rare on the Nueces River, especially in the extensive thickets along

---

[68] E. L. Deaton, "An Adventure in West Texas," in O. A. Hanscom, *Parade of the Pioneers*, p. 216; Duval, *Early Times in Texas*, pp. 70–71, mentions an instance of an unprovoked attack by a cougar; August Santleben, *A Texas Pioneer*, p. 10.

[69] William B. Davis, "Texas Cats," *Texas Game and Fish* 3 (1945): 21–22; William B. Davis, "The Mammals of Texas," *Texas Parks and Wildlife Department Bulletin* 41 (1974, revised): 130–31; Charles G. Jones, "A South Texas Big Game Hunt," *Texas Game and Fish* 4 (1946): 29, 32; Hollon and Butler, eds., *Bollaert's Texas*, p. 254; Bracht, *Texas in 1848*, pp. 43–44.

[70] W. S. Henry, *Campaign Sketches of the War with Mexico*, p. 42.

the southern part of its course." He estimated that it ranged to the Guadalupe River but was unusual north of San Antonio, where skins from the Nueces were sold.[71] In 1905, Bailey pushed the jaguar's range east to Louisiana and north to the Red River but judged it to be extremely rare. He cited four or five reports of jaguars being killed during the final thirty years of the nineteenth century. The famous "Goldthwaite" (in Mills County) animal was slaughtered on September 3, 1903, after mortally savaging a horse, killing or wounding several dogs, and being hunted by ten or twelve well-armed men.[72]

North America's only native wild pig, the collared peccary, javelina, or Mexican hog, which ranged through the brush and canyon lands of the Southwest, proved to be a feisty animal, and a menacing one when wounded or at bay. It was the smallest cloven-hoofed mammal or artiodactyl in Texas, but an early author considered it "a most furious untameable animal, dangerous to encounter, unless your weapons be sharp and sure."[73] Legend surrounding the Mexican hog has made it out to be a ferocious aggressor that made unprovoked attacks on residents. Poor Ann Coleman passed one of her first nights in Texas on the banks of the lower Brazos en route to Brazoria suffering from the mosquitos and listening to the leaping alligators (for which "I would be a dainty morsel") and shrieking panthers. Later, on the way to the home of a friend, they came across peccaries. Her friend, a Mrs. Atkinson, took to her heels; however, Coleman stayed to observe the pigs, "when presently one or two bristled up at me, gnashed their tusks which were very long and large, and came after me." She soon outraced her terrified, corpulent colleague, about whom a physician declared, "Her heart was injured by the fat melting over it" after the incident. Coleman went on to explain that Mrs. Atkinson was "very fleshy, weighed about two hundred and was only twenty years of age." The peccaries touched neither of these women.[74]

[71] Edward D. Cope, *On the Zoological Position of Texas*, pp. 8–9.

[72] Bailey, "Biological Survey of Texas," pp. 163–66.

[73] Joseph E. Field, *Three Years in Texas*, pp. 47–48. James H. Cook, *Fifty Years on the Old Frontier*, p. 27, reported an old Texan's term for javelinas: "a ball of hair with a butcher knife run through it." Ikin, *Texas*, p. 42, noted their ferociousness.

[74] C. Richard King, ed., *Victorian Lady on the Texas Frontier: The Journal of Ann Raney Coleman*, pp. 22–23, 64–67.

Mary Ann Holley contributed additional information about the "menacing" peccary. Occurring in gangs, they "will boldly attack a man, and are considered more dangerous than any other wild animal in Texas," Holley stated, adding that the "wild hog," a descendant of domestic swine, also became a ferocious and formidable animal when provoked.[75] Pigs were not to be trusted and were given a wide berth except by hunters and sportsmen.

Immigrant literature was more measured in judgments about peccaries and hogs. The young animals made suitable, affectionate pets. However, the squeals of a wounded peccary induced others to rush to its aid, so "it behooves man or beast speedily to escape by flight or climbing a tree." This is what James Nichols claimed that he was compelled to do on one occasion in 1846 in South Texas (near Los Olmos Creek, south of Kingsville), where he shot into a band of foraging peccaries. The wounded animal was killed by other peccaries, which then set upon Nichols, "poping their teeth, their haire turned the rong way, makeing a turable grunting, squeeling, or howling nois." He climbed a mesquite tree, which the animals surrounded and began to gnaw down. Only the arrival of twenty sharp-shooting men put the animals to flight and saved Nichols from an untimely death: the tree was cut "two-thirds through!"[76]

Undoubtedly, such exciting tales were fabricated or at least exaggerated; however, both wild hogs and native peccaries could be dangerous. They killed hounds (as did bears), and it required excellent marksmanship to bring them down. These swine proved agile and hardy and were able to inflict terrible wounds with their tusks and teeth. Principally because they were challenging targets and provided meat, sportsmen enjoyed tracking and killing them. Hogs were most menacing to persons, like Nichols, who were out on hunting forays (and who needed good tales for evening conversation).

Texas' long list of more than 150 native mammals, almost four times that number of birds, and numerous reptiles and invertebrates grew as natural scientists collected and cataloged them. The larger, conspicuous mammals and birds were well known to resi-

[75] Holley, *Texas*, pp. 95–96.
[76] [Lawrence], *Texas in 1840*, pp. 185–86; McDowell, ed., *Now You Hear My Horn*, pp. 131–33. Santleben, *A Texas Pioneer*, p. 11, mentions being treed by a herd of javelinas after a companion shot at them.

dents who valued them for material reasons or who feared them because these creatures killed or threatened livestock. Often, however, the appearance, movements, colors, songs, and calls of native wildlife attracted the attention of persons who liked, for example, the early morning chorus of the Texas nightingale—the mockingbird—so much as to declare it the state bird. Such animals attracted attention because they were interesting or unusual and part of the mystery and challenge of the frontier.

Settlers recalled encounters with strange or dangerous animals such as predators and bears. They explained how they had driven them off their crops or from their pastures, how neighbors had assisted, and how their hounds had pursued them. Such tales about wild animals were part of daily life, like the vagaries of weather, and most folk accepted and dealt with them. Frequent stories were told about the best places to hunt and about the ways of getting good results, so newcomers learned quickly about the useful, strange, and beautiful animals that helped to make Texas unique.

CHAPTER 3

Wildlife for Recreation

THE abundance of wild animals such as deer, antelope, waterfowl, prairie chickens, and other species that associated in numbers interested many early Texans. Some were astonished by the animals' sheer abundance and took it to be a sign of nature's bounty and a fertile environment. Others had seen such huge numbers before, perhaps in Louisiana or further east, so they viewed skies blackened by water birds or clearings dotted with deer as commonplace. Nearly everybody, however, loved to hunt these birds and mammals; most residents would have forgiven Bracht's boast about Texas abounding in game animals "beyond any other country in the world."[1] There was much fun, indeed, in this "make-do" early life, where wildlife existed for the taking, and one of the major pleasures was setting out, alone or with friends, for a day's shooting. A string of ducks or a choice buck to show for the outing made this kind of recreation extremely gratifying: some of the birds could be dressed for the evening meal or given to the neighbors as a favor or bartered.

Hunting, therefore, like free land, was one of the lures of the frontier, making it an attractive place to be. Such field craft satisfied more than immediate, material needs; it promoted camaraderie and solidified community ties and the bonds between young and old. Elders instructed youngsters in the techniques of woodcraft. By accompanying older kin or friends into the wilderness, young people learned about the movements and habits of mammals and birds, and they grew skillful in handling dogs and using traps, firearms, and other weapons. John H. Jenkins (1822–90), for example, remembers that as a boy, "I could imitate every sound one ever hears upon the broad plains or in the dense forest." Wolves investigated

[1] Viktor Bracht, *Texas in 1848*, p. 41.

his howling and turkeys his gobbling; owls answered his hoots; his "squall of a young bear" attracted any adults in the vicinity. Boyhood life in the woods was free, and Jenkins, like thousands of other youths in his day, was fascinated by outdoor experiences. He would join a gang of people in June or early July with provisions for several days and set out for "venison, honey, and 'fun,' and it was seldom, if ever, that we failed."[2]

By learning about animals and hunting them, youngsters like Jenkins expanded their geographical knowledge of home and hinterland. Field sports were also useful, exciting ways of relieving the monotony and drudgery of rural life. Frontier residents were expected to be able to ride a horse, to handle a gun, and to cope with the isolation, sudden changes in weather, and aches and fevers that characterized surviving in Texas. The variety and abundance of native plants and animals across a spectrum of environments served as magnets for many foreign-born travellers and immigrants who took up residence in the state. These folk and others entered Texas to experience for themselves "the frontier"—which meant having to identify and secure different animals. They had to develop the qualities of the "hunter," who was skilled in woodcraft; they also assumed characteristics of the "sportsman," who savored the act of killing and received credit for the accurate shot and its resulting spoils. These outdoor pastimes consumed available leisure time and were occasions for enjoyment as well as profit.[3]

In November, 1831, William Dewees penned a letter from the Colorado River that summed up the use of free time in such "an excellent country for game and fish." He devoted many hours to the pleasures of hunting, describing parties of men, women, and children that with a few provisions would set out on expeditions lasting several days. "These excursions are very pleasant," noted DeWees, "as we are able to find plenty of honey, kill game, catch fish, and amuse ourselves in looking at our beautiful country."[4] Tracking foraging wild bees back to their homes in trees was a major source of enjoyment (for the honey they provided) and a test of skill. Settlers

[2]John Holmes Jenkins, ed., *Recollections of Early Texas: The Memoirs of John Holland Jenkins*, pp. 200–201.

[3]Frank Wilden [Captain Flack], *A Hunter's Experiences in the Southern States of America*, p. 10.

[4]William B. Dewees, *Letters from an Early Settler of Texas*, p. 137.

acquired reputations for understanding the subtle ways of these introduced but wild insects, which were widely distributed throughout Texas by the period of Anglo-American settlement. A commonly held and often-repeated opinion referred to the honeybee as a precursor of civilization; reportedly Indians regarded the bee as a sign of the coming of the white man.

An ability for locating bee trees was a source of pride, as it enabled local residents to demonstrate their woodcraft and provide honey for the home. John H. Jenkins's assertion, "I never saw a man who could beat me coursing bees," demonstrated this keen competition. Foreign explorer and scientist Berlandier, when presented with a honeycomb along the Medina River in June, 1834, noted admiringly, "The people of the countryside have the ability to follow, on horseback, a single bee flitting from flower to flower, until they find the hive where it collects its honey"; "lining" bees, as it was called, was a widespread practice.[5]

Noah Smithwick's first meal in Texas was "dried venison sopped in honey." The customary method of combining these nutritious foods was to dunk a strip of venison into a honey bowl, take a mouthful, hold the meat between the teeth with the left hand, and saw off the piece with a hunting knife held in the right. Smithwick found that the boredom of life in DeWitt's Colony was relieved by the excitement of finding and cutting into bee trees and of killing the game that was "plenty the year round." However, life in the rough log cabins was drab, uncomfortable, and tedious for the women, with "nothing to break the dull monotony of their lives, save an occasional wrangle with the children and dogs." Smithwick agreed with one old woman's sentiments that Texas was "a heaven for men and dogs, but a hell for women and oxen."[6]

In San Felipe, Smithwick used to make excursions with tinner Bob Matthews to see which of them could bag more game. "Our favorite sport was picking the squirrels from the tall pecan trees in the river [Brazos] bottom." He and other settlers would also gather for shooting contests and make wagers for marksmanship. In 1861, on the trail to California, Smithwick scolded the "boys" in an emi-

[5] Jenkins, *Recollections*, p. 200; Jean L. Berlandier, *Journey to Mexico During the Years 1826 to 1834*, trans. Sheila M. Ohlendorf, 2: 559.

[6] Noah Smithwick, *The Evolution of a State: Recollections of Old Texas Days*, pp. 13–16.

grant party for "emptying their revolvers at everything and nothing, just for the fun of shooting. Many pounds of lead were thrown away in the vain attempt to kill a prairie dog." So keen was everyone to fire their weapons in the small thirty-five-man party that, if Comanches had shown up, most firearms would have been empty.[7]

In the same backcountry a generation earlier, George Kendall noted how plains travellers invariably shot at prairie dogs as they passed through the rodents' "towns." The urge to test one's skill by hitting these small but vocal herbivores was irresistible. In Kendall's case, the discovery of this "commonwealth" of prairie dogs held out the promise of meat. He and others in the Santa Fe Expedition shot as many of the "wild, frolicsome, madcap set of fellows" as possible. Unfortunately, many wounded animals dragged themselves into burrows and escaped. Kendall was filled with remorse after seeing a prairie dog drag a dead companion away: "There was a touch of feeling in the little incident—a something human . . . I did not attempt to kill one of them, except when driven by extreme hunger."[8] His colleagues continued to shoot, however, and the rodents furnished important food to the expedition in late August, 1841.

Josiah Gregg later referred to Kendall's narrative about prairie dogs and included it with details about his journey westward along the North Fork of the Canadian River. Gregg's party shot impulsively at the first prairie dogs they encountered; then he was astonished by the aim of a young Comanche, who was able to curve an arrow into a partially concealed "dog" that sat yelping some forty or fifty paces away. This seasoned trader also described how "buffalo fever" infected companions unused to the sight of the huge animals. People careered after the lumbering beasts; even the wagon drivers, "carried away by the contagious excitement of the movement, would leave the teams and keep up a running fire after them." When "all is as level as the sea, and the compass was our surest, as well as principal guide," any animal on the horizon became the occasion and excuse for an exhilarating chase in order to break the monotony of travel.[9]

[7] Ibid., pp. 78, 336.
[8] George Wilkins Kendall, *Across the Great Southwestern Prairies* 1: 201–207.
[9] Josiah Gregg, *The Commerce of the Prairies*, pp. 59, 187–88, 200–201.

The urge to improve skill, to test marksmanship, and to compete for coveted trophies by bagging big game was taken to an extreme by officials, foreign dignitaries, and aristocrats who journeyed through the bison-filled country of the High Plains, including Texas, in search of sport and adventure. From 1832, when Washington Irving hunted buffalo in central Oklahoma with Indian Commissioner, Henry L. Ellsworth, to about 1872, when the Grand Duke Alexis, son of Czar Alexander II, with an entourage of illustrious names such as General Phil Sheridan, Colonel George A. Custer, and William F. Cody, shot down these beasts along the North Platte River and in the Colorado Mountains, a number of high-placed American officials, British gentry, and other well-connected persons took a toll of big game. In 1868, the Union Pacific Railroad ran summer excursions across Kansas and Nebraska for hunters.

An insight into this practice of killing for pleasure comes from military officer Richard Irving Dodge, who travelled with three English gentlemen to Fort Dodge in October, 1872. Dodge admired his cavalry escort's dash and verve in using pistols to kill as many bison calves as possible in a short run. Ten minutes of flurry and noise were sufficient to unleash in his companions "all the English love of sport, and long before the game was disembowelled and put in the waggons my three friends were off, each for himself, in rapid pursuit of some of the numerous herds." Dodge assured his readers that great sport was to be found southeast of the fort on the tributaries of the Cimarron, where in October, 1872, he and five companions (three were "English gentlemen") bagged 1,262 mammals, reptiles, and birds, including "1 blue bird, for his sweetheart's hat." A year later in the same area Dodge and four men killed another 1,141 animals.[10]

This wanton killing was not the prerogative of elites, although better-equipped nimrods had the money and means to make large kills; it was commonplace in newly settled areas of the West, including Texas. William Bollaert enjoyed hunting in Texas and provided well-heeled readers with suggestions and instructions about dress and decorum in the outdoors. A tanned hunting shirt with leggings or trousers, which were to be replaced by apparel made

[10] Richard I. Dodge, *The Hunting Grounds of the Great West*, pp. 61, 118; Wayne Gard, *The Great Buffalo Hunt*.

from cotton in summer and from flannel in winter, made up the sportsman's habit. A rifle, bowie knife, and pistols were preferred weapons, as was a dark horse (in Indian country), which should be tethered especially close to camp at night. The hunter should use his saddle as a pillow and keep the bridle near his head, said Bollaert, so that he could mount his horse quickly in an emergency. He admonished every hunter to place his rifle and pistols beneath a blanket in wet weather. At night a guard should be posted for one- or two-hour shifts, and nodoby must ever discharge a gun or hunt in the dark. Finally, a hunter should "put fire out after cooking."[11]

Bollaert's advice was based on experience from several hunting excursions and from the sage example of Tom Hancock, famous Texas woodsman, who acted as this Englishman's guide in a journey to the Kennedy Grant in South Texas. Hancock had a remarkable life. As a boy he was taken captive by Winnebago Indians and was returned "wild" to his kin so that he had had difficulty in learning English. He came to Texas after the battle of San Jacinto, was captured by Comanches but escaped, accompanied the Santa Fe expedition, and was released finally in Mexico City in 1842. After many hardships, Hancock returned to San Antonio, where Bollaert hired him as guide and hunter on May 29, 1844. Hancock steered Bollaert's eight-man party through the remote country between the Frio and Nueces rivers for about a month. Bollaert, who admired and respected the skills of this quiet, modest, truthful man, judged that Hancock's days were numbered. The small man had contracted a severe bout of "consumptive fever" in Mexico and admitted that he was "used up" at the age of twenty-three.[12]

Kendall's description of Tom Hancock before his captivity in Mexico reveals a true "leather stocking." Hancock had been hired by another Englishman, Thomas Falconer (who possibly recommended him to Bollaert), in San Antonio in the spring of 1841 to accompany him on the Santa Fe Expedition. Falconer and Kendall owed much to this man's talents. Hancock's eye missed nothing; his spare, loose frame became taut and his body became a "wiry, knotty embodiment of action" when he caught a hint of something strange or unusual in the landscape. Kendall admitted that he owed his life

[11]W. Eugene Hollon and Ruth L. Butler, eds., *William Bollaert's Texas*, pp. 246–47.
[12]Ibid., pp. 372–73.

to Hancock, whom no Indians could outmaneuver nor any wild animals surprise. Hancock was a laconic person, neither boastful nor ostentatious, who carried a long, heavy flintlock rifle of simple but solid workmanship. He could hunt, fish, and line bees superbly and understood the ways of the Indians and Mexicans as no other person of his day.[13]

Travellers like Bollaert, Falconer, and Kendall (who became a Texas resident) drew upon the expertise of guides and local woodsmen for their hunting excursions. These natives often gathered together, as Dewees suggested, to engage in exciting sport. Much of the booty they obtained was materially useful, and outdoorsmen were able to coordinate movements and adopt tactics necessary to make substantial kills of preferred species. Many settlers kept and trained dogs to chase after deer or wolves and to "tree" raccoons, bears, and cougars. Some used hounds to follow foxes and even caught, relocated, and released these animals in order to maximize sport. All agreed that Texas provided health for the invalid, interesting sights for the tourist, and "unsurpassed hunting grounds for the sportsman." Frank Wilden, an Englishman who became a professional hunter known as Captain Flack, wrote articles and books about his hunting exploits over a twenty-year period (from the time of the republic through early statehood). Flack used the theme "Texas Prairies as the Hunter's Paradise" to interest British readers in the state's geography and biota.

This Rolling Prairie area appeared to Matilda Houstoun's educated eye as a "finely-kept English park, where the landscape gardeners and studiers of the picturesque had expended their utmost skill in beautifying the scenery." It was like parts of Windsor Park, she declared. According to Captain Flack, it was a wilderness filled with wild cattle, feral swine, bears, panthers, alligators, and other unpleasant creatures. He wished to subjugate them (thereby making Texas as secure as Windsor Park). Promotional literature picked up this theme of hunting for adventure and sport. Advice about weapons and information about the most appropriate and entertaining methods for killing specific animals filled books and journals.[14]

After crossing the Sabine at Gaines Ferry, the Olmsted broth-

[13] Kendall, *Southwestern Prairies* 1: 55–56.

[14] Pacific Railroad Company, *Texas Statistics and Information*, p. 25; Frank Wilden [Captain Flack], *The Texas Rifle-Hunter*, p. viii; and Matilda Charlotte Fraser Houstoun, *Texas and the Gulf of Mexico; or Yachting in the New World*, p. 226.

ers passed their first night in Texas listening to "huntsman's stories of snakes, game, and crack shots."[15] Their host proudly displayed an old Kentucky rifle and proved a formidable shot with it. Frederick and John Olmsted had taken the trouble of selecting for their journey into Texas a Sharps rifle, a double fowling piece, some Colt revolvers, and several hunting knives, and they advocated these weapons for others.

Both men learned about the consuming interest in all kinds of hunting, which provided meat for the table and amusement. But they remained unimpressed by East Texas, and they stated condescendingly, "We did not see one of the inhabitants look into a newspaper or a book." The brothers' patronizing attitudes toward life in the South, particularly the social conditions and hard circumstances of resident Texans, are well known. They preferred the lot of the thrifty, hard-working German stock to the "lazy poverty of East Texas." In their opinion, a Southerner was more willing to stick a hog than shoot a buck, and relied on coffee and corn pone when game was plentiful. There were exceptions, however, to the dim view they took of hospitality and accommodations. When they asked for a little venison near Centerville, "the man cut off a whole haunch," said Frederick, and charged merely twenty-five cents.[16]

Part of the problem was that the Olmsted brothers were unused initially to living rough. Coping with free-running hogs, quirks of their draft animals, dangerous river crossings, alligator holes, and "northers" made the landscape and its inhabitants seem niggardly and abject. They were much better able to cope with novel surroundings by the time they reached the Brazos River and entered more open country. Many conversations with settlers in the none too wholesome (but improving) lodgings between the Sabine and Colorado rivers were about firearms and hunting. They shot several quail in Leon County, where the species occurred abundantly. Residents around Nacogdoches and to the east netted these birds; they also shot turkeys as they lured them from roosting trees by mimicking the calls of the fat birds. A common practice was to shoot squirrels for the pot and to use hounds to drive deer past another man's stand. These animals provided most of the sport.[17]

[15] Frederick Law Olmsted, *A Journey through Texas, Or, A Saddle-Trip on the Southwestern Frontier*, pp. 65, 73–74.

[16] Frederick Law Olmsted, *Cotton Kingdom*, pp. 301, 304–305.

[17] Richard W. Haltom, *The History of Nacogdoches County, Texas*, pp. 54–55.

White-tailed deer provided both meat and fun, especially in the coastal and rolling country of Texas. Settlers enjoyed "fire hunting" or "night lighting" them; that is, a hunter carried a fire pan (a frying pan fitted with a long handle), which was filled with combustible cottonseed, tar, or pitch-pine knots, about three feet behind his left shoulder. On a dark, damp, and calm night the hunter and a companion would set out with a favorite dog with a muffled bell on its neck so that they could follow as the hound tracked a wounded animal's scent. They walked slowly into a brushy area until the light from the fire pan caught the eyes of an animal. In the reflected glare, a deer's eyes appeared bigger, more brilliant, and wider apart than those of other species. Wolves and bears tended to look about, not stare at the fire; a colt's eyes were not as bright. Experienced hunters could bag ten or more deer in an hour or two; they would place a flag beside each carcass to alarm scavengers and to help relocate dead animals the following morning.

Many outdoorsmen found night-hunting to be an entertaining but dangerous pastime, for they knew many stories about people being killed or injured because hunters had mistaken them for a deer. Purists like Flack condemned fire-lighting as "a cowardly, treacherous method of killing deer," to be resorted to only when venison was scarce. However, this avid hunter admitted that he had made many excursions with the fire pan. Hounds notably greyhounds, could outdistance and pull down grown deer, but the commotion they caused frightened game. "Still" shooting, that is, selecting a stand for an early-morning wait, was Flack's preferred method of killing deer, and it was least disturbing to other animals. A hunter could also position himself near a salt lick or drinking place and ambush deer. Sometimes horsemen would jump them from places of concealment in thickets or from spots in the prairie where the animals rested up during daylight.

On the frontier a man had to learn the easiest and quickest way to obtain meat. At the same time he could derive entertainment and pleasure from this enterprise and also felt duty-bound to rid the countryside (thereby assisting his neighbors) of noxious panthers and wolves. These activities against more dangerous species were undertaken for adventure and for good-natured competition. Friends or neighbors tested each other's familiarity, knowledge, and understanding of favorite quarry; they also endeavored to outwit prey by anticipating its movements. Running hounds after deer, bear, raccoons, and felines was part of this endeavor, and Texas became "a land of dogs and dog stories." Although strangers believed they were an ill-bred, shiftless, and flea-ridden lot, good dogs were courageous, dependable, sometimes resourceful companions, and many woodsmen took pains to select good-looking puppies. Even rough, callous characters had respect and affection for their dogs, and many became well known for fine, well-trained hounds. "Ben K.," whom Flack befriended on Caney Creek in Matagorda County, developed a habit of repeatedly instructing companions "about the parentage, birth, education, and exploits of each of his hounds" (he had more than twenty-five!), so friends grew weary of the fellow's "dog-worship." Dog owners like Ben K. customarily schooled individual, usually cross-bred, hounds to chase specific game or predatory animals, so the appropriate dog was made the pack leader for bears, panthers, or other quarry.[18]

Living near Webberville, east of Austin, always-adventurous Noah Smithwick enjoyed "rare sport" by chasing black bears with his pack of dogs. Bears were his specialty in that cedar-brake country because they were the biggest game: "the Indians were gone and likewise the buffalo." When his dogs brought the bear to bay, Smithwick usually shot it; however, if the dogs pressed too close, he was forced to kill it with a knife. Often his pack put up a panther, which was easy to shoot when cornered. Peccaries, however, were another matter. They could cut up and inflict terrible wounds on his animals before he had a chance to call the dogs off, so he avoided these bands of vicious swine with their razor-sharp teeth.[19]

Another old-timer living in the same area was John H. Jenkins, who showed similar affection for his dogs. Watch, the best of five bear dogs, was deadly at tracking bruins in Hornsby's Bend (south of Austin) and in the Eblin Bottom (twelve miles below Bastrop). Jenkins claimed, "When Watch was in sight I could tell even on a cold trail the size of the bear they were after." This dog would stick to a bear's trail through any terrain for hours, crossing streams and rivers in all weathers; he gave his master the pleasure of shooting many bears. Jenkins recalled that sometimes on freezing nights Watch would come to his bedside and beg his master to go out hunting.[20]

[18] John E. Baur, *Dogs on the Frontier*, p. 119; and Wilden, *Texas Rifle-Hunter*, pp. 67–72.
[19] Smithwick, *Evolution of a State*, pp. 308–309.
[20] Jenkins, *Recollections*, p. 234.

Tracking the big cats and doglike predators was dangerous, and dogs were vulnerable to poisoned meat set out for lobos. These carnivores were hunted because they raided the hog pen and poultry yard or killed calves and colts. Hunting them was also a test of skill, courage, stamina, and a dog's ability to follow a scent well. Jenkins's friend, Colonel Abraham Wiley Hill, showed reckless courage (and attained notoriety for it) by combating at very close quarters a cougar and a bear; both would maul dogs without hesitation. One night he stabbed a previously wounded and thus very dangerous cougar after crawling after it into a dense patch of cedar. Hill ended a bear's days by knocking it out of a tree by pelting it with rocks, as he had no gun.

Black bears, noted prizes of the Indians, were hunted in most wooded areas of Texas. The only authenticated record of the fearsome grizzly bear, however, comes from a spot in the Davis Mountains about fifteen miles southwest of present-day McDonald Observatory. There two hunters shot one in November, 1890. In the early 1890s several families, numbering forty to seventy-five persons, gathered together annually for a week's sport. Horses, dogs, children, tents, equipment, and wagons made up these caravans, and each day members of all ages set out to hunt, invariably bagging three or four bears. C. O. Finley, whose family pioneered settlement in the Davis Mountains about 1885, recalled that "every day or so some one would get lost from the bear chase, and kill a deer or two. While this was all good sport, especially if you got in the chase and got to the killing of the bear . . . it was awfully hard on the horses and men who rode hard and reckless in the rough country to follow and keep up with the hounds." On the fifth day of the 1890 Davis Mountain hunt, Finley and John Z. Means caught up with and killed the only grizzly bear recorded from Texas. It was a large and very old silvertip male, which had seized and partially fed off a cow, and it weighed approximately eleven hundred pounds. The dogs tracked the enormous bruin, albeit reluctantly (the bear savaged one), for about five miles through very rough country. After the two men shot it, four men were reportedly needed to lift the skin, complete with head and feet, onto a pack horse for the journey back to camp.[21]

[21] J. G. Burr, "A Texas Grizzly Hunt," *Texas Game and Fish* 6 (1948): 4–5, 16; Vernon Bailey, "Biological Survey of Texas," *North American Fauna* 25 (1905): 192.

Olmsted presented another adventure with bears, though not grizzlies, from west of New Braunfels (between the Cibolo and Medina rivers): "While in the mountains, the Settlers told us, with fresh excitement, the story of a great bear-hunt, which had but recently come off. The hero was one of the German hermits, named P———, a famous sportsman." Mr. P. had been mauled once by a wounded bear but had stabbed it to death. On the occasion described by Olmsted, this doughty hunter had discovered a bear's den in a long, narrow cave. After crawling into it several times in order to combat the inmates, Mr. P. had succeeded in killing one bruin after another. "Imagine the cheers, when the *five bears* were carried by his neighbors, on poles, into the settlement," said Olmsted admiringly. Mr. P. entered the community "striding modestly at the rear" of the trophy-bearing procession, and a three-day feast was declared. Olmsted concluded that his name would "live long in local tradition."[22] This "world of bears" in the Hill Country west of New Braunfels furnished provisions and, importantly, status for certain foolhardy pioneers. The exploits of this hunter and others made it certain that the wilderness could be conquered.

A more recent reference to bear hunting, "the hardest work a man ever did on earth," comes from the forests between Kountze and Sour Lake in the southeast Big Thicket where Carter Hart (1889–1973), a well-known bear hunter, lived for the sport of tracking down East Texas bruins. Hart, a long-time resident of Hardin County, knew all about the habits of bears, and about killing and feasting on them. He found, too, that cubs "aren't hard to tame and you can just feed 'em scraps like you would a puppy." Bears were finished off, however, in the lower Big Thicket by 1910, so Hart and companions only hunted when local residents notified him of occasional bears. While it lasted, bear hunting "was the greatest sport on earth."[23]

Like bears, cougars or mountain lions proved to be tough, wily loners and in some instances were prepared to stand and fight when threatened, cornered, or wounded. Usually they made off, so huntsmen loosed their hounds to follow and tree the big cats. Numerous tales existed about the fun, excitement, and adventure (and

[22] Olmsted, *A Journey through Texas*, pp. 224, 226.
[23] Campbell Loughmiller and Lyon Loughmiller, eds., *Big Thicket Legacy*, pp. 105–108.

usefulness) of shooting these hardened killers of stock. Oscar Williams provided an account of a cougar hunt in West Texas on Livingston Mesa, northeast of Fort Stockton, in the first years of this century, when bears and cougars were rapidly becoming "outlaws in the domain over which they had once reigned as chiefs." The panther hunt he enjoyed lasted more than three hours of a hot August day and covered rough country. The dogs followed a cougar that had killed a calf, then eventually cornered it so that the men were able to get close enough to fire at the big cat repeatedly (with No. 6 shot!). As the animal got near, Williams caught the whiff of the terrified beast's exhausted breathing: "Any animal that carries such a breath might also carry the plague," was his damning comment. Cougars had nothing to redeem them.[24]

Some of Randolph Marcy's comments about exploring North and West Texas typified the response to panthers. A Delaware scout notified colleagues in camp that a cougar had just crossed his path. This "piece of intelligence, as may be supposed, created no little excitement in our quiet circle," was the comment. Men were up in an instant; they grabbed firearms and, "followed by all the dogs in the camp," made after the animal. A cougar presented the chance for sport and was a welcome break to the daily routine. Marcy did not frown on such impulsive behavior because it made his soldiers practiced and reliable in the use of weapons. In general, hunting perfected accuracy and helped persons to overcome "buck ague or fever," that is, the nervous excitement that caused otherwise competent marksmen to miss their targets.[25]

These accounts of cougars, with descriptions (and later photographs) of impressively large teeth, heads, feet, or bodies (up to eleven feet), enliven books and diaries about travel, exploration, settlement, and daily life in outdoor Texas. Certain fish, like the alligator gar, reportedly equaled mountain lions in length; of course, alligators were much longer. What people were interested in was the size and number of different specimens and the various hair-raising encounters individual hunters had had with dangerous beasts. Killing high numbers of large-sized and predatory species drew recognition and respect.

[24] Oscar W. Williams, *Pecos County Panther Hunt Around Livingston Mesa*, p. 10.

[25] Grant Foreman, ed., *Adventure on Red River*, p. 19.

Mustangs provided opportunities for sport, and capturing them could be lucrative. The abilities of Indians and Mexicans and the methods they devised to capture and break wild horses was a source of considerable interest, and many people sought to develop similar skills. "Creasing" a mustang—that is, temporarily stunning the animal so that it could be roped—consisted of shooting a bullet across the base of its neck, and ranch hands and others placed wagers on their marksmanship. A miss by a fraction of an inch resulted in a colt thrashing out its last moments with a broken neck or bolting out of range, terrified but unscathed.

"Walking them down," or keeping a certain herd of horses constantly on the move day and night, was another approved way of capturing mustangs. Because of their habit of keeping to a home range, mustangs described a wide circle; thus, the tracking horseman (who practiced a relay system for following the animals) could anticipate the band's movements and remain close. One by one, the animals tired and permitted humans to close and lasso them. However, Stiff recognized in his *Emigrant Guide* that the "lazo" was the "harbinger of misery and servitude, in the republic of horses." Agile riders would mount newly captured horses and, by placing a rawhide noose tightly around their necks, would ride them until they became exhausted (or died). This brutal handling "gentled" horses, which kicked, bit, and lunged at these handlers.[26] Men admired skillful horsemanship and recognized the Indians' dexterity on horseback; they placed great stock in a fellow's ability to judge the character and behavioral traits of steeds that were available for purchase.

The hunting of horses had functional and material values; chasing foxes, however, was pure fun and foolishness. Holley told her readers that fox hunters would find much sport in Texas because "Reynard peeps from every brush and brake." Bollaert killed a fox that dogs had started and treed near Huntsville in East Texas in December, 1843. "We had no time to spare to bother with him," claimed this traveller, for the dogs were off after other game, so thinking only about shooting other animals, the party "scampered" excitedly over the ground. They shot an opossum, "after amusing

[26] Edward Stiff, *The Texas Emigrant: Being a Narration of the Adventures of the Author in Texas*, pp. 39–40.

ourselves sometime with it" and bagged a bear. In an unhurried moment later, Bollaert noted that the gray fox, smaller than its russet counterpart in England, was able to run for a chase of one hour or two until dogs made it climb a tree so that the hunter may "pop a bullet thro' his head."[27]

The red fox was introduced locally into parts of East and Central Texas for purposes of sport. Dissatisfied with the gray's inability to keep well ahead of his hounds, T. H. Brown imported in 1891 ten red foxes from Kentucky and Tennessee and released them four miles from the confluence of the Bosque River with the Brazos. He released an additional thirty animals until 1895 and discovered that some individuals scattered widely through Bosque and Erath counties. Approximately one hundred red foxes were set loose in five or six counties in Central and East Texas in the 1890s.[28]

Curiously, the practice of transporting red foxes to East Texas for sport has continued. In 1959, thirty-eight foxes from Brown and Coleman counties were reportedly shipped into eastern counties, where they were to be placed in artificial dens and "trained to race hounds in that part of Texas." The report suggested that red foxes would give a swift, stamina-testing account of themselves when hunted by hounds.[29]

Settlers and travellers in early Texas enjoyed encounters with animals and were excited by the difficulties and dangers of culling seemingly limitless numbers of many game species. In time, however, questions about what constituted "game" and by what methods or ethics of conduct it should be hunted were more frequently asked. George J. Durham of Austin published an article called "Game in Texas" in the *Texas Almanac* of 1868. His article named and described briefly most animals and birds that he believed were appropriate game species. This noted Austin ornithologist was interested in comparing European, particularly British, varieties (Durham was born in England) with others in Texas. Prairie chickens, which teemed in Texas' northern wheat region, were the equivalent of the red grouse from the Yorkshire moors or the heather-filled uplands of Scotland. "His name is legion," exclaimed Durham, "and there

[27] Mary Austin Holley, *Texas*, p. 99; Hollon and Butler, eds., *Bollaert's Texas*, pp. 253, 288–89; for another instance of hunting, see also p. 273.

[28] Cited in Bailey, "Biological Survey of Texas," pp. 178–79.

[29] Curtis Carpenter, "Trained Colonists," *Texas Game and Fish* 17 (1959): 9.

the grouse-shooter, glutton or battue-lover though he be, can fill his wagon till his cheek should mantle with shame at the ruthless and often useless slaughter of so many innocents."[30]

The whooping crane and the more familiar, numerous sandhill crane were noble and majestic targets in the winter months as well as palatable foods. Captain Flack claimed to have shot twenty whoopers (although he revised this number downwards to fifteen) in about fifteen years of active hunting in Texas. He had knocked down more than 150 sandhill cranes. The larger, more attractive-looking and -sounding whooping species was extremely wary and haunted open, wet places, where it had unobstructed view of anything in the vicinity. George Durham's father-in-law, Gideon Lincecum, had equal trouble with whooping cranes. Wishing to obtain a skin or two of these beautiful birds for George, he made an effort to shoot one on the coast, but said ruefully: "Well, I didn't kill any, but speaking in the bounds of reason, I think I came in two miles of it."[31] The two birds, according to Durham, occupied the same place that the bustard did in Europe. However, that large bird had vanished "as an ornament to the open grounds of the British Isles," where chalk downlands and sweeping vistas had been enclosed by fields.

In Durham's interpretation, "game" referred to any animals that sportsmen considered edible and worthy of their attention. It was an open-ended definition, and one that promoted Texas mammals and birds as desirable to the elitist hunting fraternity in Europe. He had few qualms about killing to excess, and this "battue" approach, reflected by "belting" snipe wholesale because of the birds' tenacity to favorite wet spots and by coming away festooned with diminutive cadavers, was unremarkable. Large kills, easy shots, and interesting morsels were Durham's delight, and his approval of sport hunting guided readers in ways of maximizing enjoyment of them.[32]

Earlier, the Houstouns' activities certainly fitted this image of foreign gentle persons besporting themselves with excursions across the prairies or along the shores. Matilda Houstoun, like many other travellers, enjoyed leasing a mount or a horse and trap from Cap-

[30] George J. Durham, "Game in Texas," *Texas Almanac for 1868*, pp. 92–94.

[31] Wilden, *A Hunter's Experiences*, p. 220; Wilden, *The Texas Rifle-Hunter*, p. 277; Lois W. Burkhalter, *Gideon Lincecum, 1793–1874*, p. 188.

[32] George J. Durham, "Game in Texas," *Texas Almanac for 1869*, pp. 105–110.

tain Cary's livery stable in Galveston and trotting off in pursuit of fish and game. Her husband concentrated on bagging geese and snipe, but results were mixed. Deer proved to be very scarce on Galveston Island, as were turkeys, so best results were obtained from hunting water birds. Matilda Houstoun, like George Durham, enjoyed prairie hen meat, but the more knowledgeable and accomplished hunter Durham esteemed other "savory friends," such as eskimo curlews, which "rained down" when fusilades were discharged into dense circling flocks. Willets, yellowlegs, sandpipers, godwits, and pigeons were all suitable quarry because they were abundant, amusing to shoot, and edible. The lowly squirrel, "which a European sportsman would scarcely classify with game proper," rounded out the catalog of game mammals that included—conventionally—bison, deer, and antelope (not mustangs or wild cattle).[33]

Approximately twenty years passed before this kind of enthusiasm for unlimited shooting and big kills became more muted. Severe declines in populations of preferred species resulted in effective demands for bag limits. For early settlers and sportsmen, however, the state's animals were a free, superabundant natural resource to be used according to an individual's preference. Questions about the role of hunters in causing the disappearances of animals were raised very infrequently.

[33] Ibid., p. 107, for curlews, and Durham, "Game in Texas," *Texas Almanac for 1868*, p. 93, for the squirrel.

CHAPTER 4

Declines in Game and Fish

IN the 1830s and 1840s, several authorities alerted the public about declines in certain populations of animals, brought on, they argued, by overhunting. Some writers began to speak out for the protection of game and other preferred species. They recognized that deer, turkeys, fur-bearing animals, and even predators had begun to disappear from the vicinity of settlements; as agriculture had expanded in the Rolling Prairies and Coastal Plains, these creatures and other species had become less plentiful. Useful creatures were declining, however, at different rates and for a variety of reasons related to the exploitation of them and to changes in their habitats.

Mexican official Juan Almonte mentioned the disappearance of otters and beavers in East Texas and urged protection for them; in his opinion trappers were taking too many pelts. In her treatment of the zoology of Texas, Mary Holley commented that game animals and predators, too, "are now found in those parts of the country which are thinly settled, and very rarely below San Felipe." Cougars, bears, wolves, and peccaries, she believed, had retreated to the "forests and brakes of the northwest," the abode of Indians where few white settlements existed.[1]

Similar opinions appeared in Muir's edited book on Texas. Written in the same decade of the 1830s as Holley's, his work noted that game, especially deer, although still common, was on the decline. Settlers caused "great havoc" among deer, and he had heard that one hunter, who was killing them for commercial gain, was shooting fifteen hundred animals per year. Bison, too, were "fast disappearing" from the "plains of the lower country," although they

[1] Juan N. Almonte, "Statistical Report on Texas," ed. and trans. C. E. Castañeda, *Southwestern Historical Quarterly* 28 (1925): 214; Mary Austin Holley, *Texas*, pp. 94–100.

maintained high numbers in the still largely untapped mountain region.

This remote zone was not immune to human pressure on animals, but most of this pressure came later as hunting by Indians and the excursions of explorers and white hunters resulted in large kills of bison and other animals. Dewees made an early note that food animals were disappearing along the Colorado River because "Indians and hunters" had driven the animals away. His party suffered from hunger after it exhausted its provisions and was forced to subsist on acorns, unripe persimmons, and the like because game was so scarce.[2] Likewise, deeper into the unsettled area, Thomas Falconer drew the same conclusion in the summer of 1841 by arguing that animals had vanished from a region crisscrossed by the tracks of Indian and Mexican hunters. The decline in animal populations in these remote places came to be seen as a problem that more and more people talked about as time passed; the land beyond the edge of permanent settlement was beginning to be drained of its native wildlife.

As might be expected, the better-known, more heavily settled central and coastal regions lost their animals first. With a hint of nostalgia, David Edward recorded in 1836 how "animals once so numerous . . . are either pretty much destroyed, or retreating to the upper region of the country, from whence they are fast taking their final leave."[3] Even the symbol of the remote country, the bison, "seldom seen below the mountains," was under assault and had been banished from central and coastal Texas. Ferdinand Roemer, it may be recalled, was forced to go further up the Brazos beyond the isolated Torrey Post before he came upon this beast that he had come so far to see; that was ten years after Edward's complaint.

Immense herds of mustangs, according to Edward, had "almost deserted the lower prairies," and the deer, although it was still common, was falling in large numbers "under the rifle of the white man and the red." This Scottish immigrant judged that these conspicuous and useful animals were taking "their final leave," so besides "worthless" peccaries and a few bears holed up in isolated

[2] Andrew F. Muir, ed., *Texas in 1837, An Anonymous, Contemporary Narrative*, pp. 75, 125; and William B. Dewees, *Letters from an Early Settler of Texas*, p. 127.

[3] David B. Edward, *The History of Texas*, p. 74.

places, the larger vertebrates were represented by troublesome wolves, wildcats, cougars, and "myriads" of hawks. Near farms and settlements rats and mice were "common annoyances," to be despised along with venomous snakes.[4]

Edward's comments are unusual because they cover a variety of animals and suggest that preferred species were being culled heavily; he was also convinced that considerable declines in native species had already occurred. He had entered the United States in 1819 and had opened a school in Alexandria, Louisiana. He made a tour of Texas in 1830 and became principal of an academy in Gonzales, where he prepared his widely read *History*. Although pro-Mexican leanings forced him to leave Texas, Edward's book is a solid depiction of the physical geography and animal resources of that region. There is little reason to regard his opinions about animal declines as untrue or unduly exaggerated.

One reason for this increasing toll on native species was the evolution of the American hunting gun. The long-barreled, dependable flintlock "Kentucky" rifle constructed by German gunsmiths from Pennsylvania through the Carolinas was the chief weapon for bagging game, although it proved most effective on smaller animals because of its relatively low velocity. Farmers also used a smoothbore musket, which they loaded with ball or shot in order to kill large predators and waterfowl. During the 1830s, however, the Plains rifle came into vogue, and it remained popular for more than twenty years. This weapon, a modification of the Kentucky rifle, was developed by Jacob Hawken in Saint Louis; a caplock, it had a short barrel and a thick stock and threw heavy bullets up to three hundred yards. The Plains rifle proved formidable against big game; it had power and accuracy and could be reloaded quickly. A similar Sharps .50-caliber bison weapon, developed before the Civil War, also proved effective.

Breech-loading shotguns for water birds appeared about 1850 and became used commonly in the 1870s. Repeating rifles were developed before the Civil War, but they were short-range weapons until the introduction of smokeless powder in the 1880s increased bullet velocities and metals for cartridges were developed to handle the high pressures of the new gunpowder. The Winches-

[4] Ibid.

ter Model 1873 high-velocity hunting rifle became extremely popular and reportedly killed more game (and Indians) than any other
rifle in the West.[5] Higher velocity, reduced caliber, and repeater
characteristics proved successful for killing all kinds of animals from
the 1870s onward, so market hunters after meat, skins, and feathers
had a variety of good firearms to choose from, and could maximize
their harvests.

Market Hunting

Improvements in firearms led to the large-scale slaughter of a range
of species to be sold as meat in urban places such as Galveston,
Houston, and Corpus Christi, where fishermen and other residents
turned to gunning down waterfowl in winter months. A glimpse of
the Galveston meat market in the spring of 1891 revealed stalls
laden with pintails (the most abundant type of duck), redheads,
lesser scaups, and half a dozen other waterfowl, including geese
and coots in abundance. Vendors sold a variety of shorebirds, too,
such as plovers, yellowlegs, and sandpipers. The attractive-colored
buff-breasted sandpiper, a long-distance migrant that was shot on
the coastal grasslands as it headed for nesting grounds in Alaska,
was reportedly readily available.[6]

These birds and many other species were obtained in the surrounding prairies, marshes, and swamps by market hunters who
had hard, lonely, often impecunious lives. John Reid's judgment in
1857 that "game is ever in season" remained true into the 1900s,
and commercial hunters supplied wholesale fish and game establishments in growing urban places with the meat, skins, and feathers of wild animals. After the Civil War some persons like Nat Wetzel
began to ship game from distant points by rail.

Nat Wetzel, who was called "the King of the Market Hunters"
in the late 1890s, adopted various ruses in order to work within
range of ducks, geese, and other game to ensure killing them in
large quantities. His weaponry was normally five-shot pump guns,

[5] Charles F. Waterman, *Hunting in America*, pp. 92, 150, 158, 175; Dave
Bennett, "Guns of the Cattlemen, the Winchester," *The Cattleman* 46 (1959): 36–
37, 62–74; and C. P. Russell, *Guns on the Early Frontier*.

[6] J. A. Singley, "Contributions to the Natural History of Texas," *Fourth Annual Report of the Geological Survey of Texas*, pp. 345–75, especially 357–59.

but one of the most remarkable methods he used was to "thresh" ducks—that is, to swing hand-held wire flails at passing flocks of low-flying waterfowl. This way of obtaining water birds was commonly used by Mexican hunters, who positioned themselves in marshlands along the border and swung into the compact flight of ducks as they swept through openings in tall reed beds or in riparian vegetation.

Sometimes a hunter could ride a horse up to game or gain partial concealment by walking beside docile horses or cattle. On other occasions he would lie down on a crude sled, which oxen then would pull to within a few yards of mammals and birds before the hunter would jump up and blast them. The techniques for capturing these animals depended on weather conditions, season, lay of the land, and the kinds of prey that a hunter wished to secure. Frequently, farmers were compelled, said Wetzel, to guard their rice and other grain fields from ducks and geese, which could devastate a hundred acres in a single night. Meat appeared on the market in these instances because too many wild animals threatened to overwhelm cultivated areas.[7]

Local men who worked the "flag marshes" along the Gulf had their peculiar "hunter's geography" of descriptive terms for special landscape features. Their purpose was to describe with accuracy and certitude the places they intended to frequent so that rescuers could find them if they failed to come back from an evening or early morning hunt. Tracks or distant landmarks could be lost easily when sudden changes of weather reduced visibility and obliterated footprints; by knowing details about local landmarks ("split-tree knoll," "goose-neck swale," and so on), however, friends could track a market hunter whom they believed was in trouble. Wetzel knew of one water-bird gunner who was so disoriented in the extensive marshes near Beaumont that he became crazed before friends caught up with him after several days.[8]

Hunting birds for plumage as millinery adornment was important on the coast, too. The storm in August, 1886, that destroyed Indianola also capsized near Saluria a fifteen-ton schooner called

[7] Nat Wetzel, "Cunning Wiles of the Hunter and the Hunted," *Texas Game and Fish* 11 (1953): 8–9, 29–30; Jay Vessels, "King of the Market Hunters," *Texas Game and Fish* 10 (1952): pp. 12–14.
[8] Wetzel, "Cunning Wiles," p. 30.

The Flower of France, which had recently arrived in Matagorda
Bay for the purpose of "hunting sea gulls for their plumage, used in
millinery." The vessel was based in Louisiana, and its six-member
crew had secured about six hundred birds before the hurricane struck
and destroyed the ship, which carried three hundred dollars' worth
of guns and ammunition. Ten years earlier herons and other water
birds had been nesting in great numbers on the lower coast. By
1889, breeding herons proved difficult to find: the snowy egret,
preferred by "plumers," was unavailable even for "cabinet specimens," for colonies with their "innumerable numbers" had been
blasted away.[9]

An important collection of articles on bird protection, which
appeared in 1886 as a supplement to *Science*, called readers' attention to the "sad havoc . . . wrought with the egrets and herons along
our southern shores, the statistics of which, could they be presented, would be of startling magnitude." Plume hunters on consignment to millinery firms in the North had attacked Florida's
rookeries first and had then proceeded westward along the Gulf
Coast. "One of our well-known ornithologists, while on an exploring trip to Texas, heard an agent of the millinery trade soliciting a
sportsman to procure for him the plumes of 10,000 white egrets,"
an ornithological report declared. In this instance, the sportsman
had "too much humanity to become the abettor of such a heartless
scheme." In 1900, however, Florence Merriam Bailey, a noted writer
and authority on birds, discovered that "settlers" near Corpus Christi
were busily killing birds for the millinery trade.[10]

As local residents took Bailey gradually into their confidence,
she learned that the poor folk had taken a large toll of water birds.
One man claimed that in 1889 he had shot during one week more
than one thousand birds, mostly terns, avocets, willets, and yellowlegs. Another claimed that he knew a fellow who could skin six
hundred birds per day (that is, water birds and "any white-breasted
birds," which went to eager dealers). Egg collectors had raided

[9] "The Storm of August 20, 1886," in *Indianola Scrap Book*, p. 139; George B.
Sennett, "Notes on the Ornithology of the Lower Rio Grande of Texas," *U.S. Geological Survey Bulletin* 4 (1878): 58–59.
[10] "Destruction of Birds for Millinery Purposes," *Science* Supplement 7 (1886):
196–97; Witmer Stone, "Report of the Committee on Bird Protection," *The Auk* 18
(1901): 74–76.

nesting places, and plume hunters had destroyed herons, gulls, skimmers, curlews, and other shorebirds because agents were prepared to pay up to forty cents for a good heron skin and twenty cents for a tern. Pelicans, too, had ceased to breed because of heavy persecution; the skins of brightly colored buntings, flycatchers, and other small birds also went to the market.

Florence Bailey believed that the millinery firms were the real culprits, because they provided the monetary incentives to residents who eked out a bare living around the lagoons of the Coastal Bend. Middlemen, however, reaped the "real profits of the trade." Therefore, it was imperative, according to Bailey, to bring the full force of law to bear on stamping out illegal shipments and sales of birds' skins and feathers. There is no doubt that severe and lasting declines in water birds in coastal Texas resulted from the fashion for ornamental plumage.[11]

To supply meat to a settlement or facility away from the coast called for other strategies. Professional hunter Captain Flack and three companions made a living by supplying venison and turkey meat to a local community. One hunter's responsibility was to carry the venison (packed in bags) and the turkeys to town every day in order to prevent them from spoiling. He would sell meat to merchants or make house-to-house calls and then return to camp with provisions. The second hunter was the cook and camp caretaker. The third and fourth spots went to marksmen who would leave separately before dawn and kill two deer or two turkeys each before coming in for breakfast. They were also expected to shoot an additional deer each before supper.

Turkeys were carried back to camp immediately, but it was usually necessary to return for a pack horse to pick up a deer, which the hunter had gutted wherever he had felled it. The men rotated the duties of killing animals for the market, concentrating on various species. Deer proved optimum in summer, bears were fattest in October, and peccaries or hogs made good eating after they had filled out on fall mast. A professional hunter lived cheaply, but he did not expect to grow rich. The best-quality bucks or gobblers fetched one dollar apiece; does and hens about fifty cents; ducks (in

[11] Stone, "Report of the Committee on Bird Protection," pp. 75–76; and Robin W. Doughty, *Feather Fashions and Bird Protection: A Study in Nature Protection.*

season) up to twenty-five cents; and quail, plover, or snipe about a dime. The rule was to minimize disturbance and maximize the off-take. As soon as the animals became scarce, the hunters shifted their campsite a few miles and began again. Flack instructed that dogs should not be kept in camp except for unusual occasions, or else the deer cleared out of the area.[12]

Pigeons and Prairie Dogs

Authorities tended to generalize about changes in the status of wild animals. Most people had the impression that many species were declining because of exploitation, but many of them failed to document their opinions. However, some animals did attract interest and attention, and a considerable amount of data was collected about them. One of these, the passenger pigeon, deserves special mention because, like the bison, its numbers were so large that they were barely calculable; this bird was a superb embodiment of nature's fecundity in all North America, not just Texas.

Harry Church Oberholser (1870–1963), ornithologist and authority on Texas birds, gathered much detailed information about the "wild pigeons," as folk named the species, including accounts from people who had marvelled at vast flights of the birds before they disappeared forever.[13] The pattern of the birds' movements and the destructive activities of settlers around roosts were much the same throughout the oak woodlands of the eastern and northeastern counties. Passenger pigeons arrived in Texas from northern nesting areas from September through November. "Spies," or advanced flocks of several dozen birds, supposedly located suitable foods, such as acorns, berries, and nuts gleaned from beneath oaks and other deciduous mast-producing trees and bushes. Enormous flights of these swiftly moving, gregarious, and noisy birds descended on localities with abundant food. They occurred westward into the Edwards Plateau and southward into counties along the central coast.

Observers agreed that passenger pigeons were impressive an-

[12] Frank Wilden [Captain Flack], *A Hunter's Experiences in the Southern States of America*, pp. 25–32.

[13] Harry C. Oberholser, *The Bird Life of Texas*, ed. Edgar B. Kincaid, Jr., 1: 415–22.

imals, because large numbers would arrive suddenly, often unpre-
dictably, in various places, where they became attached to specific
roosting sites. Trees and plants in these localities suffered heavily
from nightly concentrations of the highly gregarious birds. Some
roosts were unmolested, but local residents, visiting entrepreneurs, and sportsmen attacked many others, shooting and thresh-
ing down enormous numbers of pigeons for home consumption,
commerce, and recreation.

Captain Flack presented an early, interesting account of these
attractive birds, whose swift passage produced a thunder of wing-
beats in Washington County about 1853. Flack noted that the pigeons, following a northeast-to-southwest path and travelling above
shotgun range, passed overhead for a period of three consecutive
days. When residents discovered a roost where untold thousands
of birds congregated, the carnage commenced. They set up tents
nearby and fitted out a campsite with sacks of salt and a collection
of barrels, and other containers for storing the carcasses. Then one
night people moved into the woods and stood under the slumbering pigeons. Using flares to illuminate the scene and fumes from
sulfur pots to confuse and stupefy their prey, they began to cut
down pigeons with guns, poles, and long clubs. Pandemonium
quickly broke out in the colony as dead, dying, and maimed pigeons dropped down or scrambled about. In a short time enough
birds had been heaped on the ground to occupy a whole day in
plucking, gutting, salting down, and packing. Flack recorded that
one hunter shot down eighty-seven pigeons with one blast from his
double-barreled gun.[14] Sometimes after the hunts hogs were herded
into roosting places to root up the rotting cadavers.

Charles V. Terrell's memories of boyhood days provide similar
details about a wild pigeon roost on Sandy Creek, Wise County, in
1870. Townsfolk from Decatur headed for the large congregation
and were dumbfounded by the numbers of pigeons and the noise
they made. Vast ranks of birds settled in trees and knocked down
branches. In some places whole trees toppled down under the weight
of the pigeons as they poured into the roost in the early evening
hours. Terrell saw the sky made dark as a dust storm by circling
birds, and after they had departed, the ground under the roost

[14] Frank Wilden [Captain Flack], *The Texas Ranger*, pp. 222–24.

looked as though a whirlwind had passed over it. Too young to use a gun, this youngster's task was to retrieve fallen birds.[15]

In the same decade, passenger pigeons appeared around Austin several times; when they did, restaurant owners put them on the menu. A large flight of birds passing over the city toward the Hill Country took place in the fall of 1878. "String after string of many thousands of birds passed over; many lit in the tall trees along Barton Creek just above its mouth and in the trees along the south side of the [Colorado] River just above the creek, literally loading down the limbs," was the report. The stomachs of birds that were shot were crammed with large acorns.[16] The species was never again seen in such numbers over the capital of Texas, although in the 1880s flocks occurred in Travis County and further west on the Edwards Plateau, in Real, Uvalde, Lampasas, and Edwards counties.

In these and other areas farmers grew exasperated by the passenger pigeon's thieving ways. It filched grain and water from stock tanks, and it loafed about hog pens and gobbled down corn. Some settlers destroyed pigeons because they feared losing their crops to the birds. German immigrant and longtime resident Max Krueger (1851–1927) remembered large flocks of birds in the cedar brakes around San Saba, possibly about 1880, which had flown in to gorge on cedar berries. "For many weeks nothing could be heard but the reports of guns," said Krueger, who was a young cowhand in that area. The pigeons proved useless, however, because after feasting off juniper berries, they tasted like turpentine! According to Krueger, the following spring the local farmers set the cedar (juniper) brushlands on fire because they feared that the wild pigeons would consume their crops. "For weeks and even months the sky was black with clouds of smoke," grumbled Krueger, as men torched prime wood so useful for fence posts.[17]

One or two stories refer to the pigeons as nesting in Texas (near Goshen, Henderson County, for example) until the early 1890s, when the wild pigeon disappeared. "Little heed was paid to the disappearance of the pigeons at that time by a great many people, like myself, who had extensively participated in killing and destroying

[15] Wayne Gard, *Rawhide Texas*, pp. 45–46.

[16] George F. Simmons, *Birds of the Austin Region*, pp. 85–86, and *Austin Democratic-Statesman*, December 31, 1872, p. 3.

[17] Max Krueger, *Pioneer Life in Texas*, pp. 143–44.

them by the millions merely for sport," stated J. D. Goodgame, who lived near one of the larger, most frequented, and better-known roosts on Coon Creek, south of Athens.[18]

By 1900, however, the passenger pigeon was finished in Texas and across the nation as well, although an odd bird or two was killed in that year. It was about then that seventy-year-old Alvin Jones took a lad named Dolph Fillingim, who became a trapper and geographer of the Big Thicket, to visit "pigeon roost prairie" south of Hardin. There Jones pointed out a place of about 150 acres where pine trees had been killed when they were the roost for millions of passenger pigeons.[19] A generation earlier, these speedy pigeons had swept over and into the East Texas woodlands regularly; this dead place where they had nested was their only marker.

Another animal as gregarious and numerous as the wild pigeon but lacking that bird's itinerant nature and mobility was the prairie dog. Dog towns proved interesting places, and shooting them up was sport for many travellers, explorers, and surveyors in West Texas and elsewhere. Gregg, Kendall, Bartlett, Marcy, and others were fascinated by these creatures, whose bustling activities had many human qualities. Travelling through the enormous expanses of grasslands that were homes for millions of prairie dogs and associated animals was an especially impressive experience.

Prairie dogs were commonly encountered in the Trans-Pecos region. A comment by John C. Reid about 1857 of marching through "the principal thoroughfare of the immense prairie dog town" beyond Fort Davis, as he pressed on for El Paso, typified many comments about huge numbers. In this case, Reid estimated that the "town" extended for twenty-five miles along his route; he also passed several smaller ones, each extending several miles. Drawing from persons like Reid and previous government surveys, Vernon Bailey summed up the distribution and numerical strength of this ground-dwelling rodent in his "Biological Survey." At the turn of the present century, the black-tailed prairie dog's range occupied more than one-third of Texas, principally its northwest quadrant of about ninety thousand square miles. Concentrated in these short-grass prairies, the prairie dog population may have topped eight hundred million

[18] Oberholser, *Bird Life of Texas*, 1: 420.
[19] Campbell Loughmiller and Lyon Loughmiller, eds., *Big Thicket Legacy*, p. 82.

(consuming enough grass for over three million head of cattle), and the dogs had reportedly increased through the destruction of natural predators. State geologist S. B. Buckley noted an extension of range from a survey he made in the summer of 1875: "Fifteen years ago we saw them a few miles south of Camp Colorado [Coleman County]; now their towns are in the northern part of San Saba."[20]

These herbivores were not permitted, however, to remain in such colossal numbers for long, not because they presented free food and sport to hungry settlers, as the pigeons had done, but because they competed with incoming cattle and sheep for the grass. Ranchers and government agents in West Texas and throughout most of the Southwest set about poisoning dog towns so that the rodents were eradicated quickly and comprehensively. Some stockmen, however, claimed later that the destruction of prairie dogs led to the encroachment of brush into good pastures; the precise economic status of prairie dogs as competitors for forage has been the subject of considerable and lasting debate.

The Fishery

In addition to exploiting terrestrial animals, settlers took an increasing toll of native fishes and other aquatic creatures from the rivers and streams and from brackish lagoons along the coast. By the late 1870s it was clear that the state's fishery required protection. Under instruction from the legislature, Joseph Dinkins, the first fish commissioner, whom Governor O. M. Roberts appointed in 1879, was to examine the freshwater fishery, which had been impaired by dams and weirs. Such obstacles fragmented fish populations and altered water conditions. Overfishing, too, including the common use of seines and even explosives tossed into likely spots for large catches, had also depleted fish stocks around riparian settlements.[21]

Dinkins applied to federal fisheries personnel in Washington for supplies of exotic salmon, shad, and other anadromous species, believing that one method of rehabilitating the state's freshwater fishery was by "improving" it with new edible species. A fad cen-

[20] John C. Reid, *Reid's Tramp*, p. 124; Vernon Bailey, "Biological Survey of Texas," *North American Fauna* 25 (1905): 89–90; Samuel B. Buckley, *Second Annual Report of the Geological and Agricultural Survey of Texas*, p. 89.

[21] Texas, *First Report of the Texas Fish Commissioner for the Year 1880*.

tered on the introduction of the hardy, prolific "German" or European carp into American waters, and Texas figured prominently in early (and successful) efforts to provide a home for this "brain food." Further information about the carp experiment, which set back conservation efforts for coastal fish and other marine organisms for a decade, is given in another chapter. By the time the authority of the fish commissioner was broadened in 1895 to include marine resources, many common food fishes, oysters, and sea turtles had been heavily exploited.[22]

The commercial harvesting of sea turtles illustrates the original fecundity yet vulnerability of coastal organisms. Intensive netting of these large marine reptiles quickly depleted the population, and efforts to protect this fishery in the 1890s met with little success. Five species of marine turtles occur along the Texas coast. One of them, the green turtle, which gourmands prize for its flesh and "turtle soup," was for twenty or thirty years the basis of a sizable fishery. Fishermen netted turtles from Matagorda Bay southward, then shipped them live to the local markets and as far as New Orleans and possibly New York. Fishermen sent other turtles to be processed into meat and soup in several canneries located at Indianola, Fulton, Corpus Christi, and Port Isabel. The cannery at Fulton, a little north of Rockport in Aransas County, for example, operated for almost fifteen years (beginning in 1881) after a dozen or so meat-packing plants there had been phased out as the longhorns were trailed northward to markets in Kansas.[23]

In 1890, the facility in Fulton processed about nine hundred green turtles, totalling 243,000 pounds—that is, 42 percent of the state's reported catch of green turtles for that year. The quantity of turtles landed in Texas, namely 585,000 pounds, exceeded similar poundage for Florida (468,256 pounds) and had grown by more than twenty-five times over the preceding decade.[24] Turtles ranked fifth behind oysters, sea trout, channel bass, and sheepshead in the value

[22] Robin W. Doughty, "Wildlife Conservation in Late Nineteenth-Century Texas: The Carp Experiment," *Southwestern Historical Quarterly* 84 (1980): 169–96.

[23] Robin W. Doughty, "Sea Turtles in Texas: A Forgotten Commerce," *Southwestern Historical Quarterly* (forthcoming).

[24] Charles Stevenson, "Report on the Coast Fisheries of Texas," in U.S. Commission of Fish and Fisheries, *Report of the Commissioner for 1889 to 1891*, p. 412.

of fishery products. These data represent a meteoric rise in the take, which was concentrated primarily in Aransas Bay, where fishermen deployed nets designed to snag green turtles as they swam through the network of channels in the shallow bays and into the open sea beyond the barrier island chain.

What was initially a subsidiary enterprise to operations for slaughtering cattle became a considerable industry. Techniques were perfected for holding the marine animals and canning them. Rough stockades fashioned from stakes placed together and driven into submerged mud and sand confined the marine reptiles until they were hoisted onto wharves and butchered or trussed for shipment. One fishery expert noted that several beef packeries that had pioneered techniques for preserving and shipping meat, including ice-making and mechanical refrigeration, had a line of turtle canning as well.[25]

The huge growth in the state's turtlery was ended by the mid-1890s, however. In 1897 the catch barely exceeded one-third of Florida's turtle fishery, which was prosecuted in Escambia, Levy, Franklin, and notably Monroe counties, where marine turtles had become noticeably scarcer. Statistics reveal that landings of green turtles in Texas shot up between 1880 and 1887, held steady through about 1892, then plummeted by more than one-half in 1897 and were virtually ended by 1908.[26]

Regulations governing this harvest came too late. An 1895 law made it illegal to sell or ship green turtles weighing less than twelve pounds. However, enforcement was difficult, perhaps unnecessary, because of the decrease in turtles, which "supported in former years five or six turtle canneries, besides large shipments of live turtles." Texas Fish and Oyster Commissioner Kibbe recognized that the turtle fishery, "once a growing industry in our State," was doomed. He blamed its decline, however, on the lack of protection "in their semi-tropical breeding grounds" and appealed for international

[25] "Productions for Texas," *Texas Almanac for 1869*, p. 104; and Hugh M. Smith, "Statistics of the Fisheries of the United States," *Bulletin of the U.S. Fish Commission* 13 (1893): 389–417, especially p. 411.

[26] Charles H. Townsend, "Statistics of the Fisheries of the Gulf States," in U.S. Commission of Fish and Fisheries, *Report of the Commissioner for 1899*, pp. 105–69, especially pp. 127, 161–62, 169.

agreements to protect this migratory marine creature. His explanation is unsatisfactory. There is no doubt that the state's gill net fishery, which took the most sea turtles, had declined sharply; federal fishery expert Charles Stevenson noted that the Fulton cannery, for example, had closed "on account of increasing scarcity of green turtle on the Texas coast." The plant's consumption of approximately one thousand animals every year for a decade or more (perhaps as many more again were landed elsewhere) appears to have wiped out the turtles. The capture of perhaps thirty thousand green turtles from 1881 through 1896, particularly if they were breeding animals, as some circumstances suggest, thus destroyed the population. In later years more turtles were captured in southern waters, including Mexican, to prolong the industry. Such speculation helps to account for the shift of landings to the Laguna Madre, centered on Port Isabel and Corpus Christi, late in the 1890s. By 1908, Texas ranked twelfth of fourteen states reporting turtles (not all were marine species), and after that year the Fish and Oyster Commission ceased to publish data on turtle catches.[27]

In general, concern about the numerical declines of wild animals, particularly after 1850, and an apparent unwillingness to face up to the loss of important and useful species led individuals and organizations to warn that soon there would be little remaining of a fauna that was once so abundant. Among the first group of persons to actively alert others about the increasingly precarious status of several mammals were travellers, especially those government officials who travelled widely across the Southwest to gather information about its physical geography and natural resources. Randolph Marcy, William Emory, and John Bartlett represented three different but complementary views of Texas in the 1850s. Marcy led an expedition to explore the upper reaches of the Red River; Emory was chief astronomer for the United States Mexican Boundary Survey; and Bartlett was a boundary commissioner who journeyed from Indianola to El Paso late in 1850 and returned through South Texas in the winter of 1852–53.

[27] I. P. Kibbe, *Report on the Coast Fisheries of Texas*, p. 6; Charles H. Stevenson, "The Preservation of Fishery Products for Food," *Bulletin of U.S. Fish Commission* 18 (1898): 341; United States, Department of Commerce and Labor, Bureau of the Census, Special Reports, *Fisheries of the United States, 1908*, p. 43.

Each of these men became excited by encountering rare or unusual animals. Marcy, however, recognized most clearly that changes were occurring in the character and composition of fauna, and he sought to explain them. About deer, he remarked:

In passing through Southern Texas in 1846, thousands of deer were met with daily, and, astonishingly as it may appear, it was no uncommon spectacle to see from one to two hundred in a single herd; the prairies seemed literally alive with them; but in 1855 it was seldom that a herd of ten was seen in the same localities. It seemed to me that the vast herds first met with could not have been killed off by the hunters in that sparsely-populated section, and I was puzzled to know what had become of them.

He was not puzzled, however, about the reason for the bison's decline. People had simply shot too many: "Not many years since they thronged in countless multitudes over all that vast area lying between Mexico and the British possessions, but now their range is confined within very narrow limits, and a few more years will probably witness the extinction of the species."[28]

Such explanations, warnings, and prophecies, however, are rare in early surveys. As the end of the century drew closer, others enunciated the claims Marcy had made about overhunting. Englishman Captain Flack, an experienced hunter, despaired, knowing that the days of limitless game were over. "The home now of roving, fighting Indians, and of nearly as wild buffalo, black-tailed deer, elk, and prairie dogs; will it ever be brought under cultivation? Yes!. . . and how few years will it be before the free wilds I gaze upon will become 'improved'? Thank heaven it will not be in my day."[29] A well-travelled Frenchman, Benedict H. Revoil, launched a blistering attack in the mid-1870s on settlers who destroyed animals:

The variety of game is, in America, threatened with destruction. In proportion as civilization extends into the vast wilderness of the West, men increase in number, and the human race, which everywhere reigns despotically, and permits no restraint upon its tyranny, gradually destroyed the community of animals. Already the deer, the goats, and the great horned

[28] Randolph B. Marcy, *The Prairie Traveller: A Hand-Book for Overland Expeditions*, pp. 234, 239.

[29] Frank Wilden [Captain Flack], *The Prairie Hunter: A Book of Adventures*, pp. 162–63.

cattle which peopled the ancient colonies of England, have disappeared in the principle states of the Union. The herds of bison which, a hundred years ago pastured peacefully on the savannahs of the Mississippi, see their ranks thinning daily; while the skeletons of their fellows, slain by the trappers and emigrants and Indians, whiten on the ground and mark the gradual advance of man. Everything leads to the belief that the pigeons, which cannot endure isolation, forced to fly or to change their habitats as the territory of North America shall become peopled with the overplus of Europe, will eventually disappear from this continent; and if the world endure a century longer, I will wager that the amateur of ornithology will find no pigeons except in select Museums of Natural History.[30]

New Englander Olmsted joined in commentary about animal disappearances by informing readers that "large game" was retreating as settlement pushed into the hinterland of Texas and beyond. Near Curry's Creek, which flows through Kendall and Comal counties, for example, a man had run his hounds after sixty bears in only two years and had sold honey worth two hundred dollars from bee trees growing in the area. A German carpenter had delivered eleven thousand pounds of wild meat in less than a year to someone who was setting up a collection of skins from native animals.[31]

Naturally, such European travellers and Easterners like Olmsted, familiar with the track record of human agency that had whittled down plant and animal communities back home, were greatly impressed by the numbers and variety of biota west of the Mississippi River. Europeans and widely travelled Americans such as George Perkins Marsh, U.S. ambassador to Italy, recognized just what a heavy hand had been laid on the mammals, birds, and landscapes in general in the Old World's Mediterranean region and in temperate Europe. History had repeated itself in North America, where colonists had eradicated many important game species in most states east of the Mississippi River. Flack, Revoil, and others became indignant, then despairing, about these activities. Settlers, who were often foreigners like themselves, were thoughtlessly terminating the existence of so many interesting, beautiful, and useful creatures along the frontier in the Southwest and in Texas.

[30] Benedict H. Revoil, *The Hunter and the Trapper in North America; or Romantic Adventures in Field and Forest*, pp. 137–38.
[31] Frederick Law Olmsted, *A Journey through Texas, Or, A Saddle-Trip on the Southwestern Frontier*, p. 223.

Habitat Change

U.S. statistics demonstrate that a major and sustained expansion took place in the acreage under farmland and in numbers of livestock after 1850. In the forty years between 1850 and 1890, land in farms increased by 347 percent from 11.5 to 51.4 million acres or to about one acre in four. "Improved" farmland had the most remarkable growth, from 644,000 acres to 20.75 million acres, an increase of more than 3,000 percent, as a veritable river of new Texans poured into the state, topping 2.3 million persons by 1890. "Unimproved" acreage, always larger than the former category, also increased, but not as dramatically. The 30.7 million acres classed as unimproved farmland in 1890 did not reflect the same degree of human activity as improved land did. Much of unimproved land consisted of woodland or range that was connected with a farm and upon which livestock were grazed.[32]

Marshals for the 1850 census defined improved farmland, however, as "cleared land used for grazing, grass or tillage . . . connected with or belonging to a farm." Such land supported cotton, grain, and other crops, and Texans planted more and more acres of wheat, barley, and corn as the century progressed. Wheat acreage shot up by more than 10,000 percent in the forty-year period, reaching 352,000 acres in 1890. Oats, too, grew by over 6,000 percent to about 530,000 acres. Corn increased by a mere 1,046 percent in comparison; however, this staple food was the most extensively cultivated grain, and in 1890 more than 3 million acres in 204 counties were planted in corn, which averaged 22 bushels per acre. All five of the leading corn-growing counties of Texas and most of the other major ones were in the Blackland Prairie belt and showed yields of more than the state average. The first two, Collin County and Grayson County, had yields of 32 and 33.5 bushels per acre, respectively.[33]

[32] United States, [Census Office], *The Seventh Census of the United States: 1850* pp. 512, 515; United States, Census Office, *Report on the Statistics of Agriculture in the United States at the Eleventh Census: 1890*, pp. 228; and United States, Census Office, *Report on the Population of the United States at the Eleventh Census*, pp. 41–42.

[33] United States, [Census Office], *The Seventh Census*, p. xxiii; and United States, Census Office, *Report on the Statistics of Agriculture: 1890*, pp. 385–87.

If one projects back the 1890 average yield, then about 275,000 acres were planted in corn, compared with just over 3 million acres forty years later. Until after the Civil War, most of this area in corn was located in the East Texas pine-oak woodland. Harrison, Rusk, and Cherokee counties dominated production, but these older political units took a subsidiary place when the fertile blackland counties further west expanded production in the 1870s and 1880s as new farmers put in corn and cotton.[34]

Only Washington County, with soils "generally rich and mellow, and of different colours, dark-grey, red, and chocolate" and numerous prairies that lay parallel to the Coastal Prairie lowland, continued to be a major contributor to the state's corn crop. The yield increased there from 162,000 bushels in 1850, when the county ranked sixth, to exceed 650,000 bushels in 1870, when it ranked second, an increase of 23 percent over the previous decade's total. Washington County, one of the earliest and most populous political divisions, was intensively cultivated; improved farmland grew from less than 20,000 acres in 1850 to 258,000 acres in 1890, which represented a sizable 66 percent of the county's entire area. By that latter year, however, the land in corn, namely 43,610 acres, lagged behind new, larger acreages in Collin, Grayson, and Fannin counties. All in all, seventeen counties, mostly in the wedge of blacklands from San Antonio to the Red River east of the Balcones Escarpment and the Cross Timbers, produced in excess of 1 million bushels each at the beginning of the final decade of the nineteenth century, and the state's total corn production of 69 million bushels was 138 percent more than a previous record yield ten years earlier.[35]

This dramatic increase in farmland in East Texas and then on the Blackland Prairie for the cultivation of corn, with additional

[34] United States, [Census Office], *The Seventh Census*, pp. 515–18; United States, Census Office, *Agriculture of the United States in 1860: Compiled from the Original Returns of the Eighth Census*, pp. 141, 145, 149; United States, Census Office, *The Statistics of the Wealth and Industry of the United States*, 3: 87, 251, 255, 259; and *Report on the Productions of Agriculture as Returned at the Tenth Census (July 1, 1880)* 3: 205–208.

[35] United States, [Census Office], *The Seventh Census*, p. 516; United States, Census Office, *Statistics of the Wealth and Industry* 3: 259; United States, Census Office, *Report on the Statistics of Agriculture*, p. 387; and William Kennedy, *Texas: The Rise, Progress, and Prospects of the Republic of Texas*, p. 155.

food plants and domestic livestock becoming more widespread in the interior region, meant that habitat for existing native animals was lost through the clearing of land. Any such transformation generally results in the overall reduction in the number of native animal species in a given biological community. The actual extent of that reduction, however, depends upon the character and extent of the changes that human activities bring about through colonization and permanent settlement. In the case of grain cultivation environmental transformation is profound; native bunch grasses are plowed under, and lightly wooded or even densely forested lands are cleared for fields.[36]

In general, the size and distribution of an animal population is affected by those factors that alter the size and distribution of its habitat. Some rare organisms, which we euphemistically call "over-specialized," have developed an ability to adjust to extreme and very specific conditions. Others are rare because their small populations exist over a large geographical area or because they are widely dispersed in certain biological communities.

The disadvantages of competitive specialization or low numbers are quickly apparent when conditions change suddenly and dramatically. The arrival of agriculturalists, the rapid clearance and cropping, plus new livestock, for example, in the blacklands, doubtless increased local and regional extinction rates for native bison, prairie chickens, antelope, and turkeys, which were not able to adjust to new patterns and types of disturbances, including unregulated hunting. On the other hand, those organisms that can adjust—that is, those that are mobile, reproduce quickly, and have highly flexible patterns of behavior, such as grain-eating birds like doves—tended to prosper.[37]

Recent studies of the bird communities of the U.S. eastern hardwood forest, which has been cut over and markedly fragmented by agriculture and urban expansion, suggest that these present-day "islands" of oak-hickory, like those occurring in the woodland belt of East Texas, have lost many neotropical insectivorous warblers and vireos, which migrate from Central and South

[36] Discussion of the blacklands appears in "Game Regions of Texas: The Blackland Prairie," *Texas Game and Fish* 10 (1952): 6–8.

[37] David W. Ehrenfeld, *Conserving Life on Earth*, pp. 27–31, 200–204; and William H. Drury, "Rare Species," *Biological Conservation* 6 (1974): 162–69.

America in order to nest. Grazing pressures on understory plants
in such remnants of hardwood forests disrupt breeding; predatory
mammals, grackles, jays, and other animals also depress reproductive success, so today these once-extensive woodlands are losing
native warblers, which may comprise over 90 percent of the terrestrial bird species. Additionally, year-round residents such as chickadees, titmice, and wrens, which are also more "generalist" feeders—that is, capable of subsisting from a range of plant and animal
foods—may be replacing warblers as these adaptable birds prosper
in more disturbed habitats.[38]

Animals that have prospered through habit change and disturbances brought on by the expansion of human settlement and human population include those that are small (such as raccoons and
opossums, which are relatively inconspicuous), that have short ges-
tation periods, and that produce several young at once which become rapidly independent. Such animals prosper if they are gra-
zers, scavengers, or insectivores, whereas predatory felines or canids
suffer persecution. The practice of nesting or reproducing in pairs
or in small groups instead of in aggregations or colonies, as used by
the extinct passenger pigeon or endangered green sea turtle, makes
adaptable species less vulnerable to exploitation. Successful animals also show a wide tolerance of habitats and are widely distributed as a consequence. They are tolerant, too, of human beings,
and some of them, like quail and deer, which thrive in brushy growth
rather than in dense woodland, may also be game species that humans protect and manage for recreational hunting.[39]

One defense against extinction is the ability of individuals of a
species to move between centers of naturally occurring populations. In birds, for example, there often exists a mobile pool of
"wanderers," which are capable of colonizing new areas by taking
advantage of new foods. Some animals have cycles of population
built up that result in "eruptions," enabling some individuals to move,
sometimes long distances, and to occupy suitable environments.

In sum, the potentially successful organisms, such as rodents
and sparrows, capable of thriving in new agricultural situations are
those adapted to colonizing disturbed environments; these species

[38] Robert F. Whitcomb, "'Island Biogeography' and 'Habitat Islands' of Eastern Forest," *American Birds* 31 (1977): 3–5.
[39] Ehrenfeld, *Conserving Life on Earth*, p. 202.

are short-lived but have high rates of increase and disperse rapidly into new environments. Extinction-prone species, however, are either highly localized or specialized or both. They make effective use of stable situations but are incapable of adjusting quickly to human-induced disturbances or changes. These types of animals are often long-lived and have slow rates of reproduction; once habitat is disrupted, they become vulnerable. Settlement disturbed the latter, more specialized mammals, which, like the bison, bighorn sheep, and pronghorn antelope, were big game that also competed with domestic livestock. Settlement assisted the other, opportunistic animals, such as smaller furbearers, rodents, seed-eating birds, crows, jays, and others. The bison, pronghorn, and greater prairie chicken disappeared from the blacklands, and the latter game bird became totally extinct in Texas, although a remnant population of its subspecies, the so-called Attwater's prairie chicken, has continued to hold out in several counties on the Coastal Prairie.[40]

Relatively few of the early authors related fluctuations in animal populations to the loss of habitat through changing patterns of land use and the expansion of cropland. One reason why this situation was not associated with animal declines, as overhunting was, is that people regarded the use of fire, axes, and plows as important for the process of environmental improvement that settlement created. Cutting down forests, burning away brush, or draining swamps in order to establish fields helped to foster and reinforce the image of the "garden"—that is, a domesticated landscape where certain agrarian myths could be fulfilled.

Edward Stiff's optimistic picture of Texas emphasized the favorable climate, the soils and grand landscapes, and especially the prairies, "the most extensive and luxuriant in the world." He admonished readers to "go and go at once, to Texas!" Herdsmen and cultivators were rapidly settling the mighty Plains, and newcomers were finding "ready markets and high prices, and many of them are satisfied, and fondly look forward to superior ease, comfort and wealth."[41]

Persons interested in this new state were urged by Melinda

[40]Ibid., pp. 200–204; and John Terborgh, "Preservation of Natural Diversity: The Problem of Extinction Prone Species," *BioScience* 24 (1974): 715–22.

[41]Edward Stiff, *The Texas Emigrant: Being a Narration of the Adventures of the Author in Texas*, pp. 134–35, 202.

Rankin's *Texas in 1850* to join the flood of immigrants; "Forests are being leveled, prairies are being fenced, farms are being opened and inproved [sic], villages are springing up, and towns are increasing in population, throughout the State, to an extent not surpassed by any other portion of the Union." The existing beautiful places of Middle Texas were becoming more numerous as forest stillness reverberated to "the constant hum of civilization." Civilization's benign influences included new crops and livestock, improvements in building styles, and beautification through the use of flowers and shrubbery, so that the "looks of the country is fast improving." East Texas was "the most perfect garden of nature," to be tended and preserved by the mental and moral improvements Rankin so ardently desired. School instruction, religious faith, and prayer were her principal instruments for assuring that "a brilliant prospect would open through the darkness of the future!"[42]

Such examples of promotional literature enumerated the benefits to be accrued from a settler's dedication to honesty, industry, and thrift. Accordingly, a number of other authors echoed Rankin's views. Benjamin Lundy, for instance, wished to fill the country's vales with farms and thriving industry. Texas was, therefore, the raw stuff from which to create the "best of all possible worlds," characterized by landscape that had been transformed and improved through human agency.

In their reminiscences and anecdotes several old-timers, however, recognized that many types of native plants and animals had become less numerous and that "civilization" was in reality simplifying natural ecosystems by reducing the number of plant and animal species. James Hampton Kuykendall (ca. 1820–82), a member of a Kentucky family who came to Texas from Arkansas with the establishment of the Austin Colony, noted in his later years how much the face of the land in the original colony had been changed, unfortunately for the worse. Fine native grasses in the bottoms of the Brazos and Colorado rivers had disappeared; so had the extensive canebrakes. Vegetation had suffered especially heavily from overgrazing and from discontinuation of annual burning, so unpalatable weeds and woody plants had invaded many pastures. Kuykendall complained that poor husbandry had also caused soils to wash off

---

[42] Melinda Rankin, *Texas in 1850*, pp. 24, 25, 88, 91, 128.

and muddy the numerous streams, which failed to support food fishes. "The wild honey-bee, which once hoarded its sweets in thousands of trees in these bottoms, has nearly disappeared," and with it had gone the venerable art of bee-lining, noted this early pioneer, whose keen eye also recognized that deepening gullies and more numerous floods were the negative effects of careless farming over thirty years of permanent Anglo-American settlement.[43]

Was it possible that the immigrant farmers whom Bollaert so admired for their initiative and hard work had failed somehow to fulfill the yeoman myth? The answer depended upon the responsibilities that one felt farmers owed to succeeding generations and to the land, their "Texas heritage." Working out of their wagons, newcomers would arrive and hack down trees to build log cabins, enclosures for stock, and split-rail fences around plots of cotton or corn. Generally, they were unconcerned about the soil exhaustion from repeated harvests of twenty, thirty, or more bushels of corn per acre, or as much as two thousand pounds of cotton per acre from the bottomlands in East Texas. Farmers did not stop to calculate the results of negligence, at least not for a generation or more.[44]

The Olmsted brothers ticked off more deserted plantations than occupied ones as they passed through Houston County in December, 1853. One establishment at which they stopped had recently harvested an exceedingly poor corn crop; owing to a dry spell, cotton totaled only fifty bales. Residents explained the unkempt appearance of the countryside by reporting that "after Annexation the owners [of the deserted homes] had moved on to better lands in the West." Census statistics, however, show that every person who may have left was replaced by three others. Houston County's improved farmland grew more than four times in the decade after 1850; yields of corn increased by a similar amount, while cotton production rose sharply by almost ten times.[45]

Land was so cheap that many judged husbandry unnecessary. And that was Kuykendall's complaint. Too much stock on the uplands had caused floods in the river bottoms, where soils had be-

[43] J. H. Kuykendall, "Reminiscences of Early Texans," *Quarterly of the Texas State Historical Association* 7 (1903–1904): 52.

[44] W. Eugene Hollon and Ruth L. Butler, eds., *William Bollaert's Texas*, pp. 117, 286–87.

[45] Olmsted, *A Journey through Texas*, p. 82.

come exhausted and readily washed away. That an area as rich as the Austin Colony had proved susceptible to such erosion and degradation disappointed him. But rather than keep their lands in good order, many folks had "upped and left" for better areas.

Noted botanist Gideon Lincecum (1793–1874) reflected this concern over poor husbandry. In the early 1860s he penned two articles in the *Texas Almanac*, drawing attention to the detrimental effects of overgrazing and of the expansion of plow agriculture into the Texas prairies. The problem is "cotton, cotton, first bale of cotton!" declared this remarkably informed and perceptive resident. Because people were bringing new lands under cotton and because they ran too much stock on pastures around the increasing number of farms, native plants, especially grasses, were becoming less available. Lincecum objected vehemently to recommendations for importing grasses from foreign lands or from states in the north and east ("a Yankee trick!") in order to improve Texas pastures. "The grasses best suited for meadows in Texas are already here," argued this well-traveled resident; what was needed was a more intelligent, thoughtful, and regulated use of them.[46]

Farmers who had plowed up lands could reset them in native grasses by collecting seed from plants located in the corners or edges of their fields. "It is our avarice that overstocks and exhausts our pasture grounds" so that they are grazed too close, admitted Lincecum.[47] He experimented with a thirty-five-acre unfenced and unplowed meadow for about a decade, and discovered that the pasture produced from thirty thousand to fifty thousand pounds of hay annually. The point he was intent on making was that farmers should not exhaust the land and should develop patterns of cropping that took account of the qualities and capacities of soils and pastures for renewal. The "get in, get out" approach, he said, was destroying agriculture over the long term.

By the mid-1860s, cotton dominated most counties east of the San Antonio River, and yields from extensive river bottoms were expected to continue to average about one bale (four hundred to five hundred pounds) per acre, with one-half or three-quarters of a

[46] Gideon Lincecum, "Native or Indigenous Texas Grasses," *Texas Almanac for 1861*, p. 139.
[47] Gideon Lincecum, "The Indigenous Texian Grasses," *Texas Almanac for 1868* p. 76.

bale from upland places. In a tier of thirty counties around Dallas, wheat was prevalent; sugarcane persisted in a few districts in the lower Brazos, Colorado, and Trinity rivers, although most of it was grown in Brazoria County.

Cotton production increased almost eightfold from 1850 to 1860 (431, 463 bales were produced in the latter year), wheat jumped thirtyfold, and corn almost tripled in the same decade. These crops and many new ones were destined to increase enormously again after 1870, even though people like Gideon Lincecum and James Kuykendall before the Civil War had perceived the disastrous effects of monoculture in producing erosion and soil exhaustion.[48]

Promotional tracts and official documents tended to place stress on areas that were still empty, such as rangelands from the Grand Prairie and Balcones Escarpment westward. However, by the end of the century, stocking practices had degraded pastures even there, and the story of environmental decay beyond the Colorado River, especially in the northern Edwards Plateau and on the South Texas Plains, is a sad chapter in the state's agricultural history.

H. L. Bentley, federal agent in charge of an agricultural station at Abilene, presented an account of pasturage exhaustion over an area of twenty thousand square miles in Central Texas situated in the northern portion of the Edwards Plateau and in the Rolling Plains. This was originally buffalo country; located from fifteen hundred to nineteen hundred feet above sea level, it consisted of oak-timbered ridges, mesquite-dotted upland, and a variety of native grasses in open country plus riparian vegetation along numerous watercourses. The region filled with big game was relatively undisturbed until after the Civil War; then incoming stockmen coveted this rolling upland, seeing in it opportunities for free grass "sometimes . . . as high as a cow's back." After thirty years of continual occupancy and heavy grazing pressures from cattle and sheep, stocking rates had declined from approximately one cow per one and one-quarter acres to one cow per ten or twelve acres. Newcomers had speculated heavily in cattle; however, the bubble burst in 1884. After crowding the range brought about overgrazing and after an influx of sod-busting "nesters" planted cotton and corn in fertile

[48] United States, [Census Office], *The Seventh Census*, pp. 516, 518; and United States, Census Office, *Agriculture of the United States in 1860*, pp. 141–49.

localities, many ranchers went bankrupt as their cattle died of starvation on the denuded and ruined ranges.

Bentley argued that "the people of Texas are not different from
those of other States. They are all alike grass destroyers. Not only
has the stockman been reckless in this direction, but even the farmer
has been his ally. The latter still wages a war of extermination on
the grasses he finds growing in and about his fields; and in his anx-
iety to make more room for cotton he ruthlessly breaks the sod."
He noted that experienced ranchers in Central Texas recognized
"that the injury has gone almost past the point where redemption
is possible." The remedies were, in his opinion, to reduce stock
numbers permanently, to propagate high-quality native grasses in
order to improve the range, to cultivate meadows for hay as winter
feed, and to provide permanent water in tanks for times of drought.[49]

Four hundred miles south on the Rio Grande Plain an epoch
of overgrazing, with sheep instead of cattle as the chief culprits,
commenced in the late 1860s and lasted for a similar thirty-year
period. Through the gradual buildup of stock numbers, the South
Texas Plain was home for about 730,000 cattle and 2 million sheep
by the early 1880s. More than two-thirds of them were south of the
Nueces River—the aboriginal range of antelope, wild cattle, and
mustangs. Wildlife authority Valgene Lehmann's thesis that sheep
were "an important environmental influence in a period of great
ecological change" on the Rio Grande Plain is supported from travel
literature, county histories, and census materials that point to "a
type and degree of grazing pressure which range authorities agree
can be, and often are, destructive."

As sustained ranching began after about 1850 in South Texas,
signs of poor pasturage were quickly evident. Conditions further
deteriorated in the following decades, so open rangelands supported fewer and fewer livestock, which grazed palatable grasses
hard. By the turn of the present century, federal agronomist Jared
G. Smith noted that bermuda grass, grassbur, and certain other
grasses were widely distributed in South Texas. However, Lehmann maintained that several of them were noted indicators of range
deterioration: "Every grass which Smith described as common in

[49] H. L. Bentley, "Cattle Ranges of the Southwest: A History of the Exhaustion of the Pasturage and Suggestions for its Restoration," *Farmers' Bulletin* 72
(1898): 6–7, 10.

South Texas in 1899, therefore, was typical of rangelands from which the most productive native grasses [Indian grass, bluestem, joint grass] had disappeared." And the carrying capacity of the range had declined in little more than a generation from about one animal unit per two to five acres, to one per twenty or twenty-five acres; too many animals trampled new growth and intensively grazed surviving forage. Heavy brush—that is, shrubby growth unsuited to cattle and sheep—invaded pastures, so cactus, mesquite, catclaw, huisache, blackbrush, and other "brushy" plants grew more densely and were more widely distributed than before. One resident noted that much of the once open country between Corpus Christi and the Rio Grande had become filled with thorn thickets, often impenetrable to horsemen. Smith had no doubt that this brush and cactus would take over many of the remaining tracts of open range.[50]

Another way of avoiding the environmental decay posed by settlement and the expansion of agriculture was to emphasize the suitability of the land for specific farming practices. Kennedy, for example, noted that "a native of a southern clime, devoted to tropical agriculture and anxious to obtain quick and large returns from capital," should establish a plantation on the coast or even on the Red River "bottoms." Others from more temperate regions should locate their mixed farm holdings in grain, cotton, and livestock on the Rolling Prairies, and northerners and industrialists would prosper best in the mountain region of Texas, where they could introduce merino or saxony sheep, irrigate grains, and develop the mills and machinery for processing wheat. Texas also provided a good return from poultry and mast-fed hogs, and there was a promise of numerous and growing markets for agricultural produce in Louisiana, Mexico, Cuba, and the West Indies. Kennedy's suggestion, therefore, was to fit people and economies into localities most suited to their abilities and interests. The state's size and position were well able to satisfy sundry enterprises, so new residents were advised to accommodate themselves to its geography. However, the impulse was to alter the geography to fit human preferences, and little recognition was given to the blighted landscapes that were the

[50] Valgene W. Lehmann, *Forgotten Legions: Sheep in the Rio Grande Plain of Texas*, p. 121; and Jared G. Smith, "Grazing Problems in the Southwest, and How to Meet Them," U.S. Department of Agriculture, Division of Agrostology, *Bulletin* 16 (1899): 33.

end product of careless stocking and cropping practices and to the effects of such transformations on native fauna.[51]

In practice, Texas fulfilled the images of both an Arcadia and an Eden. Except for protecting stock from predators (which were eliminated by crusades against such scourges) and burning the prairies periodically to stimulate growth, stockmen could leave goats, sheep, and cattle to populate the ranges and fend for themselves. In 1835 Lincecum had noted how healthy and fat cattle and horses were in Central Texas, so the simple advice to turn stock loose, sit back, and watch it multiply was frequently believed. The adage "It costs more to raise a brood of chickens in Texas than an equal number of cattle" was repeated. Cattle thrived on their own, away from human vigilance, but hens and roosters had to be hand-fed and kept close to the house, away from stealthy predators. Native mammals and birds would survive somehow or die off, so in the popular mind it made little sense to have any regard for them except as objects for recreational hunting, and no sense at all to preserve them or their habitats, for there was ample room for both settlement and wild creatures. Besides, environmental transformation was a kind of messianic activity—Texas was being reclaimed.

[51] Kennedy, *Texas*, pp. 132–34.

CHAPTER 5

Mediterranean Metaphor: Old World Plants and Animals in Texas

THE expansion of settled areas and a continued reliance on game and other animals brought about a slow but growing awareness that many species were declining and becoming very scarce. Until this concern was expressed by laws for wildlife protection, however, settlers were wedded to the idea of "improving" Texas by introducing new plants and animals, not rehabilitating native ones.

One motif that they pursued energetically was to transform the wilderness into a "garden," especially the type of landscape consisting of family farms with orchards, vineyards, and herds of goats and sheep so typical of Spain, Italy, and other areas in the Mediterranean Basin. The eminent natural scientist Alexander Von Humboldt (1769–1859) drew an early optimistic picture by characterizing Mexico's temperate zone (30°–38° north latitude) as a region where "German winters succeed to Neapolitan and Sicilian Summers." Referring specifically to Texas, Von Humboldt saw in this immense "wild desert, still more thinly peopled than the governments of Asiatic Russia," a climate, soils, and natural resources with great opportunities. Promotional literature from the 1830s and 1840s bolstered this view of Texas as a land of unparalleled bounty and promise; authors mentioned repeatedly the similarities between Texas landscapes and Mediterranean environments. In 1832 Friedrich Ernst, the state's first German settler, likened the climate of Texas to that of Sicily.[1]

[1] Alexander Von Humboldt, *Political Essay on the Kingdom of New Spain*, 2: 273; and Caroline Von Hinueber, "Life of German Pioneers in Early Texas," *Quarterly of the Texas State Historical Association* 2 (1898–99): 227–32.

This idea of a new and expanding landscape conflicted with what actually existed as the natural habitat in Texas. This rural scene, similar to the landscape paintings by Salvatore Rosa or Nicholas Poussin in which orchards, flocks of sheep, and rustic cottages were surrounded by trimmed copses and tilled fields, had great visual appeal. Its open parkland was a symbol, too, of the cultural hearth of Western civilization; Texas was, as Lieutenant Maury put it, a neoclassical landscape where Western religion would find its renaissance.[2] This Mediterranean image of Texas was also the basis for a series of individual experiments with plants and animals to turn a high profit. The natural equability in this Texas-to-be meant that useful Old World biota could be introduced successfully and become even more vigorous in North America. Consequently, such "improvements" on nature made native biota of incidental interest and concern; undisturbed sections of woodland, prairie, or marsh became less common, and their indigenous bears, deer, waterfowl, and other species lost a fundamental requirement—habitat for food, rest, and reproduction.

New grasses, shrubs or trees, and livestock strengthened the garden image and its Mediterranean expression, so native species, although initially abundant, were subject to "improvements," too. Either they fitted into this new environment as adaptive or opportunistic elements or they did not. If they were unable to adjust to the presence of increasing human numbers, they were relegated to the periphery of settled areas. If they were noxious or dangerous, people eradicated them.

The general healthfulness and fertility of this new land made it the "golden mean" between the colder, harsher climes of northern Europe and North America and the tropical, hot ones to the south, in Africa and northern South America. Olmsted termed this equability an "Arcadian preeminence of position among our States," characterized by a balmy climate, "soil unmatched in any known equal area," and "a front on the highway of the world."[3]

The middle or Rolling Prairie zone, especially the land between the San Jacinto and San Antonio rivers, was considered the best place. It had warm winters and hot summers but received rainfall

[2] Lieutenant Maury, "Great Commercial Advantages of the Gulf of Mexico," *DeBow's Review* 7 (1849):522.

[3] Frederick Law Olmsted, *A Journey through Texas*, p. 411.

throughout the year. The coastal zone in the southeast and the outer mountain region to the north and west were more given to extremes. Hot, humid conditions persisted on the coastal lowlands in summer, although they were relieved in places like Galveston by cool sea breezes. Winter snows, freezing spells, and chilling northers occurred across the northern distant plateaus and plains.

Taken as a whole, however, Texas was blessed by variable weather within a moderate climate, so, according to Colonel Stiff, the "climate of classic Greece is not more favorable to the development of the intellect." Stiff called upon classical ties with Greece and with Rome in his promotional *Texas Emigrant*, which was published after his short sojourn in Houston in 1840. He appealed to young and vigorous persons, "who must be the architects of their own fortune," to carve out a new civilization in Texas: "The eagles of Rome in all their glory, soared not over so fine a country." Moreover, exclaimed Stiff, "Spartan mothers never nestled to their bosoms better materials for heroes" than could be nursed in this "beautiful inclined plane." Once they were settled in Texas, these immigrant "heroes" would find that they were "beyond the tormenting jingle of sleigh bells in winter"; they would be wafted by sea breezes and enjoy balmy temperatures beneath groves of newly planted trees.[4]

Similar hyperbole is found in other tracts and may have had practical consequences. A "visionary speculator," wishing to provide considerably more than new shade trees and fully cognizant of the evocative value of classical expressions, decided to invest in this "best region," between Austin and Brushy Creek, some time before George Kendall's misadventure with the Texan Sante Fe Expedition. According to Kendall, this land promoter drew up plans for the city of "Athens," where "there were colleges and squares, city halls and penitentiaries, public walks and public houses." However, it seems that Comanches scared the builder away; "thus fell a modern Athens," concluded Kendall piously.[5]

David Edward presented a more cautious, less hortatory version of this "garden" image. He included the "causes of disease," which he attributed to climate (heat), soils (location), and rotting

[4] Edward Stiff, *The Texas Emigrant: Being a Narration of the Adventures of the Author in Texas*, pp. 135, 136, 198, 202.
[5] George Wilkins Kendall, *Across the Great Southwestern Prairies* 1: 73–74.

vegetation (miasma), and he listed the sites people should avoid. After his initial caveat, however, Edward argued that if the new republic was not a "second paradise," it could certainly be made into one. Neighboring Louisiana and Mississippi had more diseases from the miasmas because of their abundant stagnant waters and swamps. Regions further north in the United States suffered from frost and other inclement weather. But the moderate conditions of Texas were kind, especially to those inhabitants of interior "Texas Kentuck," that is, to persons recently settled in the Rolling Prairies. There people were able to harvest and store bountiful supplies of corn ("more bread stuff than they well know sometimes what to do with") after planting a little seed. Milch cattle increased, too, faster than they could be managed, and with the abundant supply of varied wild game ("as wild animals decreased, the domesticated ones will increase"), the livelihood of Texans was guaranteed. Indeed, many people had become somewhat indolent through effortlessly picking over the "condiments and relishes" of nature.[6]

William Kennedy also presented an attractive picture of this "Italy of America," with a temperature "delightful to the sense, and favorable to life." The only "ungenial" months were winter periods when stormy northern winds occurred. Ice and snow were transient, however, making winters usually pleasant, so that unlike New Mexico, which Albert Pike called the "Siberia" of North America, Texans could plant two gardens—one for the summer, the other for winter. Under such healthy conditions, Kennedy argued, no malady was really endemic to the republic. By acclimatization and self-restraint (notably in the consumption of alcohol), a stranger could quickly cope with the "febrile diseases." And excepting coastal places, where people became sickly, "no part of the globe is more friendly to the regular action of the human frame" than Texas.[7]

Obviously, the fertile soils supported a varied plant and animal life, and early writers judged that they offered ever greater prospects for gain. It did not surprise Edward, for example, to learn that the black, sandy alluvial, cotton-bearing soils yielded several

[6] David B. Edward, *The History of Texas*, pp. 78–79, 86.
[7] William Kennedy, *Texas: The Rise, Progress, and Prospects of the Republic of Texas*, pp. 66, 69, 71; Olmsted, *A Journey through Texas*, p. 412, substantially agreed that Texas was "Italy" in terms of climate, and likened spells of hot dampness to the sirocco (p. 275).

hundred pounds more per acre than did similar lands in the South, and more sugarcane, oats, and even wheat. Corn yielded thirty to forty bushels per acre in an "open woody bottom with a marlinspike" and needed very little husbandry except to keep vermin off.[8]

Arthur Ikin's *Texas*, published in 1841, discussed all aspects of these soils in glowing terms. Deep, very rich, stone-free alluvia characterized the Coastal Plain, making it like a vast "bowling green" or "a wilderness of flowers" in summer. Citrus, pomegranates, and even pineapple matured there. And the lands adjacent to the Trinity, Colorado, and Brazos rivers and their tributaries were extremely rich (although unhealthy), "not surpassed in fertility in the far-famed lands of the Delta of the Nile."[9]

Fertile loams, mixed with sands, typified the "most enchanting" second division, that of the Rolling Prairies. The silica content or limestone substrate seldom inhibited "the culture of the most exhausting products," with promise for olives, almonds, apricots, and pawpaws. "The country is probably destined to the occupation of a mixed population of herdsmen and planters," declared Olmsted, who judged that the thick soils west along the Red River system (some termed this northwest region the "Egypt of Texas") were superbly adapted for wheat; others in the east were good for sugar, and those in the south produced much cotton. Finally, the "mountain" zone of West Texas (beyond the Colorado) boasted fertile valleys with well-timbered slopes in its eastern sections. It became a "waste region," however, from the Hill Country westward. Olmsted declared the Rio Grande Plain "a region so sterile and valueless, as to be commonly reputed a desert" and the Staked Plain "an immense desolate, barren table-land." This unsettled and incompletely known tableland was not unlike the steppes of Central Asia, but more fertile.[10]

Access to Gulf Coast ports such as Galveston added a new spatial dimension to the prospect of marketing exotic agricultural produce. The north-to-south drainage pattern, protecting harborages,

[8] Edward, *The History of Texas*, pp. 45–47.

[9] Arthur Ikin, *Texas: Its History, Topography, Agriculture, Commerce, and General Statistics*, pp. 19–21; and D. L. M'Gary, "Central Texas," *Texas Rural Register and Immigrants Handbook*, p. 39.

[10] Olmsted, *A Journey through Texas*, pp. 421, 424–25, 447–48; "Texas," *Texas Almanac for 1878*, p. 11; Ikin, *Texas*, pp. 20–21.

and ready markets along the Mississippi watershed in the east and beyond, and to Mexico in the west, made the commercial geography of Texas very appealing. The physiognomy and position of the Gulf of Mexico compared favorably with that of the Mediterranean Sea.

Lieutenant Maury of the U.S. Navy argued that navigation in the Mediterranean Sea was impeded in places by deep bays and promontories that lengthened sailing distances by a factor of ten compared with those in the Gulf of Mexico. "There are no such interruptions to navigation in the Gulf of Mexico," he declared; ships sailed directly across its 4.3 million square miles, a body of water larger than the Mediterranean, India, and Western Europe combined, and could proceed through a drainage system four times longer than that in the Mediterranean. Maury argued that the "physico-commercial" characteristics of the Gulf of Mexico and Caribbean Sea, which he termed "our Mediterranean," were unique.

Western Europe had no rivers like the Mississippi or the Amazon. The hinterlands of these mighty rivers, and similar large waterways, offered "production upon production, in such luxuriance and profusion that man without changing his latitude may in one day ascend from summer's heat to winter's cold, gathering, as he goes, the fruits of every clime, the staples of every country."[11] This "new Mediterranean" was located in the southern portion of the temperate zone, and residents could draw freely on the resources of the adjacent torrid and frigid zones. Man was neither pinched with cold nor starved with hunger in this land of the golden mean— the new nursery for civilization and Christianity.

Maury expanded his geopolitical treatise by arguing that God had intended "inland basins" as the secluded places for human development. As the residents of the River Jordan basin had fallen into a "semi-barbarous state," the inhabitants of the Mississippi watershed, which bound the United States together, were the new standard-bearers of civilization. Texas was linked into this Gulf heartland where, Maury concluded, the promise of a Mediterranean-type renaissance in the Americas was anticipated.[12]

The strategic place of Texas in the Gulf Coast "Mediterranean"

[11] Maury, "Great Commercial Advantages of the Gulf of Mexico," pp. 515, 523, 517.

[12] Ibid., pp. 520–22.

evoked historical analogy because of its central position. Texas was like "the Byzantium kingdom of old"; it was at the crossroads for the agricultural and industrial produce of North American states and for the mineral wealth of Old Mexico (and the city of Austin was its central market).[13] The image persisted. The *Corpus Christi Caller* (December 23, 1883), for example, referred to that port city as "the Gibralter [sic] of the Gulf"; its elevation kept the city healthful and protected from storms. Additionally, Corpus Christi, like Gibraltar, was positioned to serve a number of nations. The city provided the port of entry to the continent's interior, especially for the Southwest and California.

Other states, too, were likened to the Mediterranean region of Europe. Image-makers compared the sun-kissed southern valleys of California with Italy, Greece, or Spain. John Charles Fremont, for example, promoted the image of Italy in his writings about California. He wanted his estate "to glory in California-as-South, California-as-Mediterranean," challenging settlers to "embrace beauty and escape the Puritan past." This politician and charismatic personality celebrated the same vestiges of a Latin culture that occurred in Texas, but he was prepared to extend and embellish them. The landscapes of the Golden State were ordered, gardenlike, and daily described as an interaction of fact and imagination.

Riding horseback on the Los Angeles plain through man-high mustard abloom in vivid yellow under a Levantine sun, travelers recalled the Holy Land, and perhaps even the parable of the mustard seed. As they sailed off the coast, they thought of Morocco, Sicily, or Greece. Silhouetted at sunset, a row of cypresses outside of Fresno in the San Joaquin brought to mind a similar day's end in Lombardy or the Campagna; and, of course, the vineyards of the Bay counties suggested the south of France.[14]

Quite frequently, travellers and others in Texas were reminded of these Mediterranean landscapes as they passed from one region to another. Muir noted that near San Antonio "something in the fresh and beautiful appearance of the valley" served to uplift the spirits of weary travellers entering the city from the east. From a distance the environs seemed "covered with works of art, that re-

[13] George A. Ferris, "Stock Raising in Texas," *Texas Rural Almanac*, p. 99, and W. Eugene Hollon and Ruth L. Butler, eds., *William Bollaert's Texas*, pp. 193–94.
[14] Kevin Starr, *Americans and the California Dream, 1850–1915*, pp. 367, 370.

mind one of Washington Irving's description of the green valleys of Granada." As Muir drew closer, however, the image changed; the ruins of the churches reminded him of Italy.[15]

Other visitors discovered Mediterranean, particularly Italian, images in other urban scenes. Austin, "like the ancient city Rome," was built on seven hills, so "it is impossible to conceive of a more beautiful and lovely situation," declared George Bonnell, who came to Texas in 1836 and settled in Austin, where an eminence overlooking the Colorado River in the city is named after him. Although William Bollaert found Austin like a ghost town in August of 1843, when the seat of government was temporarily located in Houston (bats infested the President's house, and the Capitol was "the abode of bats, lizards and stray cattle"), he nevertheless liked Austin's situation and its site "abounding in game, and bees as numerous as the swarms of Hybla, and blessed with a climate fit to yield the Hesperian Fruit." "If Rome was celebrated in song for her 'seven hills,' Austin may well boast of her 'thousand mounds,' covered with bowers equal in splendor to the Arcadian groves," eulogized Bollaert, who predicted that as emigrants propelled "the car of enterprize to the West," the wildernesses beyond Austin would "'bloom and blossom as the rose.'"[16]

This capital of Texas was on the edge of the mountain zone where the wilderness, not the garden, prevailed. Some writers found the Mediterranean metaphor in that region, too. When George Kendall, for example, decided to break away from the Santa Fe expedition in late August, 1841, he climbed out of a deep canyon in West Texas and looked down on the tiny white-topped wagons, silvery waters, and greenery, a scene that later caused him to exclaim: "Almost the whole valley was bordered by the yawning chasm that had impeded the progress of our waggons, now brought more plainly to view by the elevation upon which we stood, and the whole scene forcibly reminded me of one of Salvator Rosa's beautiful landscapes, framed with rough, gnarled, and unfinished oak."[17] There in West Texas this well-read, widely travelled gentleman was able

[15] Andrew F. Muir, ed., *Texas in 1837, an Anonymous, Contemporary Narrative*, pp. 94, 98.

[16] George W. Bonnell, *Topographical Description of Texas*, p. 65; Hollon and Butler, eds., *Bollaert's Texas*, pp. 193–95.

[17] Kendall, *Southwestern Prairies* 1: 231–32.

to discover a perfect example of the sublime and beautiful landscapes that were much beloved by late-eighteenth- and early-
nineteenth-century tourists who wished to take in and admire the
alpine scenery of France or Italy.

The juxtaposition of prairie and sky and the awful emptiness of
Texas filled many travellers with feelings of both admiration and
fear. In respect to skies, a promotional tract on West Texas, published by the Galveston, Harrisburg, and San Antonio Railway
Company, included comments about the remarkable clarity of the
night skies in the dry, underpopulated region. In the evening the
sun became "a huge ball of fire falling amidst the grass of the prairie" and suffused the open plains with a golden hue that darkened
as the night advanced to reveal a sky studded with bright stars.
"Poets have often sung of the beauty of the Italian skies, but those
who have seen both pronounce ours equally beautiful," was the
conclusion. Olmsted agreed, too; the nebulae were agreeably brilliant in Texas; they shone more brightly there than in other places
he had visited. "The Germans," who were Olmsted's experts in most
matters Texana, "have a saying that the sky seems nearer in Texas
than in Europe," he noted.[18]

New Crops

In Texas, as in California, the Mediterranean motif was expressed
most clearly through similarities in climate and in the crops that
replaced native vegetation and consequently the habitats of many
native animals. The metaphor endured in references to grape culture. In Spanish times, Bishop Marín de Porras likened South Central Texas to Spain's Old Castile because of its climate and native
vines. Similarly, El Paso and the production of wine and raisins
there reminded him of Spain. Von Humboldt also likened this locality in the Southwest to areas he had seen in the Mediterranean.
The dry heat, the maquis-like xeric vegetation, and the Spanish-
speaking peasantry made the metaphor simple and compelling.

The native mustang grape (*Vitis candicans*), a widespread vigorous vine, was especially thought to represent similarities with

[18] Galveston, Harrisburg and San Antonio Railway Co., *A Description of Western
Texas*, p. 6; Olmsted, *A Journey through Texas*, pp. 308, 412.

wine lands in the Old World and the promise for commercial wine-making. "It is found on every timbered hill side and by every running stream," stated an immigrants' handbook with customary hyperbole. The plant's tiny purplish sweet fruit (despite a bitter rind) was expected to equal the best "of France and Italy."[19] Burke's *Texas Almanac* for 1878 predicted fame and fortune for a wine industry, and T. V. Munson's research into grape culture, including the mustang variety, at Denison, on the bluffs of the Red River in Grayson County, drew national recognition and international acclaim.

Munson obtained varieties of American grapes from his friend and instructor Robert Peter in Lexington, Kentucky, in 1873. Testing seeds as a nurseryman in Nebraska proved fruitless; then Munson moved to the rough "dark limestone, timbered land" of Denison, Texas, in April, 1876. Munson scoured the area for wild grapevines and discovered "six or eight good species of wild grape" previously unknown to him. Denison proved to be "my grape paradize!" This native son of Illinois, who developed an interest in Texas as a student in the Agricultural and Mechanical College of Kentucky, pioneered long and extensive investigations of native grapes in the 1880s; his research and classification of grape varieties in 1885 was well received and generally accepted.

Munson exhibited all of the American and many Asiatic grape species at the Columbian Exposition in Chicago in 1893; however, his major effort was directed at collecting and testing the best wild and cultivated grapes in order to improve viticulture in the United States. Every year after 1880, Munson planted one to five acres in grapes, including native and introduced stock as well as hybridized varieties, and tested and developed scores of grape species. He was only the second American to receive France's prestigious medal of the Legion of Honor, for saving French vineyards from the scourge of *Phylloxera*.[20]

More than fifty years earlier, commentators had lavished praise on the state's natural vines. Mary Austin Holley eulogized the variety and flavor of grapes, emphasizing that "no country can be better adapted for the culture of the vine than this." She predicted that vineyards would become important commercially because experi-

[19] M'Gary, "Central Texas," p. 39.
[20] Thomas Volney Munson, *Foundations of American Grape Culture*, pp. 6–8, 230.

ments in wine-making were proving successful. Others supported
the idea of growing grapes for wine-making. David Edward, who
also published his guide in 1836, agreed that "every sort of fruit
seeds adapted to the temperate zone, have been found to want only
that persevering industry, and particular attention"; moreover, for
producing the grapevine, "Texas excels." Edward had a definite
preference for Texas grapes, claiming that the new republic exceeded all other places in the variety and quality of them. Wild
vines were more plentiful and widespread in Texas than in Louisiana and Arkansas and were healthy and flavorful. He echoed Holley's opinion that even the poorest lands were suited for vineyards.
Wine promised to become as common as honey from the bee trees,
so Texans would soon be well fortified physically and commercially
by this "profitable concern" and would produce beverages equal to
those of Switzerland, Italy, or France.[21]

In practice, however, it appears that viticulture was not widely
established in the eastern counties of Texas by southern Anglo-
American settlers or by German immigrants, many of whom originated from northern Germany, where grape cultivation did not occur. Some German settlers, however, did establish vineyards near
Houston and in Fayette and in Colorado counties, selling and even
exporting wines. Several discussions of the best grapes and places
for setting vines were reported in meetings of the German-pioneered
Cat Spring Agricultural Society, the first agrarian society in Texas.
In February, 1885, for instance, it was noted that the Hebremont
grape was "recommended as the variety best suited for this area."
Making wine from local, native grapes was more common, however, and the mustang variety was the principal source. After initial
fermentation, the new wine received large quantities of sugar in
order to make it palatable.[22]

An authority on German settlement has noted that in the west,
around New Braunfels and in the Hill Country, vine cultivation was
more common, and apparently profitable, partly because immigrants came from wine-making localities in Alsace, Hesse, and Nas-
sau. Some persons settled by the Verein carried vine cuttings into

[21] Mary Austin Holley, *Texas*, p. 65; Edward, *The History of Texas*, pp. 71–72.
[22] Cat Spring Agricultural Society, *Century of Agricultural Progress, 1856–
1956*, p. 108; Terry G. Jordan, *German Seed in Texas Soil: Immigrant Farmers in
Nineteenth-Century Texas*, pp. 76–79.

Hill Country settlements. A notice in the *Southern Cultivator* (March, 1868) confirmed the practice of wine-drinking in German settlements, where "a very palatable table wine, equal to good ordinary Claret, is made from the Mustang grape, and used habitually as we use coffee."[23]

Viktor Bracht reported that "many varieties of European grape vines" were being planted in Castroville, where wild grapes also grew "luxuriantly," and that they had produced fair wine, excellent vinegar, and some brandy. It seems, however, that immigrants turned once more to local grapes as imported European stock faded. Some commerce in wines was recorded from Fredericksburg and Boerne, but the unimproved, abundant native grapes appear to have been the mainstay of the wine industry, which was geared mostly for home consumption and for vinegar.[24]

Cotton and Sugarcane

Overwhelming interest in cotton and corn, authorities have argued, tended to inhibit the development of other crops, such as orchard fruits, until after 1850. But cotton expansion in eastern counties was one significant enterprise that resulted in sizable transformations of native bottomland vegetation and its dependent fauna. The cotton industry developed quickly under the *empresario* system, as exemplified by Jared E. Groce's plantation along the Brazos River (about 1821). There a cotton gin was constructed, and bales began to be exported to New Orleans. Planters and their slaves quickly enlarged cotton acreages, and in 1834 Colonel Almonte reported to the Mexican government that the Nacogdoches Department was expected to export about two thousand bales (in that year the Texas crop sold for about six hundred thousand dollars). Assuming that an acre of cotton produced one bale weighing between four hundred and five hundred pounds (a generous estimate), the area under cotton expanded at least fivefold between 1829 and 1839— to about five thousand acres. It increased by almost the same again, to twenty-three thousand acres, by 1845, and by a similar amount

---

[23] Jordan, *German Seed*, pp. 140–141; and *Southern Cultivator* 26 (1868): 69.
[24] Viktor Bracht, *Texas in 1848*, p. 101; Jordan, *German Seed*, pp. 140–41.

a decade later. Most of it grew in southeastern counties along the Brazos and Colorado rivers and in East Texas.[25]

By the late 1870s Texas was a leading state in cotton, growing in excess of one million bales. A year or so later, however, when officials made the Tenth Census, cotton production had dropped below that of Mississippi and Georgia. The state's 2.2 million acres also made it a close third to Georgia and Alabama, which had 2.6 and 2.3 million acres, respectively, under cotton. The acreage in Texas, however, represented 15 percent of the national total, whereas the slightly larger area under corn, 2.5 million acres, comprised merely 4 percent of the land under that crop nationwide.

In Texas, cotton, like corn, represented about one acre in six of improved farmland, and the blacklands in Fayette and Washington counties as well as that major blackland wedge cutting through McLennan and Ellis counties were planted in cotton. In 1879 these four counties had in excess of fifty thousand acres each under cotton—more than the amount under corn. By the 1890 census the area under cotton surpassed the area sown for corn by almost one million acres and was close to doubling again by 1900. Soil exhaustion and erosion through constant monocropping caused a shift away from exclusive dependency on cotton as influential persons pushed a number of plans to improve crop husbandry, including the diversification of agriculture.[26]

In his keynote address to the first annual Texas State Fair, held in Houston in May of 1870, the Honorable John H. Reagan (1818–1905) lambasted cropping practices in antebellum Texas as overly committed to cotton. Not enough effort, he argued, had been given to orchard fruits and forage crops. The congressman declared that: "While diversifying our crops, we should cultivate less land to the hand, fence it better, manure it more, drain, and especially underdrain it better, give more attention to the proper rotation of crops,

[25] Lewis C. Gray, *History of Agriculture in the Southern United States to 1860*, 2:825; "History and Status of Cotton Production . . .," *Texas Department of Agriculture Yearbook 1909*, pp. 33–70, 47; Jordan, *German Seed*, p. 68.

[26] United States Census Office, *Report on the Productions of Agriculture as Returned at the Tenth Census (June 1, 1880)* 3: 276–78; United States, *Report on the Statistics of Agriculture in the United States at the Eleventh Census: 1890* 1: 396–97; and John S. Spratt, *The Road to Spindletop: Economic Change in Texas, 1875–1901* pp. 70–73, present a favorable view of cotton as a nonexhausting crop.

rest our land . . . our land ought to be broke in deep, and thoroughly pulverized."[27]

Reagan concluded that comfortable homes on well-tended farms with orchards, vegetable plots, and flower gardens reflected true artisanship. There was a need for such husbandry and the "mechanic arts" to accomplish these improvements. Reagan was against too much cotton. For him, Texas was the home for independent yeomen farmers, not for those given over only to "cash-cotton," squalor, and fecklessness.

Warm-weather-loving cotton was the first of many subtropical and tropical fruits, grains, and livestock, many of them from Mediterranean Europe, that farmers tried and tested in Texas. Some of them, like cotton, were intended to supply markets in north-temperate urban and industrializing areas at home and abroad. As such, they fitted into a plantation system geared to extensive agriculture because land was cheap. This crop was an essential item of pioneer agriculture that planters and farmers established as they entered a new region. Significantly, it was also a crop that required major changes in natural plant and animal associations. An agricultural historian has called pioneer planting a "transition stage . . . between herding and systematic agriculture," whereby a variety of staple foods, including free-ranging hogs and cattle, were raised with cash crops like cotton; both livestock and plantation crops exerted pressures on indigenous fauna. Most food and clothing was produced on the plantation, where "pioneer planters were frequently little behind pioneer farmers in degree of self-sufficiency."[28]

With cotton in the central and eastern counties and with corn, which "will grow indiscriminately and in the greatest abundance, in every portion of the State," people also expected sugarcane—another crop requiring clearing for new fields—to expand greatly in the East Texas bottomlands from its traditional base in Louisiana. They argued that the "still more congenial soil and climate of the level region of Texas" would yield bumper quantities of molasses. Long, balmy days in Texas enabled a large number of joints on the cane (reportedly brought by Columbus from the Canary Islands to the West Indies) to ripen before the onset of light frosts, which

[27] Mechanical and Blood Stock Association of Texas, *Report of the Texas State Fair*, pp. 12–26, quotation pp. 17–18.
[28] Gray, *History of Agriculture* 1: pp. 438–40, quotation p. 439.

substantially injure the crop. Kennedy believed that Texas cane was superior to that further east, and that it would yield up to thirty-five hundred pounds per acre. Both ribbon and Creole varieties were apparently well suited to the heavy lands of the Brazos bottoms and supplied copious amounts of sugar while proving excellent fodder for cattle and horses.[29]

Early authors like Kennedy eulogized cane in its incipiency: the "comparative superiority of Texas sugar over that of the United States, is declared by so many witnesses, and those of such reputability as to remove all doubt of its truth." The prospects for the commercial success of sugar in riparian areas, and even in the moister uplands, were considered to be bright; additionally, one source noted that many planters set aside a small plot near the house where children were permitted to cut and consume cane, because juice, syrup, and sugar had proven healthful to persons engaged in cutting, gathering, pruning, and boiling cane extract. The production of molasses was not necessarily the prerogative of rich planters; family farmers working around a single mill could earn a good livelihood.[30]

The lower reaches of the Trinity, Brazos, and Colorado rivers became the focus for most cane growing. A visitor in 1831 reported that people on Judge Williams's estate on the Trinity had raised forty hogsheads of quality sugar, apparently from "ribband" or ribbon cane (which had been planted in Louisiana first in 1817 to replace indigo), a hardy, early-ripening cane, and also from the more durable Creole variety. Another writer, however, noted in the late 1830s that "cane had been successfully cultivated" in the vicinity of San Antonio. And Viktor Bracht mentioned it as successful at Castroville, located twenty-five miles west of San Antonio, a decade later.[31]

In the late 1840s Texas ranked low in sugar production (only Alabama, South Carolina, and Arkansas harvested less), reporting a mere twenty thousand pounds. After 1850, when Brazoria and Mat-

[29] United States, Patent Office, "E. F. Gilbert, Matagorda County," *Report of the Commissioner for 1853*, p. 124; Gray, *History of Agriculture* 2: 749, 751; and Kennedy, *Texas*, p. 88.

[30] [A. B. Lawrence], *Texas in 1840 or, The Emigrant's Guide to the New Republic*, p. 117.

[31] *A Visit to Texas; Being the Journal of a Traweller Through Those Parts Most Interesting to American Settlers*, p. 92; Gray, *History of Agriculture* 2: 749; Muir, ed., *Texas in 1837*, pp. 99, 120; and Bracht, *Texas in 1848*, p. 101.

agorda counties dominated production, however, cane growing increased greatly, and the state's production grew to exceed nearly all of the other six states except Louisiana, which dominated the market. After the Civil War, sugarcane growing was revived along the upper coast and cane was planted in the lower Rio Grande Valley. But the yields from this soil-exhausting crop never attained Kennedy's optimistic figure for them, although some places in its traditional center, Brazoria County, produced well. Geologist S. B. Buckley spent the early part of January, 1860, on a well-run plantation with about seven hundred acres under cane near Ellerslie, Brazoria County, where the crop was planted anew on a rotated basis every three years. He explained the cultivation process:

The planting begins from the middle to the last of January, with joints of cane; for this plant never matures its seed either in the United States or Cuba. He plants in drills seven feet apart; but in Louisiana, the distance between rows is often less by one or two feet. There also a hogshead of 1000 pounds is considered a good yield per acre; but as much as one and a half hogsheads are occasionally made. In Brazoria county, two hogsheads of 1200 pounds each have been made from one acre in one season, the average in good seasons being from 1200 pounds to 1500 pounds per acre. The cane is worked with the plow until the last of July, when its tops meet and shade the ground, so as to prevent the growth of weeds; then the crop is "laid by." The grinding of cane begins from the 10th to the 20th of November, and lasts until it is time to plow for a new crop. The molasses is considered as generally sufficient to defray the expenses of cultivation.[32]

Horticulture

Well before 1600, the Spanish carried to the Indies apples, pears, plums, apricots, mulberries, oranges, lemons, and limes—plants that demanded, for the most part, carefully prepared plots or fields and assiduous attention, including protection from diseases and thieving birds. Early imports required a lengthy sea crossing, which made the transfer of plants difficult because of exposure to saltwater, tropical temperatures, and high humidity. However, orchard crops with a distinctively Mediterranean character, such as peaches and citruses, were promoted in Texas under Anglo-American and

[32] Gray, *History of Agriculture*, 2: 748–49, Table 29; and Samuel B. Buckley, *A Preliminary Report of the Texas Geological Survey*, pp. 60–61.

"civilized" Indian colonization from the late 1820s.[33] Peaches, which were natives of Persia and South Asia and had become so familiar in gardens and orchards in southern Europe, made new settlements attractive, and certain varieties of them became profitable. Ikin and other early writers characterized peaches as "commonly cultivated fruits," and several noteworthy peach orchards were planted in coastal areas.[34]

Promotional literature judged that these quick-growing peach trees gave fruit in the third year where orchards were free of disease. It was argued that varieties "of unrivalled size and flavor" would be enhanced by new strains, and approximately a hundred of these varieties are attributed to horticultural research in Texas. Many resulted from Gilbert Onderdonk's pioneering work at Nursery, in Victoria County, during the 1860s. Onderdonk drew national applause for his classification of peach varieties according to locality and geographical position. The "Peen-To" or Chinese peach group grew in the most southern latitudes of the nation and was replaced northward by cold-tolerant varieties, namely South Chinese, Spanish, North Chinese, and Persian races. Peach growing became widespread in the southern through north-central counties of Texas. Delicious fruit, for example, existed around Austin from late June into October and could be put into reusable "self-sealing cans," so that "instead of bringing canned fruit from the New York market, we should have a surplus to send there."[35] By the 1890s, horticulturists were tending almost 4.5 million peach trees, and in 1909 the orchard inspector in the newly formed Texas Department of Agriculture noted that 2,991 acres of orchard nurseries held 17 million trees, including 7.1 million peach, "the most important fruit grown in Texas."[36]

[33] James A. Robertson, "Preliminary Notes on . . . Plants and Animals to . . . Colonies Overseas," *James Sprunt Historical Studies* 19 (1927): 7–21. For early references to horticulture, see Holley, *Texas*, p. 65; Muir, ed., *Texas in 1837*, p. 124; and Stiff, *The Texas Emigrant*, p. 10.

[34] Ikin, *Texas*, p. 47; and Euroda Moore, "Recollections of Indianola," *Indianola Scrap Book*, pp. 94–132.

[35] Buckley, *Texas Geological Survey*, p. 62; and Gilbert Onderdonk, "Pomological Possibilities of Texas," *Texas Department of Agriculture Bulletin* 9 (1909): 5–55, especially 28–33. See also Kennedy, *Texas*, p. 94; [Lawrence], *Texas in 1840*, pp. 144–45; and Holley, *Texas*, p. 66.

[36] R. H. Porce, "Pruning and Training Peach Orchards," *Texas Agriculture Experiment Station Bulletin* 58 (1900): 27; also Onderdonk, "Pomological Possibilities," *Texas Department of Agriculture Bulletin* 9 (1909: 8–9.

Head of the citrus family was the orange, which reportedly reached the nation in small quantities from southern Europe and was grown in the southeastern United States for domestic use. It was, however, considered a luxury and difficult to acclimatize to freezing winters. Although oranges were grown in coastal areas from Galveston southward, this fruit did not prove to be a money-maker in Texas until late in the nineteenth century. Edward Clopper remembered planting orange and lemon seeds near the confluence of the San Jacinto River with Galveston Bay on January 2, 1828. In that same area, a traveller to the Hall plantation in mid-March of 1831 noted a "large enclosure around the house, filled with young orange and fig trees, as well as many other kinds of fruit." Later in the decade Muir judged that the orange "flourishes with proper culture and attention," unlike sickly looking apples and other fruit that he had seen.[37]

The cold winter of 1849–50 wiped out orange cultivation on the coastal plain around Galveston. Similar conditions had affected promising citrus groves in South Carolina and Georgia half a century earlier.[38] But some individuals around Victoria, Texas, persisted and revitalized orange-growing until winter "northers" again killed the trees. It is not surprising, therefore, that a note in the *Almanac* of 1870 suggested that the future of the orange on Galveston Island was not as secure as in Florida. Nevertheless, most gardens in that city were adorned with orange and lemon trees nearly every year. A hardy variety, dormant in winter, was desirable, so the Satsuma variety (a slow grower in spring, but good-flavored) grafted to the deciduous hardy *Citrus trifoliata* was tested successfully.

Gilbert Onderdonk, pomologist and pioneer in the cultivation of peaches, also experimented with oranges in order to test and improve hardiness. He believed that with careful management six or seven crops of citrus could be grown per decade in suitable locations from the Sabine River to Corpus Christi. Further south, between Kingsville and Raymondville, for instance, it was possible

[37] W. H. Ragan, "Our Cultivated Fruits—Native and Introduced," in U.S. Department of Agriculture, *Report of the Commissioner for 1888*, pp. 577–95, especially p. 583; Edward N. Clopper, *An American Family*, p. 166; *A Visit to Texas*, p. 68; and Muir, ed., *Texas in 1837*, p. 124.

[38] Gray, *History of Agriculture* 2: 826.

on average to raise seven or eight crops in a decade. Naturally, best results were to be expected from the lower Rio Grande Valley, which experienced killing frosts perhaps one year in ten. Satsuma on *trifoliata* was most recommended, but the less hardy Dugat variety prospered, too. The story of the Texas orange industry, however, must include mention of two severe winters in the late nineteenth century (1886 and 1899) that killed trees; although pioneers like Onderdonk had set citrus on a careful footing, inclement weather took its toll.[39]

Oranges met with growing success; however, some new plants never prospered in a commercial sense. The fig, for example, never did very well because it proved difficult to dry in the humid climate and was a poor shipper. Settlers grew this traditional plant from the Mediterranean as a fruit for preserves or desserts. A canning industry developed in Texas after 1900 when coastal entrepreneurs began to grow figs for distant markets.

The Magnolia, a hardy, prolific, flavorful, and early-bearing fig, proved to be a superior variety, and it did well on the coast around Alvin between Houston and Galveston. Viktor Bracht had been pleased to see fig, chinaberry, and peach trees on the streets of Galveston in June, 1845; groves of figs were laden down with yellow fruit in July, 1847, giving a lift to him, who with other townsfolk was much discomforted by mosquitos.[40] This well-travelled immigrant noted that figs were widely grown in Texas and particularly thrived around San Antonio, where they bore abundantly from mid-May through late summer.

It seems, however, that no general system of fig growing for orchards was worked out, although the Magnolia became the standard variety for horticulturists in South Texas and gave fruit in the first year. It was recommended that 193 trees per acre was the proper set, and infrequent low temperatures did not inhibit early-bearing on the coast.[41]

[39] Gilbert Onderdonk, "Orange Culture in South Texas," *Texas Department of Agriculture Bulletin* 8 (1909): 251–53; and Onderdonk, "Pomological Possibilities," pp. 7–21.

[40] Bracht, *Texas in 1848*, pp. 35, 154, 192.

[41] W. A. Stockwell, "The Magnolia Fig," *Texas Department of Agriculture Bulletin* 8 (1909): 253–54.

Silk

Desire for commercially viable new crops with which to "improve" Texas by drawing from the rich natural setting extended to the mulberry, which was the mainstay for silkworm culture. Publications in the 1830s and the 1840s reported on the advantages of silk production in Texas. The 1840 *Guide* recorded the first experiments with mulberry, which had two species native to Texas, on Galveston Island. A few hundred shoots were planted successfully in 1839, but opinion suggested that other types of mulberry for silkworms would do better. The trees on Galveston Island were able to withstand inclement winter weather, so one promotional text remarked, "If this country does not within a quarter of a century become an extensively silk growing region, the only reason will be because other branches of industry are so successful that no competition exists to seek for new ones."[42]

A principal requirement for high-quality silk production was a climate as favorable "as any part of the south of Italy, a soil transcending the finest fields celebrated in the songs of the Mantuan bard." Silkworm experiments had been initiated in Alabama and Louisiana, but Texas was expected to do better because of its "more equitable" climate and aspect and because of the enterprise and ingenuity of its residents.[43]

The culture and manufacture of silk in the United States dates from the first settlement in Virginia in 1622, where James I urged settlers and others to grow mulberry trees for silkworm culture. Silk culture was begun in Louisiana in 1718, it was practiced in Georgia in 1732, and it was first established in Connecticut in 1760. By the time of the Revolution, the South and New England had made appreciable strides in the manufacture of silk.

The British Irish and Colonial Silk Company was founded in 1825 in order to establish mulberry plantations in England and Ireland and received backing from wealthy and influential entrepreneurs. However, after lengthy and expensive field trials, the enterprise was abandoned as unfeasible. In the 1830s, the U.S. Congress and legislatures in several states promoted mulberry cultivation to feed silkworms and raise cocoons. Nurseries set out lines for supe-

[42] [Lawrence], *Texas in 1840*, pp. 141–43.
[43] Ibid.

rior mulberry and best-quality silkworms until intense speculation caused the bubble to burst in 1845. A large number of people squandered money on the rage for mulberry.[44]

In Texas, silk culture reportedly occurred in San Antonio under Spanish rule, and western districts of the city that grew native mulberries were judged to be most promising for silk, an "easy and advantageous occupation to females and children."[45] Numerous publications about silkworm cultivation were circulated in the 1830s so that immigrants and others could cash in on a novel but easily developed enterprise.

German settlers in the Brenham region developed silk culture, and one fellow in Washington County planted several hundred Japanese and Italian mulberry trees. This man may have been C. F. Herbst of Brenham, who, in the late 1870s, experimented successfully with two hundred standard Japanese mulberries and other varieties from Italy and Germany. In 1881 it was reported that Herbst had raised a "valuable race of silk worms, the eggs having been imported from Corsica." In his judgment Texas offered an unusual combination of promising circumstances for silk culture, which was still in its infancy.[46]

A short entry on silk culture in the *Texas Almanac* claimed that the state's food trees budded so early that several crops of worms could be reared at low cost. Under a balmy climate, supplemental heat was unnecessary, and "this industry can flourish where no other crop can be made, for the tree will thrive where it is useless to plant crops." The aim was to bring "idle land" into mulberry production; when cotton failed through pest or drought, it was claimed that silk would flourish. Silk was, therefore, to become a supplementary staple to cotton. Furthermore, urban residents, in Galveston, for example, could profit nicely from a flourishing trade in high-quality silkworm cocoons simply by learning "the habits and wants of the worms."[47]

[44] United States, Patent Office, "Silk," *Report of the Commissioner for 1853*, pp. 77–79; Wilson Flint, "Textile Fibres of the Pacific States," in U.S. Department of Agriculture, *Annual Report for 1864*, pp. 484–85.

[45] Kennedy, *Texas*, p. 93.

[46] "Silk Culture in Texas," *Texas Almanac*, p. 88; and M. A. E. Farwell, "Silk Culture in Texas," *Texas Almanac*, pp. 85–86. See also Edward, *The History of Texas*, p. 73; and Holley, *Texas*, p. 69.

[47] Farwell, "Silk Culture in Texas," pp. 85, 86.

People were fascinated by the prospects for silk; "a child six to twelve years of age can produce more money growing silk than any five adult persons growing cotton" and have fun doing it, exclaimed Vartan Osigian, who managed the Austin Silk Plantation and Manufacturing Company in Austin. Sericulturist Osigian believed that Texas had advantages because the long producing season made possible six or eight crops per year. With prices skyrocketing because of World War I and with "no boll weevil, hot winds, sand storms, grasshoppers, San José Scale, moths, or other pests" to contend with, he was anxious to show what could be done. "I want to make this fact plain, that this is the best country by far I have ever visited for silk growing," said Osigian, who claimed that his Austin plant was the largest silk-producing facility in the United States. With his family's knowledge of the silk industry in Armenia and France, this gentleman dedicated his energies to the diffusion of knowledge about silkworm culture.[48]

Other plants like olives, indigo, tobacco, vanilla, and cochineal were promoted in nineteenth-century literature, and in some instances field experiments were made with these crops in Texas. Buckley had tested the fruit of an olive grown in Columbia, South Carolina, and explained why olive groves could become established in Texas. Interestingly, Von Humboldt had noted that the olive tree was very rare in New Spain; he knew of a successful planting southeast of Mexico City that supplied annually about twenty-five hundred kilograms of oil. Other experiments with Mission olives had been carried out near San Diego, California; however, the Andalusian olive carried in by Cortez was inferior to a Corsican olive, which Von Humboldt reported as more resistant to cold.[49]

Onderdonk liked olives, too, except the trees that he imported from France suffered badly from frosts in 1880. "I am firm in the conviction that the entire Gulf coast of the United States will yet find the olive to be one of its more valuable resources," declared this crop pioneer. California, not Texas, however, took command of olive production, and the foothills of the Sierra Nevada, away from

[48] Vartan K. Osigian, "Address," *Texas Department of Agriculture Bulletin* 54 (1917): 81–86.

[49] Buckley, *Texas Geological Survey*, p. 64; and Von Humboldt, *New Spain* 2: 517–18.

fogs, humid air, and scale insects, and elevated enough to escape severe valley frosts, were preferred locations. Furthermore, in Texas, cottonseed oil (and later castor oil) competed with the olive, which is a slow-growing, long-lived evergreen well suited to areas with temperatures above 20°F, and where mean temperatures for the coolest month average not much lower than 43°F. Cold spells damaged olive trees in Texas.[50]

Holley scolded newcomers for attempting "to graft their own customs and comforts on the land of their adoption" instead of exploring the country and ascertaining its natural resources.[51] But that is what many agriculturalists did. They applied themselves zealously to the establishment of Mediterranean-type crops and tested many other exotic ones, including coffee and tea.

Bracht mentioned that coffee bushes seemed to be doing well near New Braunfels and that a bush had flourished for "several years" at Dimmitt's Landing, a trading post founded by Philip Dimmitt on the east shore of Lavaca Bay.[52] Tea plants were also tested in many places in Texas and the South. The French botanist Michaux successfully planted tea near Charleston, South Carolina, in about 1800, and another useful experiment was conducted in that state near Greenville shortly before 1850. In the following decade, tea specialist Robert Fortune visited China as a government agent in order to oversee the introduction of tea into the United States. As a result of his visit, about thirty-two thousand small plants were distributed in 1859 or 1860 "among gentlemen who had expressed a desire to experiment; . . . fully two thirds were forwarded to planters residing south of Virginia and Kentucky." A map entitled "Regions Apparently Adapted to the Tea Culture in the United States, 1857," depicted a broad band of the South (away from the piedmont) westward to California and Oregon as suitable for tea-growing, and Texas was the center of this zone. Except for its coastal lowland, the whole state was considered fit to supply this beverage. Problems from

---

[50] Gilbert Onderdonk, "Olive Culture in Texas," *Texas Almanac for 1881*, p. 145; and C. B. Smith and C. F. Longworthy, "Culture and Uses of Olives," *Farmers' Bulletin* 122 (1900): pp. 11–18.

[51] Holley, *Texas*, pp. 64–65; Edward, *The History of Texas*, p. 43; Kennedy, *Texas*, pp. 91–92.

[52] Bracht, *Texas in 1848*, p. 33.

plucking and blending the leaves, not growing tea plants, appear to have been serious enough to have caused the U.S. Department of Agriculture to discontinue experiments in the 1880s.[53]

Extensive tests were also made with dates and apricots. Date palms bore fruit in Louisiana until the great freeze of 1886 killed off all but a single tree in New Orleans. Florida and California had many palms, too, but few of them produced dates. However, places in Arizona (Phoenix) and Texas (the lower Rio Grande Valley) offered suitable locations for date growing, and suggestions about the likely success of dates in Texas go back to before 1840.[54]

Apricots grew well in the states of Jalisco and Saltillo, Mexico, and in most parts of Texas, too, except those much below San Marcos, but they sustained no real commerce. Plants prospered in the central and more northern counties and were locally attractive in the Nacogdoches region and elsewhere. Nectarines, pomegranates, bananas (Bracht reported a tree in Galveston "laden with matured fruit"),[55] quinces, almonds, and, after the Civil War, a number of other exotics such as canaigre (in 1886), roselle (about 1910), papaya (by 1912), kumquat (by 1914), and the guava had variable successes. Most of them were planted in Texas about the turn of the present century or before; however, none seemed especially promising or profitable.

Holley believed that rather than expend energies on such domestic plants, Texans should "unfold agricultural treasures and commercial advantages which will astound a world that has scarcely known of her existence." In each case attention was turned to transforming the face of the country, especially in tapping that most fertile Rolling Prairies zone, in order to intensify the production of foodstuffs and other crops and to expand the acreages under the most adaptable ones. Thoughts of preserving or sustaining native

[53] U.S. Patent Office, "On the Practicability of the Tea Culture in the United States," *Report of the Commissioner of Patents for 1857*, pp. 161–81, and *1860*, pp. 15, 28; and George F. Mitchell, "Home-Grown Tea," *Farmers' Bulletin* 301 (1907): 1–16.

[54] [Lawrence], *Texas in 1840*, p. 148; H. E. Van Deman, "Report of the Pomologist," in U.S. Department of Agriculture, *Report of the Commissioner for 1887*, pp. 627–52; and *1890*, p. 37.

[55] Onderdonk, "Pomological Possibilities," pp. 5–55; Richard W. Haltom, *The History of Nacogdoches County, Texas*, p. 49; Bracht, *Texas in 1848*, p. 35.

plants and animal populations were very much subordinated to desires for economic progress.[56]

Livestock Husbandry

Three domestic animals, the horse, the longhorn steer, and the Spanish sheep, are important in the Southwest's history and biogeography. "All three were gifts from Old Spain. All three modified the lives of the Southwest's men, conditioned the lives of her Indians, created her folklore and drama, determined a large part of her history," and competed with native mammals by becoming feral. The Spanish missions possessed horses, cattle, sheep, and goats, and when Captain Domingo Ramon directed a sixty-five-person group across the Rio Grande in April, 1716, more than one thousand cattle, sheep, and goats accompanied the party. Others had imported this meat on the hoof almost twenty years earlier to the missions of San Francisco and Santa Maria on the Neches River, and later, Spanish padres drove many more livestock to the twenty missions that they established between 1690 and 1791. The San Antonio missions had several thousand head of livestock in the 1730s.[57] By 1800, however, when the mission period had spent itself, sheep raising had retreated to the lower Rio Grande Plain, and the ancient churro sheep had disappeared from East Texas. Predators had picked off untended animals there and in other places.

Austin's colonists imported some quality Spanish merino sheep from the northern United States as early as 1821, and merino crosses prospered in Texas, although one report of a flock of merino-Southdown (the Southdown was a fine-wool sheep which came from the United Kingdom to the United States in about 1803) in coastal Matagorda County noted that the animals became sick and died from the "deleterious gases of the locality."[58] Vermont-bred merinos crossed with Mexican sheep grew heavier fleeces. German-derived stock was also driven into the Hill Country and prospered; how-

[56] Holley, *Texas*, pp. 64–65.
[57] Winifred Kupper, *The Golden Hoof: The Story of Sheep of the Southwest*, p. 19; Charles W. Towne, *Shepherd's Empire*, pp. 117–18.
[58] [Lawrence], *Texas in 1840*, pp. 135–36; and United States, Patent Office, "E. F. Gilbert, Matagorda County," p. 46.

ever, it was George Wilkins Kendall (1809–67) who pioneered sheep raising, largely from American-bred merino stock on five thousand acres of land he owned near Boerne. People have called Kendall Texas' greatest sheepman, because of innovations that he made in the care, management, and quality of his stock. New England-born Kendall, journalist, publisher, and rancher, remained very active in sheep raising. In 1857 he ran his stock on a ranch near Post Oak Spring, that is, in the county that bears his name. He shared his studies about the range conditions and forage requirements for sheep with other interested persons, and he discussed, in the *Texas Almanac*, for example, problems such as scab, procedures for dipping and shearing, and ways to minimize losses from predators. Kendall was an ardent admirer of Texas, frequently reporting on its agricultural life in his newspaper, the *New Orleans Daily Picayune*.[59]

Another ungulate animal with Mediterranean origins that found a home in Texas and proved to be a similar money-winner, especially in the regional economy of the Edwards Plateau, was the angora goat. Angora goats arrived in Texas within ten years of the first introduction of them into South Carolina by livestock breeder James B. Davis, whom President Polk designated as a consultant to the sultan of Turkey. Davis purchased nine angoras in Turkey, imported them to South Carolina in 1849, and five years later sold six of them to Colonel Richard Peters of Georgia for one thousand dollars each. Peters, who was a noted stock breeder, judged that his angoras would prosper in southern Blue Ridge Mountain country, and he worked for twenty years to upgrade stock in order to produce quality mohair, which found a ready market in upholstery for railroad cars. Through careful crosses with common goats, Peters established a herd of nationally renowned angora goats.

In 1858, Peters sold eight of his goats to Texas resident William W. Haupt of Hays County, who transported them to his ranch near Kyle and commenced to raise angora-Mexican goat crosses, keeping careful records of their progeny. The mohair industry in Texas blossomed after the Civil War; it was developed from the Hill Country stock of Haupt and a few others who obtained other animals from Davis or Peters. In the 1870s at least seven addi-

[59] Edward Wentworth, *America's Sheep Trails*, p. 382, called Kendall "the greatest sheepman Texas ever claimed." See also *Texas Almanac, 1970–1971*, p. 382.

tional raisers began operations. European, particularly British, firms declared that they had seen no finer mohair than that originating in Central Texas. With other transplants from California and elsewhere, Texas stock became populous. About ten goat raisers established large, profitable goat herds and made the Lone Star State the chief region for mohair in the United States, and one of three in the world.[60]

In the late 1870s and 1880s some ranchers found angoras more profitable than sheep. Providing mohair and cabrito, the animal proved to be hardy, adaptable, and cheap to keep in the rough, open limestone country where winters were not overly wet and where temperatures were, on the average, relatively mild and equitable. By the mid-1880s, mohair prices were two to three times higher than those for wool, with no greater production costs.[61]

By 1890, Texas was generally acknowledged as the leading state for angoras, and raisers increased production and began to sell their best stock to other states. A pamphlet circulated in the Midwest by William L. Black called attention to the value of angora goats for brush clearance, and it contributed to the large demand for Texas goats. From 1897 to 1900, more than fifteen thousand animals were shipped to Illinois, Iowa, Kansas, and Missouri. Census reports for 1910 show that Texas was well entrenched as the leading mohair producer, accounting for 64 percent of mohair production.[62]

Several arguments have been advanced to explain why the mohair industry succeeded so spectacularly on the Edwards Plateau. One suggestion is that much of the environment's rugged terrain and sparse vegetation is ideally suited to these Mediterranean-derived goats (their native home, Turkey, remains an important exporter) and is only marginally suited for other livestock or crops. Additionally, the availability of abundant, inexpensive tracts of land favored the establishment of large ranches where goats could be herded cheaply and rotated with cattle. These factors appear to have

[60]William W. Haupt, "The Angora Goat," *Texas Stockman and Farmer* 4 (1884): 1; William L. Black, *A New Industry: or, Raising the Angora Goat and Mohair for Profit*, pp. 46, 49, 60–63.

[61]"Goat Gossip," *Texas Stockman* 2 (1882): 4.

[62]United States, Bureau of the Census, *Thirteenth Census of the United States* 5: 504; Black, *A New Industry*, p. 12.

favored Texas, particularly the Edwards Plateau, over other areas where land was less available, more expensive, and designated for other agricultural uses.

Haupt and others provided an early, sizable nucleus of high-quality, thoroughbred angoras from which local stockmen drew. These early goat raisers pioneered a novel, diversified livestock industry that they promoted in farm journals, newspapers, and livestock reports. The proficiency of an angora buck in impressing his fleece on progeny from a female common goat was critical in developing the mohair industry. Common short-haired goats were cheap and freely available and proved to be excellent browsing animals; therefore, with a modest investment a rancher could purchase an angora male and in four or five years "breed up" a flock of lucrative, fine-fleeced goats.

Additionally, early breeders actively pursued the market for mohair; they sought out agents and manufacturers in New England who were interested in purchasing the strong, lustrous mohair fiber. Information about the demands for mohair and the various grades and prices were disseminated through local and national trade media, and successful breeders encouraged others to enter the industry.

In these ways a small group of men proved instrumental in the founding of the mohair industry in Texas. There were, to be sure, many others who played significant roles in this effort, particularly during the last fifteen years of the nineteenth century. Haupt and his colleagues, however, provided an essential pool of information, experience, and wisdom.

Efforts to build up an attractive mohair industry in Texas were complemented by another experiment with animal fibers—those to be derived from ostriches. Ostriches had been reared in captivity in Algiers and more successfully in the Mediterranean climate of southern Africa in the 1860s and had been hunted formerly along the Mediterranean coast in northern Africa. Initiatives in the 1880s in the United States led to sizable importations into California and Arizona of these giant flightless birds, both as items of curiosity and for commerce. Texas was included in early discussions about ostrich farms in the Southwest.[63] A note in the *Corpus Christi Caller* of

[63] Robin W. Doughty, "Ostrich Farming American Style," *Agricultural History* 47 (1973): 133–45.

February 11, 1883, referred to a Boston-based company that intended "to establish an ostrish farm in Southern Colorado or Texas." State Department officials abroad and agricultural experts in the United States had examined the prospects for raising ostriches—primarily for their wing and tail feathers, which could be sheared off the birds like wool from sheep, but also for meat and skins—in drier regions of the West. "It is thought that the prairies of Southwestern Texas are well adapted to ostrich farming," claimed one author. The proposition was not as far-fetched as it may have seemed. Expert T. C. Duncan wrote an essay entitled "Ostrich Farming in America" for a Department of Agriculture report in 1888, detailing the attractiveness of raising these birds and explaining how it was being accomplished in South Africa. "When domesticated in Texas, as they doubtless soon will be, we expect to hear that the cow-boys utilize ostriches in herding cattle," whimsically declared Duncan, who judged that their swift movements would be attractive to "scouts and hunters."[64]

This novel enterprise in animal husbandry was successful in Africa; it had been started in South America, too. In 1882 a "successful" ostrich farm manager from Argentina placed an advertisement in the *Texas Wool Grower* for a partner to invest ten thousand dollars for a new line in ostriches for Texas. But Orange County, California, and Arizona's Salt River Valley, not Galveston or Corpus Christi or the Nueces or Pecos valleys, turned out to be the places where ostriches became a familiar sight in the United States until a more austere period in dress that was associated with World War I made feathers unfashionable and a luxury that Western nations could well afford to do without.

Stories of using ostriches as draft animals or of cowboys mounted on these huge birds possibly may have been stimulated by earlier successes with the camel, another denizen from the Old World Mediterranean rimland, which U.S. military personnel transported to Texas in 1856 in an experiment to improve transportation in the desert Southwest. Thirty-four camels, mainly single-humped Arabian dromedaries, plus a two-humped Bactrian and hybrids of the two species, were unloaded near Indianola in May, 1856. Destined for San Antonio, the caravan reminded Kendall of a street scene in

[64] T. C. Duncan, "Ostrich Farming in America," in U.S. Department of Agriculture, *Report of the Commissioner for 1888*, p. 700.

Cairo, Egypt. The camels alarmed horses but provided a great spectacle for children.[65]

Authorities took excellent care of these exotics, which were joined by another forty or fifty animals in February, 1857 and then quartered at Camp Verde, near Kerrville. Again, Kendall, who was interested in such innovations and novelties, remarked to his friend and fellow expert on sheep, Henry S. Randall, that at the breeding station in Camp Verde, a "turbanned raskall" told him that "a 2 year old camel raised in Texas was larger than a 3 year old at home, and better formed.[66] Secretary of War Jefferson Davis was pleased with the Texas "camel experiment," which proved that these new beasts of burden were superior to mules in speed, load capability, and endurance. However, Davis left office in 1858, and his successors decreased support to the program; they transferred subordinates who were versed in the ways of camels to other duties. Some of Camp Verde's camels were included in a wagon train that set out for California in June, 1857. The draft animals performed well and ferried supplies between military posts in California and Arizona during the Civil War before being sold off and scattered. Other camels in Texas were sold, too; it seems that Confederate soldiers, who had time for horses and mules, had little use for these bizarre-looking, often unpredictable exotics.[67]

Efforts to introduce and establish novel, potentially valuable animals and plants in Texas created an agricultural landscape that massively disrupted and restructured native fauna and flora. In their zeal to tap nature's fertility, most people ignored the effects of rapid land clearing and poor husbandry; rather, they spoke glowingly of the coming new order—fashioning verisimilitudes of earlier, familiar and "safe" environments that had been molded, and that in turn had supported Western Civilization, in the Mediterranean Basin.

[65] Letter to Henry S. Randall, June 17, 1860, in Harry J. Brown, ed., *Letters from a Texas Sheep Ranch*, p. 80.

[66] Ibid.

[67] Lewis B. Lesley, "The Purchase and Importation of Camels . . . ," *Southwestern Historical Quarterly* 33 (1929): 18–33; Chris Emmett, *Texas Camel Tales*; and Frank B. Lammons, "Operation Camel . . . ," *Southwestern Historical Quarterly* 61 (1957): 20–50.

CHAPTER 6

Wild Animal Conservation:

Protection and Management

THE fifty years following the Civil War were critical for native wild animals in Texas and throughout the nation. Before the middle of the nineteenth century, descriptions of wildlife, particularly that of the unsettled places, had celebrated the abundance of different species. On the Great Plains bison numbered in the millions. The vast prairie country of Texas contained large droves of mustangs, and deer browsed the edges of oak mottes and brush; in the fall and winter months ducks, geese, and other water birds flew in huge chevrons over the marsh-filled coastal lowland. In some places, jackrabbits were supposedly so approachable that settlers killed them by simply heaving a stone or clubbing them with a stick. No doubt some stories of such high numbers were exaggerated; however, populations of many game and other animals were extremely high, certainly when compared with those remaining in the final decades of the nineteenth century.

As the wave of immigration grew, especially after the establishment of the Republic of Texas and annexation by the United States, the sustained and cumulative impact of Anglo-American farmers, planters, stockmen, and traders ended the "dominion of wild animals." Hunting practices and campaigns to eliminate predators and vermin took a large toll of animals. Environmental change from planting new crops, felling woodlands, draining wetlands, and establishing industries in expanding settlements destroyed animal habitats. Pollution in waterways and burdens of silt killed off fish. Domestic stock and other exotic animals competed with native fauna for food, cover, and space. Some species, such as the wild turkey, bison, and prairie chicken, disappeared as the wilderness receded;

others, like the bobwhite quail and the white-tailed deer, benefited from cut-over landscapes that had been cleared and cropped then abandoned to grow back new shrubs and trees. Animals that tended to build up populations in environments under second growth, however, were often overhunted and exploited locally to the point of extinction.

As the decline of wild animals became more noticeable, especially around settlements and cultivated places, a number of persons began to speak out against this tradition of thoughtless and unrestrained killing. They wished to slow down the loss of game and other preferred animals in order to prevent the eventual demise of a free, widespread, and plentiful resource, which had been whittled away through decades of exploitation. Most importantly, these people perceived that the state's incredibly fecund wild animal community, indeed the nation's in general, was not limitless, although the idea of superabundance tended to linger on, particularly in thinly populated places on the frontier.

A salutary reminder about the likely long-term effects of the unrestricted harvest of animals for local consumption and for city meat markets was penned by D. G. Elliot in the mid-1860s. Elliott admitted that wild bird meat had economic importance throughout America; however, it had become clear to him that the vendors' stalls displayed more animals than were being replenished naturally. He argued that the disappearance of the grouse, turkey, quail, and other upland game birds and shorebirds were clear examples of abuse. In New York City, "one man has been known to receive in one consignment *twenty tons* of prairie chickens" (estimated at twenty thousand birds), said this federal official. Apparently it was not uncommon for dealers to sell two hundred thousand game birds in a six-month period.[1]

All year, settlers set snares, traps, and other "besoms of destruction," which effectively swept places clean of fauna so that, according to Elliot, an absence of suitable animal targets was leading to the decline in field sports in the East. Market hunters were, in a sense, unpatriotic because the nation would soon be "degenerating into effeminacy" unless animal destruction was halted. The

[1] D. G. Elliot, "The 'Game Birds' of the United States," in U.S. Department of Agriculture, *Report of the Commissioner for 1864*, p. 383.

large quantities of animals shipped into the New York markets suf-
ficed to lower prices. A survey in early 1874 discovered that an
"immense" slaughter of deer in Wisconsin had glutted this market,
resulting in the paltry sum of six cents a pound, and whole carcasses
and quarters had spoiled. Quail and prairie chickens were readily
available; dealers were storing them in icehouses and selling them
later, contrary to state game laws. Large bags of other species such
as water birds occurred along New England's coast as well as southward and west of the Mississippi.[2]

In Kansas, deer and antelope had been largely shot out, and
sportsmen quickly killed any bison they came upon. "Wisps" of yellowlegs, entire flights of waterfowl, and whole herds of mammals
fell to farmers, market men, and nimrods. In the mid-1880s young
entrepreneur Nat Wetzel hired scores of professional hunters and
farmers to shoot geese, deer, quail, and prairie hens for the expanding game market in Kansas City. Later, this so-called King of the
Market Hunters turned his attention to Texas, where he grew rich
from several other ventures, including a line in frog meat in
Houston.[3]

Texas was initially off the beaten track for these game dealers
and well-heeled sportsmen, but rail communications and the development of refrigeration opened up the state for people like Wetzel
who had supplied local markets in Galveston, Houston, and San
Antonio with cheap meat. Saint Louis and Chicago were the principal outlets for game. Regulation that would control and finally put
a stop to this commerce was a primary objective of the Audubon
movement and sportsmen's organizations in both the Northeast and
in Texas. Even after federal laws made interstate shipments illegal,
hunters could easily procure the services of former market hunters
as guides for duck shooting around Rockport or Corpus Christi.
Gum Hollow, seven miles from Gregory in San Patricio County, was
a famous duck-shooting resort; so was Mitchell's Lake, ten miles
out of San Antonio, where in one afternoon of shooting a marksman
could easily procure teal, gadwall, or mallards for supper.[4]

[2] C. W. S. "Game in Season for January," *Forest and Stream* 1(1874): 380–81.
[3] Jay Vessels, "King of the Market Hunters," *Texas Game and Fish* 10 (1952):
12–14; and Henry Oldys, "The Game Market of To-day," in *Yearbook of the U.S.
Department of Agriculture, 1910*, pp. 243–54.
[4] *Texas Field and National Guardsman* 13 (1911): 217–18.

Early Game Laws

Incipient attempts to protect game animals were aimed at ending exploitation by establishing hunting seasons and restricting the killing of certain species. Interested citizens and sportsmen's groups pressed for laws to preserve those species that they considered to be in the most trouble. Bobwhite quail on Galveston Island received first attention. District Representative Hartley's bill on November 21, 1859, for a closed season set the precedent for stamping out wildlife abuse. Decreases in bobwhite quail and the consequent loss of recreational hunting, provided the impulse for the Act for the Protection of Game on Galveston Island, which became law in February, 1860. It prohibited the hunting of quail (or partridge) for two years and closed hunting from March through August for future years.[5]

This first state game law was not directed at wildlife protection statewide; rather, it typified the localized and spotty character of early legislation. An amendment to include turkeys and prairie chickens was not adopted, nor were deer mentioned, although they had become much less abundant in the area. Matilda Houstoun had noticed how scarce deer were around Galveston, principally because other sportsmen like her, enjoying excursions through the dune-filled landscape, had joined residents in killing off animal life.[6]

This first law for animals had little practical or long-term significance because legislators tended to shy away from measures curtailing individual privileges, especially the right to hunt. The law had, however, important implications. Restrictions on harvest reflected an acceptance that the numbers of certain wildlife had indeed become limited and that unregulated hunting was the primary culprit. The public, it was to be argued later, must understand that animals had value beyond merely filling immediate material needs. The scientific, ecological, and aesthetic values of wildlife were important, too. From the 1870s conservation-minded individuals and associations addressed these broader concerns. They insisted on the importance of animals as helpmates to horticulturists, as important in the overall balance of nature, even as "little people,"

[5] H. P. N. Gammel, ed., *The Laws of Texas, 1822–1897* 5: 120.
[6] Matilda Charlotte Fraser Houstoun, *Texas and the Gulf of Mexico; or, Yachting in the New World*, p. 138.

and as capable of fostering the virtues of citizenship, brotherhood, and patriotism in adults and especially in school-aged children.

Legislation was to scale down the rate of exploitation while reflecting a growing interest in the nonconsumptive uses of wild animals. In Texas, however, after the first initiative on behalf of bobwhite quail, almost fifteen years passed before further attention was paid to wildlife conservation, and it was about twenty years before lawmakers established closed seasons for other game species. Even then, many counties were promptly exempted from such laws.

The Civil War shifted attention to social and political issues and made wild animal conservation a low priority. Even so, Hartley's efforts for quail and other activities for other game in Texas were late. Provisions for deer in Connecticut dated back to 1677. Virginia (in 1699) and New York (in 1705) had set up closed seasons on deer, too, when colonists realized that supplies of these animals were exhaustible. Another New York game law was passed in 1709 to establish seasons for wild turkey, heath hen, partridge, quail, and woodcock.

In the mid-nineteenth century recognition of the agricultural benefits of insectivorous birds was bolstered by laws in Connecticut, New Hampshire, Vermont, Pennsylvania, Massachusetts, and Ohio. Importantly, the enforcement of these and other game and wild animal laws began to take hold, and by 1885, New Hampshire, Maine, Massachusetts, and Ohio had appointed game commissioners; Michigan and Minnesota established game wardens about the same time.[7] In Texas, however, the effective protection of native animals would have to wait until the twentieth century.

Several factors made conservation difficult in the Lone Star State. First, it was an uphill struggle to alert and interest influential persons and the public about the growing scarcity of many useful animals and to convince them that laws were necessary. One explanation for this apathy centered on the frontier situation in Texas. Three generations of Anglo-American settlement had pushed the frontier from east to west, so as game species became scarce in eastern and

[7]Theodore S. Palmer, "Legislation for the Protection of Birds," in U.S. Department of Agriculture, Bureau of Biological Survey, *Bulletin* 12 (1902 rev. ed.): 15; and Theodore S. Palmer, "Chronology and Index of the More Important Events in American Game Protection, 1776–1911," in U.S. Department of Agriculture, Bureau of Biological Survey, *Bulletin* 41 (1912): 12–13, 21–23, 57.

central counties, people took it for granted that such wildlife was abundant farther west. Moreover, as market hunters supplied city stalls with ample quantities of migratory ducks, geese, and shorebirds, residents expected that these numbers would be replenished. Incalculable flights of waterfowl would descend from northern skies and light on the coastal marshes. In short, comments about local declines and the progressive diminution of wildlife were parried by the idea that the remote, isolated frontier in West Texas was home for those same or similar species, which had vanished around settlements. When it became certain that these animals had also suffered declines and that conditions were deteriorating statewide, interested sportsmen and other groups lobbied for legislation.

Jurisdiction over wild animals proved to be a second complicating factor for conservation efforts in Texas. Many counties refused to comply with game laws and were exempted from provisions enacted by the state legislature. Most importantly, law enforcement was virtually nonexistent. Joe Dinkins, the state's first fish commissioner, discovered that an ordinance providing for fish ladders at dams and weirs had no provisions for enforcement. His responsibilities in this initially unpaid post were directed toward disseminating information about the office of fish commissioner and the need for vigilance and a greater interest in the freshwater fishery. His chief weapon was to advise Texans about conservation efforts in other states and, in a sense, shame them into improving their own fishery, which was being ruined.

Fish and Fisheries

Thirteen years after the protection efforts on Galveston Island, the legislature dealt with wildlife again, placing an emphasis on fish. In 1874 the Fourteenth Legislature made seine and net fishing illegal at certain times of the year, and in 1879 the Sixteenth Legislature proposed action on a larger scale. In "An Act for the Preservation of Fish, and to Build Fishways and Fish-Ladders," any person building a dam or weir across a river was required to construct and keep in repair devices to aid fish in returning to their spawning places. This bill also authorized the governor to appoint a fish commissioner, and Governor O. M. Roberts named Joe H. Dinkins to the post. Initially, Dinkins received no salary and lacked any authority to enforce the law; his duties as the state's freshwater fishery official were vague. At a later session, the legislature expanded the 1879 act to include a salary of fifteen hundred dollars per year and made the fish commissioner responsible for the preservation of fish and for the enforcement of the provisions of the fisheries act.[8] In the same year, 1879, the legislature introduced another measure for wildlife. It drew up closed seasons for deer, wild turkey, prairie chickens, and quail and prohibited killing songbirds. However, the importance of this legislation was reduced because eighty-three counties were exempted from its provisions.

Commissioner Dinkins, an Austin-based surveyor and engineer, notified mill owners about the requirement for fish ladders but made no inspections because of a lack of travel funds. Dinkins did, however, broaden his knowledge about fishery matters elsewhere. He contacted U.S. Fish Commissioner Spencer F. Baird's office in Washington about obtaining shad and salmon for Texas in order to augment earlier releases. Earlier transplants of shad and salmon in the Colorado, Brazos, Trinity, and other rivers had proved fruitless, and subsequent releases did not take.[9] Dinkins's letter to the nation's capitol, however, arrived at an opportune moment in respect to the edible "German" carp.

U.S. fisheries authorities embarked on a massive campaign to raise and ship the imported carp to every applicant. Dinkins received his first 151 carp in December, 1879, and distributed them to residents. It was too early to build elaborate pools or receiving ponds; nevertheless, the young carp prospered. People familiar with this exotic fish, which had been brought to the United States from Germany and bred in the Washington Monument ponds in the late 1870s, judged that Texas was particularly well suited to carp culture. Federal fish expert Marshall McDonald, who visited Austin to inspect likely sites for carp ponds, commented, "The State of Texas seems to possess extraordinary facilities for raising carp . . .

[8] Texas Game, Fish and Oyster Commission, *Review of Texas Wild Life and Conservation*, 10; Gammel, ed., *Laws of Texas* 8: 1400; and Texas Legislative Council, *Wildlife Management in Texas*, no. 53–4, p. 7.

[9] Texas Game, Fish and Oyster Commission, *Review of Texas Wild Life*, pp. 11–12; Texas Legislative Council, *Wildlife Management*, p. 15.

It is believed that carp-raising will soon become a valuable industry in that State."[10] The fish's natural fecundity was enhanced by placing it in warm-water ponds and lakes in Texas where it spawned from May through July. Growth rates in these impoundments, notably stock ponds, where the carp was reportedly well suited, were phenomenal. An article on carp culture in the *Dallas Herald* of January 5, 1882, eulogized them as "remarkable rapid growers and tablefish." It reported that Mr. J. B. Rogers's plantation north of Austin, in only sixteen months had produced a fish measuring seventeen and one-half inches and weighing five pounds. Generally, a five-month-old carp was expected to be about ten inches in length and "ready for the pan," and it was not unusual to find fish up to three and one-half pounds or even five pounds at thirteen to fifteen months.

From 1880 through 1883 prospects for the long-term, profitable culture of the Old World carp looked very bright. Many Texans, and others from the South, declared that they were making money from selling carp. In 1884 a Corsicana resident stated that his carp were worth twelve to fifteen cents a pound in the local market, and he anticipated selling three hundred to five hundred dollars' worth of fish in the coming year. Another man reported that he had sold one thousand young carp for fifteen dollars per hundred and that he could not breed them fast enough. A third fish-raiser from Navarro County put it bluntly: "I cannot raise meat half so cheap."[11]

These positive comments reassured Fish Commission officials in Washington and in state capitals, including Austin, that the production of food fishes was worth continuing. Dinkins and his successors, Commissioners R. R. Robertson and J. B. Lubbock, believed firmly that the German carp was a splendid addition to the state's fauna and was ideally suited to farm ponds and stock tanks. Dinkins noted that "unquestionably the carp is the very fish for the ponds, lakes and even tanks in the State, and with a little aid will

[10] Austin *Daily Democratic-Statesman*, December 3, 1879; Marshall McDonald, "Report of Distribution of Carp, 1881–82," in U.S. Commission of Fish and Fisheries, *Report of the Commissioner for 1881*, p. 1125.

[11] Charles W. Smiley, "Some Results of Carp Culture in the United States," in U.S. Commission of Fish and Fisheries, *Report of the Commissioner for 1884*, p. 841.

soon be abundant where fish cannot now be found."[12] The carp was, therefore, expected to augment the freshwater fishery of Texas and to complement, not compete with, other excellent food species.

The carp's fecundity, ease of handling, hardiness, food value, high growth rates, and relative docility in respect to other fish proved insufficient to maintain esteem for carp after the mid-1880s. Matters came to a head in Texas in 1885 when the legislature abolished the Fish Commission and did not reconstitute it for a decade. Although the tastiness of the fish was a much-debated matter in Texas and across the nation, problems that related more to economics and politics made carp culture a controversial subject. In April, 1883, congressional committees investigated the office of Fish Commissioner R. R. Robertson and made critical comments about poor management. Lawmakers were concerned about the accountability of carp breeding, which had become costly and time-consuming, in special ponds set up in Austin. According to the *Austin Statesman* of January 7, 1885, the Texas fish commissioner had played favorites "dealing out a few carp to those able to have private pools." It questioned whether any city fish stall sold carp. [13]

The carp, however, had fulfilled most of Baird's predictions for it. German fish culturist Rudolph Hessel produced hundreds of thousands of these fish in the Washington Monument ponds. After it was transported to almost every state, people found it hardy and adaptable to various water conditions. It succeeded magnificently in Texas, becoming locally abundant and available to most who requested it. But many fanciers mismanaged their carp, and no doubt the bad press about the carp's table qualities referred to pond and tank specimens that had been fed putrescent or other ill-suited materials.

Furthermore, the Fish Commission was open to charges of misconduct. Officials had eulogized the "domestic" qualities of the carp, arguing that it would offset losses to the state's native freshwater fishery. However, commissioners in Texas had paid more attention to the contents of ponds, that is, the carp's pleasing characteristics, than to the legality of the dams and weirs impounding

---

[12] Texas, *First Report of Texas Fish Commission for 1880*, p. 25.

[13] For an overview see Robin W. Doughty, "Wildlife Conservation in Late Nineteenth-Century Texas: The Carp Experiment," *Southwestern Historical Quarterly* 84 (1980): 169–196.

these fish, so Dinkins and his successors were accused of being overly committed to the carp-raising experiment. People identified the commission with carp promotion, so once the carp fell into disfavor, opposition was heaped on the office of fish commissioner and the state legislature declared it to be redundant.

Texas lagged behind in similar efforts for animals. Twenty-eight other states, including ones adjacent to Texas, passed comprehensive legislation for game by the mid-1880s, and many were able to enforce these laws. Legislation west of the Mississippi River had progressed steadily since 1850. Louisiana passed its first game law in 1857; Missouri's had been passed six years earlier, and the first in California was passed in 1852. All three of these states, like Texas, had very localized game laws; only later did constitutional provisions cut through such localized provisions so that game received widespread protection.[14]

In 1895, the office of fish commissioner was reconstructed in Texas under the new Fish and Oyster Commission, and the post included authority over marine resources. Commissioner I. P. Kibbe served on the new state-sponsored agency for eleven years, reporting annually about the coastal fishery and about a downward trend in populations of terrestrial game mammals and birds. The discouraged tenor of several reports made it clear that Kibbe believed that people disregarded existing laws, and the fact that many counties were exempted from provisions made conservation impossible. Many large mammal species had disappeared, ducks and geese were gunned down remorselessly, and beds of prime oysters were being damaged by overuse, silting, and the increased pollution of shallow bay waters.

Commissioner Kibbe was a "travelling salesman" for oyster management. Especially interested in protecting beds of these shellfish, he journeyed up and down the coast urging fishermen to improve methods of extraction. His efforts resulted in doubling production from good beds, but speculation in the submerged reefs set in, and he and his successors realized that oysters were being depleted.[15]

Sea fishes fared no better. No law dealing with marine fishes

[14] Palmer, "Chronology and Index," pp. 13–14.
[15] Texas Game, Fish and Oyster Commission, *Review of Texas Wildlife*, pp. 17–19.

was passed until 1887, when the legislature prohibited seines in shallow bays useful for spawning. Inland, conditions for game mammals and birds began to improve after 1903, when a five-year closed season was placed on the pronghorn antelope and bighorn sheep. Organizations worked hard to regulate overhunting and to improve laws, which had been mainly limited in the previous twenty-five years to adding or subtracting various counties from unenforceable provisions.

Bird Protection

Measures to protect insectivorous birds and others that were being destroyed to furnish ornamental feathers to millinery establishments date back to the mid-1880s when George Bird Grinnell, sportsman and natural historian, founded the Audubon Society. Grinnell's Audubon Society was principally an antiplumage league for women and children who pledged to eschew feather trim and to promote in homes and schools the study of bird life. His proposal appeared first in the sportsman's weekly periodical *Forest and Stream* of February 11, 1886. It quickly attracted a sizable number of adherents—sixteen thousand members by November, 1886. Forest and Stream Publishing Company launched *Audubon Magazine*, which printed essays on the usefulness of birds and the measures required to protect them. The meteoric success of this Audubon group strained the financial and other resources of *Forest and Stream*, so the publication was discontinued, but the American Ornithologists' Union (AOU), of which Grinnell was a founding member, established the Committee for the Protection of North American Birds and continued to work for the same cause of preservation that the popular bird-loving society promoted.[16]

The AOU's greatest activity occurred in 1886 when committee chairman George B. Sennett convened a score of meetings in order to gather data about the traffic in bird plumage and to discuss vari-

[16]"The Audubon Society," *Forest and Stream* 26 (1886): 41; "Second Meeting of the American Ornithologists' Union, *The Auk* 1 (1884): 369–70. The six-member Committee for the Protection of North American Birds was W. Brewster, H. A. Purdie, G. B. Grinnell, E. P. Bicknell, F. A. Ober, and W. Dutcher (p. 376), who became president of the National Association of Audubon Societies until he died in 1920.

ous possibilities for terminating it and other forms of wildlife destruction. The AOU bird protection committee's efforts culminated in the publication of a fifteen-page supplement for *Science* (February 26, 1886), which documented cases of bird exploitation and proposed enforceable laws to end destruction. The AOU "Model Law," which distinguished between game and nongame bird species and established closed seasons for a majority of native birds, became a concern with state legislatures, including that of Texas.[17]

Little was accomplished in Texas before 1900. Elsewhere, the Audubon Society and the AOU bird protection committee suffered reverses. A new and expanded AOU group headed by William Dutcher, who guided the revitalization of the Audubon movement and presided over the national association for more than twenty years, began efforts to rehabilitate native birds. In 1898, E. Irene Rood of Austin, a member of the AOU bird protection committee, supported "Bands of Mercy," which were aimed at stamping out mistreatment and cruelty to animals. Education was the key, especially in the South, where "small birds have been regarded as legitimate game for generations." Rood and others fought against killing songbirds, particularly robins.[18]

Bird-Lore, an illustrated bimonthly magazine aimed at bird study and protection, became the official publication of the reconstituted Audubon movement. Ornithologist Frank M. Chapman (1864–1945) owned and edited this periodical, which first appeared in February, 1899. Author Mabel Osgood Wright headed the "Audubon Department," which reported on the activities of state and local bird groups. Cecile Seixas of Galveston was the secretary of the state's first Audubon Society, which was organized in March, 1899. Nothing appeared in *Bird-Lore* about the Texas chapter, however, except to report that Seixas and her mother and two sisters were victims of the hurricane that flattened Galveston in 1900. The Texas post remained vacant, and the chapter, one of seventeen societies listed in

[17]"Notes and News," *The Auk* 3 (1886): 145; and *Science* Supplement 7 (1886): 191–205. The "Model Law" (An Act for the Protection of Birds and their Nests and Eggs), consisting of eight sections, is printed on p. 204.

[18]"Notes and News," *The Auk* 14 (1897): 116. The new thirteen-member committee was chaired by Dutcher; beginning in 1896 it published details of activities in several states. See also Witmer Stone, "Report of the A.O.U. Committee on Protection of North American Birds," *The Auk* 16 (1899): 68–69.

June, 1899, was dropped from *Bird-Lore* in June, 1901, until Hope Terhune of La Porte became secretary and Millie Lamb its president two years later. [19]

Information about the role of the Texas chapter of the Audubon Society in promoting bird (and mammal) protection is incomplete. Captain M. B. Davis of Waco, who took up cudgels effectively for the bird cause about 1905 and remained active in the Audubon Society until he died in 1912, fought hard to keep the provisions of the 1903 state game law intact after intense lobbying by professional market hunters. Henry P. Attwater, an agent for the Southern Pacific Railroad who served as a member of the AOU bird protection committee and with the advisory council of the National Association of Audubon Societies, lent clout to AOU and Audubon efforts to push the model law through the Texas legislature. [20]

An Act to Preserve and Protect the Wild Game, Wild Birds and Wild Fowl of the State, to Provide Adequate Penalties for the Unlawful Taking, Slaughter, Sale or Shipment thereof . . ., called the Wild Game and Birds—Protection of—Act, became law in April, 1903, and several sections were most important for conservation. Section 2 followed the Audubon model law, making a distinction between game and nongame species, and making it illegal to possess, purchase, or sell nongame species. Additionally, the 1903 law prohibited commerce in waterfowl and game mammals, so market men, "whose devastations have reduced the number of ducks and geese annually wintering on the coast more than fifty per cent," were forced to suspend operations or conduct them surreptitiously. A correspondent in *Farm and Ranch* noted cynically that the laws for birds resulted when sportsmen ("one-third of the present Legislators have shotguns and bird-dogs at home") recognized that bags

---

[19]"Directory of State Audubon Societies," *Bird-Lore* 1 (1899): 100, 103; "Death of Miss Seixas," *Bird-Lore* 2 (1900): and "Directory of State Audubon Societies," 166; *Bird-Lore* 3 (1901): 114. The directory in *Bird-Lore* 6 (1904): 104, listed Hope Terhune of La Porte as secretary for Texas.

[20]"Directory of State Audubon Societies," *Bird-Lore* 7 (1905): 39, listed Captain Davis for Texas; however, William Dutcher, "Report of the A.O.U. Committee," *The Auk* 20 (1903): 145, noted H. P. Attwater's efforts for the AOU Model Law in Texas, which included illustrated lectures to farmers' clubs and groups. In another issue of *The Auk* (21 [1904]: 99), he suggested that a state Audubon group was first organized in 1903.

of game had grown smaller and smaller, not when farmers joined the crusade, because the birds "are our most efficient insecticides."[21]

In 1904 the Audubon movement employed a warden in Texas, who joined a growing force nationwide to guard nesting colonies of shorebirds and water birds. The lighthouse keeper for Matagorda Bay kept an eye on tern, gull, and skimmer nesting areas. On another front, efforts were concentrated on fending off attempts to amend the 1903 law so that professional hunters, restaurant owners, and hotel keepers could continue to trade in game animals. Sportsmen, however, remained unaffected by the important game law and could bag a daily limit of twenty-five ducks per gun. In employing gun bearers, these gentlemen frequently made extremely large kills, all of them quite legal. Davis, who had become secretary of the Texas Audubon Society, joined with Attwater and Thomas A. Montgomery, a zoologist at the University of Texas and a member of the National Audubon Advisory Council, to stall any dilution of the 1903 law. They pushed the cause of bird lovers, too, by lecturing to school children, women's groups, and farmers' associations about the usefulness of birds as insect and rodent destroyers and about their aesthetic and interesting qualities.

Davis claimed to have helped organize more than one hundred chapters of the Audubon Society so that Texas could change "from a vast slaughter field of avian and mammalian life to a grand preserve." He urged interested persons committed to the cause, especially women, to speak out and rally around the "noble cause of protection." Armed with society leaflets about various species and a rationale for preserving and studying them, Davis and his coworkers urged teachers and children to spread the word about nature study and bird protection. Davis alerted colleagues in New York and Washington about bird slaughter on the Texas coast and about the plight of wintering robins, which were gunned down by the tens of thousands for food.[22]

[21] Texas, Twenty-eighth Legislature, Regular Session, *General Laws of the State of Texas*, pp. 222–26; Southern Pacific Railroad, Sunset Route, *A Few Expressions from Various Audubon Societies Regarding the Action Taken on the Preservation of Bird Life*, p. 16; and W. J. Arthur, "Legislative Sportsmen Will Not Protect Birds," *Farm and Ranch* 22 (1903): 1.

[22] "Notes and News," *The Auk* 22 (1905): 111; William Dutcher, "Annual Report of the National Association of Audubon Societies for 1905," *Bird-Lore* 7 (1905):

Such educational missions to instruct the public about birds and about the cruelty and waste associated with unregulated hunting helped stamp out market hunting and the traffic in ornamental plumage. Davis recognized that "women's clubs, educators, the newspapers and periodicals and the railroad companies" were important allies in bird preservation. Another important conservation vehicle was the State Fish and Oyster Commission, whose duties were expanded to encompass game mammals and birds.[23]

Provisions for state game wardens who enforced wildlife laws were important. Davis admitted that "the Texas Audubon Society estimates that the old law [of 1903], without the warden system, reduced the slaughter after the enactment fully 50 percent annually." Wardens in Texas were paid from nonresident hunting license fees (hunting cost residents nothing), and it was clear that there was dire need for law enforcement. Game was being shipped by rail to Saint Louis and Chicago. Davis discovered that market men had even chartered a small coastal vessel to carry the carcasses of wild ducks and geese from Texas waters. With new game wardens such practices would be more difficult.[24]

The Texas Audubon Society continued to fashion links with political figures such as Governor Tom Campbell and Attorney General R. V. Davidson, with educators, and with professional associations. Women's groups, youth clubs, and local organizations sponsored lectures about bird preservation and supported efforts to interest members in bird study. With this groundswell of sympathy, bird life reportedly increased toward the end of the first decade of the present century, although many game species, especially doves, continued to suffer from "inveterate butchery." On the coast near Houston and Beaumont, local clubs assisted with law enforcement, and Davis praised the efforts of sport hunters. In his report for 1911, Secretary Davis, who was one of eight salaried field agents of the New York–based National Association of Audubon Societies, judged that the Texas society was "coming very near mastering" the situation. Six lecturers were actively promoting the bird cause, and an affiliation with the Texas Farmers' Congress had proved ex-

343; and "Annual Report of the National Association of Audubon Societies," *Bird-Lore* 8 (1906): 272–73.
[23]"Annual Report of the National Association, p. 273.
[24]"The Audubon Societies," *Bird-Lore* 9 (1907): 57, 143.

tremely important in reaching those folk who were in the day-to-day position of protecting and managing the state's wildlife.[25]

The Farmers' Congress encouraged Davis and his colleagues, who were crisscrossing the state to urge an end to killing birds for plumage (some plume-bearing egrets were reappearing in Jasper and Sabine counties). So the Audubon group spearheaded a major effort to control the destruction of migratory shorebirds, and Davis also inveighed against the exploitation of "among the best destroyers," horned toads, which were shipped by the crateload to millinery establishments where they were "metalized" into hat oddiments.[26]

By establishing junior Audubon clubs (each child received ten educational leaflets, ten colored plates, ten outline drawings, and an Audubon button for a dime annually), the Texas society launched an extensive campaign for education. "We believe that teaching mercy and kindness should be as much a part of the curriculum of our schools as a knowledge of spelling or arithmetic," declared Mrs. M. B. Davis, whose husband unfortunately did not live to see his pioneering activities for white egrets and other birds come to fruition. When Davis died in June, 1912, the society had taken nationwide measures to protect nineteen of the twenty-six known rookeries of nesting egrets, or about thirty-five hundred birds. Most of them were in Florida, Georgia, and South Carolina, but one breeding colony existed in Texas.[27]

The energy and enthusiasm shown by Secretary Davis rubbed off on a Central Texas Audubon group, which H. Tullsen from Taylor founded in January, 1914, and which grew to about forty members within two years. This protection group paid close attention, albeit unsuccessfully, to the status of the mourning dove, and Tullsen joined forces with conservationists Attwater; W. S. Taylor, a Texas A&M faculty member; and George F. Simmons, of the University of Texas at Austin, to argue for conserving the bird.[28]

[25] M. B. Davis, "Texas," in "Annual Report of the National Association of Audubon Societies for 1908," *Bird-Lore* 10 (1908): 315–17; ibid. 12 (1910): 304–305; and [M. B. Davis], "Report of Capt. M. B. Davis," *Bird-Lore* 13 (1911): 350–51.
[26] [Davis], "Report of Capt. M. B. Davis," pp. 350–51.
[27] "Junior Work in the South," *Bird-Lore* 15 (1913): 278; and T. Gilbert Pearson, "The Report of the Secretary," *Bird-Lore* 14 (1912): 383–92, especially pp. 386–87.
[28] "Report of States Societies, and of Bird Clubs," *Bird-Lore* 17 (1915): 510.

T. Gilbert Pearson, secretary and later president of the National Association of Audubon Societies, added his clout to the Texas movement after he made a fact-finding tour to the central and lower coasts in June, 1918, in order to determine the status of nesting water-bird colonies. Pearson visited a number of bird rookeries between Mesquite Bay and San Antonio Bay, northeast of Rockport. He discovered that several thousand pairs of herons, egrets, skimmers, and terns were breeding on islets. One important find was a single colony of the very rare reddish egret. About 1,250 pairs of these egrets, much persecuted for their plumes, frequented remote, isolated cactus- and yucca-covered islands. Pearson estimated that a few pairs of the once-abundant least tern, another victim of the plumage trade, nested "along the outer islands off the coast of Texas, especially in the neighborhood of San Antonio Bay." Millinery agents had persecuted this diminutive white "sea swallow" on its nesting beaches from Maine to Texas. Ten thousand birds had been shot in one season on Cobb's Island, Virginia before 1892; Moorehead City, North Carolina, was the trade center for terns and egrets.[29]

Pearson made a second visit to the Texas coast, accompanied by William L. Finley, field agent for the Pacific states, in May, 1920. The birdmen searched the coast and shallow lagoons near Aransas Pass for signs of breeding water birds, then Pearson proceeded south to Corpus Christi and on to Brownsville, where he investigated reports of nesting herons and seabirds in the lower Laguna Madre. Audubon executive Pearson was greatly impressed by the number and variety of birds he encountered. He ticked off brown pelicans, frigate birds, roseate spoonbills, terns, herons, and egrets and confirmed rumors about a "famous bird-island" in the Laguna Madre.

Big Bird Island, about thirty-two miles south of Corpus Christi, "proved to be one of the largest breeding-places of sea-birds on the Gulf Coast of the United States," declared Pearson. It was the summer home for thousands of gulls and terns and scores of pelicans and herons. A remarkable colony of white pelicans on Little Bird Island, one mile from Big Bird Island, proved to be the highlight of Pearson's visit. "Heretofore we have not known them to nest in

[29]T. Gilbert Pearson, "A Reddish Egret Colony in Texas," *Bird-Lore* 20 (1918): 384–85; T. Gilbert Pearson, "Least Tern," *Bird-Lore* 20 (1918): 383.

the United States at any point east of Chase Lake, North Dakota, or south of the Salton Sea in California," he explained, so he was most anxious to employ a warden to protect this unusual nesting place.[30]

Judge James B. Wells and R. D. Camp in Brownsville helped Pearson secure title to the important nesting islands in the Laguna Madre. In August, 1921, Texas lawmakers authorized the General Land Office to lease without charge Big Bird Island, Little Bird Island, and Green Island, which was about thirty miles north of Point Isabel, to the National Audubon Society for fifty years. These critical habitats in Kleberg and Cameron counties were completely protected, for R. D. Camp became the Audubon warden for Green Island. He rented a houseboat, towed it north from Point Isabel, and remained in the sanctuary from May 20, 1922, through the fledging period. University of Texas scientists George Simmons and B. L. Tharp provided encouragement by visiting his floating home. Camp kept armed trespassers off the island; however, he judged that boat-tailed grackles, more than humans, plundered eggs from untended heron nests, so he trapped, poisoned, and shot these predators, which had built about three hundred nests in the sanctuary. High water, however, flooded low-lying places and caused poor success among the nesting terns and skimmers.[31]

These islands and other breeding places along a 125-mile stretch of coastline from mid–Cameron County northward to Mesquite Bay in Aransas County were extremely important for water birds. They were the home of the nation's only breeding colony of reddish egrets; other rare birds, such as snowy egrets and terns, which had been very hard hit by plume hunters from Massachusetts to Florida, also fed in the shallow lagoons. The white egret, the snowy egret, and the American or great egret species became symbols of the Audubon Society, which worked hard to police nesting places and pushed for laws to protect them. Most of the society's successes occurred outside Texas in the heavily hunted coastal areas of the Atlantic Seaboard. In patrolling Florida's waters, several wardens were murdered as they challenged plume agents. Texas was not immune

[30] T. Gilbert Pearson, "Exploring for New Bird Colonies," *Bird-Lore* 22 (1920): 324.

[31] "New Audubon Reservation," *Bird-Lore* 23 (1921): 276–77; R. D. Camp, "Guarding the Great Texas Heronry," *Bird-Lore* 24 (1922): 319–22.

to the activities of these millinery men; however, the sheer size, configuration, and difficulties of access to the island-studded seacoast made it possible for some birds to persist. Pearson investigated the rumor that the huge, remote Laguna Madre contained sizable bird islands, and it turned out to be true. Some of the nesting places suffered the all-too-common fate of more accessible areas, which hunters seeking feathers, meat, eggs, and "sport" cleaned out.

The Audubon movement's fortunes in the Lone Star State fluctuated. Davis, Attwater, and others promoted interest in bird study, and the subsequent lease on island sanctuaries proved beneficial for nesting water birds. However, Texas' share of the national membership was never large. In the early 1920s, Texas ranked twenty-fifth; it had only 23 members (including five life members) from a national pool of over 5,700. New York had most (1,764 members); Massachusetts (869), Pennsylvania (498), and Connecticut (422) followed distantly. Twenty-four wardens guarded fifty breeding places from New England to California; R. D. Camp was the only person employed in Texas.[32]

During the early 1920s the Texas Bird and Nature Study Club, the Dallas Bird and Nature Study Club, and similar groups in Corsicana and Houston continued to push the bird cause locally. All of them were affiliated with the national Audubon movement in New York. Mrs. Clarke Burr organized the Texas bird group because "of the persecution of the native birds by the English sparrow and the boy with the gun."[33]

With assistance from the Dallas Federation of Women's Clubs, a "rigid" campaign was launched against the despicable foreign sparrow, which had been deliberately shipped into Galveston from Europe and released about eighty-five years earlier. It appears that James M. Brown, entrepreneur and public figure in Galveston after the Civil War, decided to add the City of Oleanders to a growing list of urban communities where English, or house, sparrows supposedly benefited and comforted the inhabitants. Beginning in Brooklyn in about 1850, people released a number of these small, brown, chirping sparrows in order to remind European immigrants

[32]T. Gilbert Pearson, "Herons of the United States," *Bird-Lore* 24 (1922): 306–14; "Distribution of Members," *Bird-Lore* 402.

[33]"Report of the President," *Bird-Lore* 25 (1923): 436–44, 511; 28 (1926): 479, 485; and 30 (1928): 480.

of home and also to rid the city's shade trees, which shyer, native birds had abandoned, of pestiferous insects. These "bullying Britishers," as people came to name them, fed off grain spilled by horses drawing carts and wagons. By the mid-1880s, most experts realized that this alien bird had become a serious pest. It was driving off native wrens, chickadees, martins, bluebirds, and other useful and likable birds; it fed largely on seeds, not insects; and its vermin-ridden nests in gutters and crevices caused people to regard it more as a rodent than a bird.

Brown imported English sparrows into Galveston in the late 1860s when there was little adverse comment about them. By 1880, however, sparrows' nests clogged that port's water system, and the sparrows reportedly scared away native songbirds, including even the aggressive mockingbird. Burr's drive to eradicate English sparrows around Dallas was therefore an appropriate position, even for a bird lover. Audubonists were generally embarrassed by the English sparrow's success and conspicuousness in the United States. By 1920, when Burr organized her bird group, numbers of the sparrows had diminished. The automobile had replaced the horse, so supplies of feed grains were not as readily available to city sparrows.[34]

The Corsicana bird club was also the brainchild of Burr, who laid the foundations for a similar group in Kaufman, Texas, in June, 1923. This so-called Bird Lady was extremely active in Texas and visited Austin to speak with the Governor and the Superintendent of Public Instruction about the possibility of declaring a "Bird Day" for schools. The legislature passed a resolution to have May 1 named "Bird Day," when schoolchildren would learn about bird life and assist feathered friends by constructing feeding stations and bird houses or planting food-bearing shrubs.[35]

The idea of Bird Day, which was often combined with Arbor Day, originated with school superintendent Charles A. Babcock in Oil City, Pennsylvania. Babcock interested J. Sterling Morton, Secretary of Agriculture, in the idea of improving attitudes toward native birds by instructing children about them. Several states, backed by the federal government, promoted the idea in the mid-1890s.

[34] Robin W. Doughty, "The English Sparrow in the American Landscape," University of Oxford, School of Geography, *Research Paper* 19 (1978).
[35] "Report of the National Association," *Bird-Lore* 26 (1924): 497.

Before 1930, when the Texas Wildlife Agency was reconstituted as a six-member commission and initiated significant steps for managing the state's flora and fauna, animal groups orchestrated by Burr and others held the line for conservation. Most efforts included stories for children, with bird walks, slides, lectures, and collections of old nests. A series of popular articles about birds appeared in the *Houston Chronicle*. In 1930, Texas had 103 junior Audubon chapters totaling 4,768 members. It ranked, however, twenty-second in the nation in the number of bird clubs; 8,882 were in the United States, mostly in New England and in the Midwest.

The national Audubon Society recognized the good work for birds in Texas. *Holland's Magazine* ran a campaign for increased animal protection; landowners were willing to limit or prohibit hunting on their acres, and 120,000 persons had pledged to abide by state game laws. The grassroots support that Davis, Attwater, and others had instigated during the first decade of the century had expanded and developed through the creation of local agricultural groups; educational, humanitarian, and sportsmen's associations; and outdoor clubs, which were increasingly interested in wildlife protection and the management of game mammals and birds.[36]

Game Laws and Wildlife Management

Animal conservation came of age in the 1930s after more than thirty years of stop-and-go efforts for mammals and birds. Early in the century, lawmakers ordered that lengthy closed seasons be placed on specific animals such as the pronghorn antelope and bighorn sheep, whose status people judged to be most threatened. Their intent was to permit these animal populations to recover naturally. A new game division was also added to the office of the Fish and Oyster Commissioner, so an incipient institutional structure was set up for managing mammals and birds throughout most of Texas. After about 1920, efforts were made to capture and transplant important game animals to their former ranges, where they had become depleted or extinct. Federally sponsored programs in the following decade helped to promote research into these and other native spe-

[36]"Report of the President" *Bird-Lore* 27 (1925): 443–514; ibid. 31 (1929): 447–520, especially 499–500; ibid. 32 (1930): 473, 550.

cies by assisting universities, such as Texas A&M, to conduct surveys and to study the distribution, life histories, and habitat requirements of useful animals. This set of initiatives, which moved Texans from desultory, piecemeal, and often unenforceable legislation that restricted the killing of certain animals to more far-sighted, constructive, and scientifically based management of wildlife, deserves closer scrutiny.

The 1903 Act to Preserve and Protect the Wild Game, Wild Birds, and Wild Fowl of the State was the catalyst for effective game laws in Texas. The law established a five-year closed season for antelope, mountain sheep, and pheasants; most importantly, it struck at ending commerce in wild animal meat, skins, and plumage. Wholesale meat merchants, restaurant owners, and millinery agents objected to these restrictions; initially, they had little to fear, as the 1903 law, like others before it, was poorly and incompletely enforced. Provisions about outlawing the sale of game, however, became the foundation for subsequent laws. One in 1907 added the word *game* to the official title of the State Fish and Oyster Commissioner; it also extended the five-year moratorium on hunting bighorn and antelope to include prairie chickens and it bolstered efforts for conserving deer. Section 5 of this law provided for a chief deputy commissioner with an annual salary of eighteen hundred dollars to work with the commissioner, and it required the commissioner, who was R. H. Wood, to enforce all game laws through deputy game commissioners. The 1907 law provided the teeth for enforcement, and it authorized the new Game, Fish and Oyster Commissioner to sell hunting licenses to finance necessary enforcement.[37]

One comment about the 1907 law suggested that, in passing it, the legislature built "the roof to complete the statutory shelter it had begun for protection of Texas wildlife in 1879."[38] This act was not eviscerated by county exemptions, which had nullified previous laws; rather, these local exemptions to legislation had decreased over the previous ten to fifteen years.

The 1907 act was passed, however, in the face of an indifferent

[37] Texas, Twenty-eighth Legislature, *General Laws of Texas*, pp. 222–26; Texas, Thirtieth Legislature, Regular Session, *General Laws of the State of Texas*, pp. 254–57.

[38] Texas Legislative Council, *Wildlife Management in Texas*, p. 9.

populace and judiciary, who had been unwilling to give previous game laws wholehearted or sympathetic consideration. Before lawmakers set up the game division, very few instances of game law violations had been prosecuted successfully; only one out of eleven arrests in Calhoun County in 1900 and two of thirty-one in Galveston County had resulted in convictions. Moreover, a legislative committee faulted the commissioner for neglecting to enforce game laws, implying that he had little incentive to be vigilant in the prosecution of wildlife-related laws.[39]

How much law enforcement existed is difficult to determine. Reportedly, first commissioner Kibbe employed several deputies on the coast in 1902 and 1903, under provisions of the 1895 law creating the office of Fish and Oyster Commissioner. In his final year as commissioner the number had been increased to ten. The new official, R. H. Wood, hired approximately fifteen men, and a decade later the number had more than doubled. Most of these game wardens monitored the coastal fishery. In his annual report for 1912, the commissioner complained scathingly of the "wild theory of enforcement"; it seemed that the public was not prepared to back up the laws on the books.[40]

Provisions for paying game wardens from a fund generated by the sale of hunting licenses also ran into trouble. Records suggest that fees were collected for the first time in the fiscal year ending August 31, 1910, when five thousand licenses had been sold to hunters, although no license was necessary in a hunter's county of residence. The Thirty-seventh Legislature, however, dealt a telling blow to the whole game program when it channeled the fund for other purposes.

The poor record of partial enforcement, inefficiencies, lowered morale, and unfulfilled promises resulted from, at least in part, the rapid turnover in the office of Game, Fish and Oyster Commissioner. Four men occupied that post between 1910 and 1920, and three others followed in the next decade. Commissioner W. G. Sterrett provided a reason for such a rapid turnover when he suggested that the office had been created by "the demand of a few people," so authorities "were forced not moved to respond . . . and

[39] Ibid., p. 10.
[40] Ibid., p. 11.

'let it go at that.'" A tradition of apathy and neglect had dogged the activities of the Texas conservation organization. A later comment was more pointed: "The Department had been called a joke, but the joke was on the sportsman who had bought hunting licenses on the supposition that the money would be used to protect and increase the game supply."[41]

The Game, Fish and Oyster Commission judged that "the outlook for game had never been worse, not only in Texas but in other parts of the Nation."[42] During and immediately after World War I, animal populations had tilted downward. Deer and prairie chickens, once so abundant, were noticeably lower, and by 1922 the pronghorn numbered fewer than three thousand head in Texas. Closed seasons were placed on additional species, including wood ducks and turkey hens (in 1919), and the bag limits for quail and doves were cut from twenty-five to fifteen birds per day.

An important innovation for game, namely the move toward restoring wild animals by propagating or capturing and restocking them, received initial impetus in 1911 when the state legislature provided that funds from the sale of shell and sand dredged from subsurface areas should go into a special Fish and Oyster Fund, which the commissioner could draw from in order to establish fish hatcheries and suitable places for oyster beds. In the decade after 1913, about four million freshwater fishes were distributed from a hatchery constructed in Dallas. The commissioner initiated oyster culture in 1920 and also commenced activities to purchase quail from Mexico in order to release them to interested landowners and associations for restocking. Almost one hundred thousand bobwhite quail were released in Texas from 1920 to 1940, and efforts to broaden the restocking program included turkeys, deer, and antelope.

The idea of establishing refuges or preserves for wild animals appeared in the commissioner's comments in 1912. Matagorda Island was a locality suggested for quail; later, agricultural lands around state penitentiaries were listed as suitable places where wildlife would be protected and perhaps propagated. The sanctuary or refuge concept combined the goals of preservationists and wildlife managers and had a federal precedent dating back to 1903.[43]

[41] Texas Game, Fish and Oyster Commission, *Review of Texas Wild Life*, p. 89.

[42] Ibid.

[43] Texas Legislative Council, *Wildlife Management in Texas*, p. 21.

A 1925 law for state game preserves "welded together for the first time the crusade of the conservationists, the plans of state game officials, the desires of many landowners, and the hopes of disillusioned hunters." Through its provisions a landowner agreed to introduce and protect species of game animals for "not less than ten years." Animals were introduced in order to build up numbers in these private places, which acted as reservoirs for new stock. In the first year thirty-three game preserves, totaling more than one million acres, were set up, and in its heyday in the 1930s the state system increased to fifty-three reserves covering 2.7 million acres.[44]

As more people realized that game had been literally swept away from vast areas of East and Central Texas and that useful, interesting mammals and birds had been shot out, restoration programs gathered momentum. Persistence and patience with game-related issues, including a corpus of laws that a growing force of dedicated wardens wanted to enforce, began to pay off. In 1923, lawmakers turned over additional funds to the Game, Fish and Oyster Commissioner, who employed fifty salaried deputies to monitor hunting. Their work resulted in a threefold jump in the number of fines for game law violations (598 in 1923–24), and interest turned toward preserving wildlife habitats, especially riparian and coastal wetlands where untreated sewage and industrial effluents posed significant hazards for aquatic animals.[45]

The Forty-ninth Legislature reorganized the state's conservation arm in 1929 by establishing a Game, Fish and Oyster Commission comprising a six-member board whose first executive secretary was William J. Tucker. Tucker, who served for fifteen years, believed that the new commission would help stabilize and streamline the range of conservation activities. Not one of the twelve administrators, except Kibbe, had held office long enough to fully grasp, evaluate, and address the problems and needs of wildlife over the entire state of Texas.

It turned out that many commission members were most knowledgeable about fauna and were well versed about the status of many species. Caesar Kleberg, for example, who was a member from 1929 to 1936, provided brood stock from the King Ranch for restocking deer and other species. In the 1930s, liaisons with fed-

44 Ibid., pp. 21, 23, Table 11.
45 Ibid., p. 11.

eral agencies, particularly the U.S. Department of Agriculture's Biological Survey, were strengthened, and Texas was one of nine states selected by the Biological Survey to cooperate in scientific research. Biologists recognized that Texas had the great potential for increasing its stock of game, and the state's wildlife agency and Texas A&M College provided specific interest and assistance for the effort to increase and protect wildlife.

Federal and State Relationships

The federal government has influenced wild animal conservation in Texas in three ways. First, several agencies, including the Department of Agriculture, the Department of the Interior, and the Department of Defense, own and operate tracts of land and regulate human access and activities on them. Second, national laws to protect animals and animal habitats have provided controls for the harvesting of migratory game, preserving migratory nongame species. Other laws have provided for the restoration and rehabilitation of certain animals or served as the basis for state and local controls of predatory or pestiferous ones. This set of legal initiatives protects, manages, controls, regulates, or aims to restore animal populations, thereby providing a benchmark and structure for state laws. Many of these laws provide for consultation and cooperation between federal and state wildlife authorities. Congressional appropriations for research into the biology and management of wild animals are the third important means for wildlife conservation. Monies have been and are still apportioned to state programs on a matching basis. They may also be "seed" funds for the establishment of new programs.

The U.S. government agreed to make no claims to Texas lands after annexation in 1845, so all unappropriated lands were subject to disposition under state laws. Consequently, the federal government owns less than 2 percent of the Lone Star State's 171 million acres, which make Texas second in size to Alaska. The largest federal landholders in Texas are the Department of Defense (about 1.2 million acres) and the Department of the Interior (about 1.1 million acres), whose chief components, the National Park Service and the Fish and Wildlife Service, have made a special commitment to animal conservation.

There are ten U.S. migratory bird refuges, mostly for water-fowl, which comprise prime habitat for several million ducks and geese that migrate annually down the Central and Mississippi fly-ways to winter on coastal wetlands. These refuges were established largely with funds from the Migratory Bird Hunting Stamp Act (1934), which required waterfowl hunters sixteen years of age and older to purchase a hunting stamp.[46]

The Aransas National Wildlife Refuge was the first federal ref-uge in Texas. It was established in 1937 to conserve waterfowl, in-cluding a small flock of approximately fourteen whooping cranes that was wintering on the tidal marshes of the Blackjack Peninsula in Aransas County. This large, conspicuous water bird, whose fall silhouette shimmering in the haze near Austin made Olmsted once mistake it for a llama, has become a symbol for conservation. Today, the crane represents sustained and intensive efforts to protect and restore endangered wild animals through habitat preservation in refuges, prohibitions on hunting, programs aimed at finding foster parents for eggs and young cranes, and even breeding these endan-gered animals in captivity and releasing them.

Santa Ana, another important national wildlife refuge, is the home for more rare and threatened wildlife species than any other federal refuge in the United States. This two-thousand-acre tract of subtropical woodland in the lower Rio Grande Valley is covered with ebony, hackberry, ash, cactus, chaparral, and other plants which have been cleared from most of the valley through the expansion of agriculture. Santa Ana, commonly known as the "gem" of the na-tional wildlife refuge system, was set aside in 1943. Twenty-nine mammal species live there, and many of them are unusual or rare; 326 birds, or about two-thirds of the species occurring west of the hundredth meridian, have been recorded. Many of the birds are migrants that use the refuge as a temporary home. Others are Mex-ican species and are unusual in the United States because the ref-uge is located on the northern edge of their ranges.[47]

Texas' own system of wildlife refuges for research and manage-

[46] Environmental Law Institute, *The Evolution of National Wildlife Law*, pp. 142–61.

[47] David R. Zimmerman, "Endangered Bird Species: Habitat Manipulation Methods," *Science* 192 (1976): 876–79; and Robert Murphy, *Wild Sanctuaries*, pp. 100–105.

ment includes eleven wildlife management areas, which in 1976 totaled about 190,000 acres. Many of the areas were purchased out of state funds with federal reimbursement of seventy-five cents on the dollar. Most of the management units were established before 1960, and in recent years Texas has lagged behind other states in its program of land acquisition. Oklahoma, like Texas, has only a small area (3.5 percent) that is owned by the federal government. The Sooner State, however, has set aside 57.6 percent more land for wildlife management than Texas has, although Oklahoma is only a little over one-fourth the size. New Mexico is less than half the size of Texas, but it has more reserves for wildlife and 50,000 more acres in management areas or refuges than does Texas. Moreover, the federal government owns roughly 34 percent of New Mexico's land, and the U.S. Fish and Wildlife Service controls over 316,000 acres, double the area that the agency controls in Texas.[48]

Federal laws that have helped to curb the misuse of the nation's wildlife were based on the government's authority to regulate commerce, to make treaties with foreign nations, and to control the killing or capture of animals in federal parks, refuges, or forests. As early as 1894, for example, all hunting was prohibited in Yellowstone National Park.

The government's right to regulate the interstate shipment of wildlife was first established in 1900 by the Lacey Act. Under this law, Congress invoked its powers to regulate commerce, including the importation of wild animals, by prohibiting any shipments of game animals taken in contravention of state laws. The Lacey Act helped to support and enforce state laws for wild animals; importantly, it regulated the entry of injurious mammals and birds into the United States.[49]

The treaty-making power of the federal government has been a third method of regulating wildlife hunting. A challenge to the constitutionality of a federal migratory bird act (1913), which placed migratory game and insectivorous birds under the custody and jurisdiction of the federal government, was diverted when the U.S. Department of State concluded a wildlife treaty with Great Britain. This law, the Migratory Bird Treaty Act of 1918, was judged to take

48 U.S. Fish and Wildlife Service, *Federal Aid in Fish and Wildlife Restoration, 1976*; U.S. Bureau of Land Management, *Public Land Statistics, 1976*.

49 Thomas L. Lund, *American Wildlife Law*.

precedence over the powers of individual states. Under its provisions federal agencies regulated harvests of migratory bird species such as waterfowl moving along the flyways connecting the United States with Canada, and terminated commerce in ducks and geese.[50]

Over the past eighty years federal legislation has moved from total protection to the establishment of laws and regulations governing the harvest of game on a sustainable basis. Through the imposition of closed seasons, bag limits, and a clarification of the definition of "game," including methods by which hunters may kill animals, federal involvement with wildlife has shifted from preservation to management and restoration.

Managing game mammals and birds as a harvestable resource was determined largely by hunting stamp monies under provisions of the Migratory Bird Conservation Act of 1929. Amendments to this act established the practice of hunting on many wildlife refuges, and currently up to 40 percent of national wildlife refuge (NWR) may be opened up to sportsmen. Hunting regulations and public access to NWRs remain important, though controversial, considerations in contemporary conservation discussions.[51]

The state's six-member Parks and Wildlife Commission has authority to exercise regulatory control over all or part of the wildlife resources in 239 of the state's 254 counties; current efforts suggest greater regulatory control by the commission. This power includes the establishment of bag and possession limits as well as the season, (that is, timing and duration) for hunting native mammals, birds, and fur-bearing animals. The state wildlife commission, however, does not have overall jurisdiction for migratory game.

Under the powers of the Migratory Bird Treaty Act of July, 1918, the federal government, in the person of the secretary of interior, establishes the framework for migratory bird hunting. The secretary has prohibited certain practices, such as using live decoys and setting out baits, and has placed limits on gun gauges and the number of shells a weapon can hold.[52]

Ninety-seven species within five families (Anatidae or ducks,

[50] Ibid., pp. 49–51.

[51] Defenders of Wildlife, *A Report on the National Wildlife Refuge System*; and National Wildlife Refuge Study Task Force, *Recommendations on the Management of the National Wildlife Refuge System*.

[52] U.S. Fish and Wildlife Service, *Issuance of Annual Regulations Permitting the Sport Hunting of Migratory Birds*, pp. 4–8, Appendix VIII.

swans, and geese; Gruidae or cranes; Rallidae or rails, gallinules, and coots; Scolopacidae or shorebirds; and Columbidae or pigeons and doves) are now classified as migratory game birds. Texas sportsmen adhere to the framework of regulations for hunting these birds which the federal government sets annually. Individual states may adopt more stringent regulations.

Thirty-six species of native ducks, seven species of geese, and three species of swans comprise the migratory waterfowl in North America. In autumn, these birds migrate from northern breeding areas down four "flyways" (routes that have more administrative significance than biological precision) to wintering grounds on interior and coastal marshlands of the southern and western states. Texas is the terminus for many fowl on the Central Flyway, which funnels a variable but significant fraction of the 77 million to 120 million ducks and 4 million to 6 million geese passing southward in fall months. Duck productivity varies according to the quantity of surface water on northern prairies; goose reproduction is more affected by spring and early summer temperatures in arctic Canada and Alaska.[53]

Estimates of waterfowl reproduction and overall numbers form the basis for hunting for each flyway and are derived through information exchanges between state agencies and the flyway councils, the federal Fish and Wildlife Service, and other interested groups. A flyway council is the organization of states sharing a common waterfowl resource; biologists in Texas contribute data that help formulate policy for the Central Flyway Council.

Additionally, within Texas, personnel generate data about waterfowl species by means of periodic breeding and wintering bird surveys, analysis of banding returns, and hunter questionnaires. The degree of cooperation, collaboration, and coordination between state and federal wildlife biologists is important for establishing and adjusting regulations for waterfowl hunting and for other migratory game birds such as woodcock, doves and sandhill cranes. Recent federal statistics estimate that about 110,500 hunters kill 828,000 ducks and 223,000 geese in Texas every year.[54]

Another federal statute with increasing significance to Texas

[53] Ibid., pp. 2–5.

[54] William Brownlee, Texas Parks and Wildlife Department, personal communication, November 19, 1982.

and to other states in general is the 1973 Endangered Species Act. In one sense this act ties the hands of state wildlife departments by making it unlawful for anyone subject to the jurisdiction of the United States to "take" any species listed as endangered. The act, however, has opened up a program for expenditures from the Federal Land and Water Conservation Fund for the acquisition of habitat for threatened and endangered wildlife. It has instructed federal authorities not to modify or destroy habitat "critical" to the survival of vanishing organisms.

Under the Endangered Species Act, the Fish and Wildlife Service has entered into cooperative agreements with thirty-six states (by September, 1980), which are eligible for assistance of up to two-thirds the cost of their endangered species programs in return for meeting conservation criteria stipulated by the 1973 act. New Mexico, for example, signed a cooperative agreement with the U.S. Fish and Wildlife Service in 1977 and became eligible for matching funds for work on its endangered species. New Mexico employs four biologists in its endangered species program, which has surveyed North America's most elusive and rare mammal, the black-footed ferret, and has supported research on the peregrine falcon. Under an act of February, 1974, New Mexico listed 104 species as endangered, including 10 on the federal list. The objective of the program is to conserve the biological diversity of New Mexico's flora and fauna.[55]

Texas passed its own Endangered Species Act in 1973 and has drawn up a list of endangered animals. The legislature charged the Parks and Wildlife Department with responsibility for conducting investigations on threatened and endangered animals. Recent surveys have examined eagles and falcons, the rookeries of fish-eating birds on the Gulf Coast, and certain threatened nongame species such as the red-cockaded woodpecker and the Houston toad. Finances for nongame animal research come from appropriations from the state's general fund, not from sport license monies, which sustain most efforts for game. Although Texas and Arizona appear to meet the requirements for concluding a cooperative agreement under Section 6 of the 1973 federal Endangered Species Act, they

[55] John P. Hubbard et. al., *Handbook of Species Endangered in New Mexico*; and William S. Huey, *Symposium on Rare and Endangered Wildlife of the Southwestern United States*.

have not sought to do so. Currently, revenues for state conservation agencies are static or are actually decreasing, and there is a noticeable dearth of state funds to match available federal dollars.

Important and long-term federal support for state wildlife programs dates back to the 1930s, when conservation initiatives in Texas began to be reimbursed by revenues generated by taxes on ammunition and weapons used in hunting. The Pittman-Robertson program, established by the Federal Aid in Restoration Act of 1937, was the basis for the apportionment of funds to state wildlife projects. Revenues were raised from an excise tax on sporting arms and ammunition (first imposed in 1932) which was earmarked for wildlife management, particularly for waterfowl, in 1936. In that year a White House–sponsored North American Wildlife Conference recognized the critical status of many game animals and their habitats. The International Association of Game, Fish, and Conservation Commissioners and a number of key wildlife groups endorsed key legislation that Senator Key Pittman of Nevada and House member Willis Robertson of Virginia introduced into the U.S. Congress early in 1937. The Pittman-Robertson Act, or so-called P-R, received President Franklin D. Roosevelt's signature on September 2, 1937.[56]

Some state legislatures (not Texas', however) were reluctant to pass "assent" legislation incorporating the provisions of P-R, because it was to be more than merely a conduit for tax revenues. The federal law stipulated that states must place their wildlife programs on a financially stable basis by channeling hunters' license fees toward game conservation. Also, federal authorities had to approve state projects. All states, however, finally adopted the provisions of P-R, although it took some of them almost a decade to do so.

The specifications of P-R, and a later companion act for fisheries, the Dingell-Johnson Act of 1950, are set out in Table 1. Current funding formulas are based upon the number of hunting licenses sold and the geographic size of each state. Several amendments have modified P-R; one of them in 1946 established a ceiling for total funds at no more than 5 percent and no less than 0.5 percent for any state. This formula ensured that the larger states such as Texas would not receive disproportionately large apportionments.

The mission of the P-R reimbursement program is, first, to

[56] U.S. Fish and Wildlife Service, *35 Years of Shared Wildlife Management*

TABLE 1. Funding Provisions of the Pittman-Robertson and Dingell-Johnson Programs.

	Federal Aid in Wildlife Restoration Program, P-R Act	Federal Aid in Sport Fish Restoration Program, D-J Act
Purpose	Conserve and manage wild birds and mammals	Conserve and manage fish
Funding Source	Manufacturers' excise tax on sporting arms and ammunition Sport guns—11 percent Handguns—10 percent (1970) Archery Equipment—11 percent (1972)	Manufacturer's excise tax on rods, reels, baits, etc.—10 percent
Date Initiation	September 2, 1937 fiscal year 1939	August 9, 1950 fiscal year 1951
Apportionment	Formula based on state area and the number of paid hunting licenses; 5 percent ceiling, or 0.5 percent minimum, per state amendment, 1946,	Formula based on state area (including coastal waters) and the number of paid fishing licenses; maximum of 5 percent, minimum of 1 percent, to any state.
Availability Federal Funds	Annually, and the following fiscal year 75 percent maximum	Annually 50 percent maximum, except for multistate projects.
Total	$736.97 million (1939–77)	$227.79 million (1951–77)

SOURCE: U.S. Fish and Wildlife Service, *Federal Aid in Fish and Wildlife Restoration Manual.* Rev. ed. (Washington, D.C.: Bureau of Sport Fisheries and Wildlife, 1973).

provide funds for states to protect and manage wildlife and wild animal habitats in order to meet the current and future needs of recreationists. It is anticipated that thirty-eight million acres of wildlife habitat will be under active management by 1985. Second, P-R has enabled state agencies to survey their wildlife and to conduct biological research into various species. Third, through hunter safety training programs, P-R has facilitated the provision of instruction in "safe and ethical conduct in fish and wildlife recreation," thereby reducing hunting accidents and game law violations.[57]

In the late 1930s, P-R funds in Texas were spent to survey game mammals and birds; biologists, trained frequently under another federal program, the Cooperative Research Unit Program at Texas A&M, confirmed that many species had declined and had been extirpated from former ranges. The white-tailed deer, for example, had disappeared from many places in East Texas. Pronghorn antelope numbers on the High Plains had not recovered from unregulated killing despite a closed season imposed by the legislature back in 1903, and the eastern turkey, bobwhite quail, and Attwater's prairie chicken had also suffered catastrophic drops in population.

Accordingly, P-R funds went into an ambitious and largely successful program to restock game through trapping and transplantation. The Aransas National Wildlife Refuge, the King Ranch, and other private ranches trapped wild white-tailed deer for release both inside and outside Texas. Since 1939, more than five thousand antelope have been relocated in suitable habitats in Texas, and sizable populations now occur in four ecological areas—the Trans-Pecos, the northeast Edwards Plateau, the Rolling Plains, and the High Plains. Other P-R restocking efforts have included beaver, turkey, quail, javelina, and chachalaca. Wildlife specialists continue to provide game species to landowners and have used the P-R program to introduce exotic game birds, principally ringnecked pheasants and partridges, and a foreign ungulate, the barbary sheep or aoudad (into Palo Duro Canyon in 1957), to areas where they are likely to thrive and not compete directly with indigenous animals.[58]

[57] U.S. Fish and Wildlife Service, "Draft Environmental Impact Statement: Federal Aid in Fish and Wildlife Restoration Programs," pp. 1–10.

[58] Texas Game, Fish and Oyster Commission, *Principal Game Birds and Mammals of Texas: Their Distribution and Management*; William B. Davis, "The Mammals of Texas," *Texas Parks and Wildlife Bulletin* 41 (1974, rev.).

Research conducted under P-R on the eight big game animals and on the score or so of upland and migratory birds (see Table 2) has determined population dynamics, interspecific relationships, and habitat requirements of key species in order to establish effective regulations for hunting. The Parks and Wildlife Department's Wildlife Division has been reorganized to focus on the species concept in management, moving away from single, disaggregated projects.

In absolute terms, however, P-R has made a minute contribution to habitat retention. Of the estimated 1,785 million acres of big game habitat in the nation, only 33.5 million acres, or 2 percent, are under the full or partial control of state wildlife agencies. However, P-R is vitally important in providing the funds for animal surveys and biological research; as a consequence, recommendations for hunting seasons and cropping limits are much more meaningful.

Over the past forty years, federal influence over state wildlife programs through P-R and other programs has tended to diminish as amendments to these laws have helped to broaden the scope of state activities. Presently, funds may be used to aid in the development of a "comprehensive fish and wildlife resource management plan," an amendment in 1970, and some nongame conservation initiatives are siphoning off P-R monies.

The mid-1930s was the time for another important measure that strengthened federal-state relationships. The federal and state Cooperative Wildlife Research Units program was begun in 1935 to build back dwindling stocks of game mammals and birds in the United States. The program was the achievement of Jay N. ("Ding") Darling, chief of the Bureau of Biological Survey, who inaugurated the training of wildlife scientists by cooperative agreements with state land-grant colleges and conservation departments. The objective was to staff game and fish agencies with technically competent personnel, to develop research programs, and to educate the public about the needs of wildlife. The Cooperative Wildlife Research Unit program was expanded in 1960 through agreements with universities and colleges for training programs in wildlife and fisheries science. There are twenty Cooperative Wildlife Research Units and twenty-five Cooperative Fishery Units at twenty-six universities and colleges across the nation. Congressional appropriations provide annual funds for the Cooperative Research Unit program, in which eighteen states participate.

The Texas Cooperative Wildlife Research Unit was organized

TABLE 2. Pittman-Robertson Funding for Game Animal Transplanting and Restoration in Texas.

Species	Area	Past Status	Present Status	Remarks
Big Game				
Aoudad sheep	Introduced to Palo Duro Canyon	44 introduced in 1958	600–800 (1981)	Hunted since 1963
Bighorn sheep	Virtual extirpation in Trans-Pecos; introduced to Black Gap Management Area		about 50	Predation has been severe since 1970, when 68 captive sheep existed.
White-tailed deer	Restocked statewide	much reduced	about 2.98 million	Aransas NWR and the King Ranch supplied stock after 1938.
Mule deer	Restocked in Panhandle	much reduced	150,000	Hunted
Pronghorn antelope	Restocked in four ecological areas of its former range in West, Central, and North Texas	down to 2,407 (in 1924)	about 12,000	Hunted since 1944
Elk	Extirpated; introduced in the Guadalupe Mountains		300 wild, 969 penned	Transplanted to other uplands in the Trans-Pecos; a few are hunted by permit.
Javelina	Formerly north to Red River and east to Brazos River; limited restocking and exchanges for stock with other states	reduced	locally common in southern one-third of the state	More than 150 transplanted since 1953; decline through brush clearance continues

Upland Game				
Turkey	Restocked east of 97th meridian; some propagation		estimated 300,000–500,000 (6,000–8,000 of eastern race)	Eastern race extirpated by 1930; restocking continues
Bobwhite quail	widespread, including East Texas	Restocked; some propagation statewide from a hatchery at Tyler, 1956–68	locally abundant; 2.9 million harvested by 267,000 hunters (1981)	Stronghold in Central and South Texas
Prairie chicken (Lesser)	Native to the North Texas Plains	much reduced in High Plains	about 8,677 in North Texas (1981)	Habitat destruction, pesticides, and draught cause declines; some hunting.
Prairie chicken (Attwater's)	Endemic to Gulf Coast Prairies (originally over approximately 6 million acres)	much reduced to about 8,700 in 1937	about 1,500	An 8,000-acre national wildlife reserve established near Eagle Lake, Colorado Co., in 1972.
Pheasant	Releases in Gulf Coast Prairie, Post Oak, and Panhandle	about 31,500 released 1964–78	36,000 harvested on High Plains 1981	Hunting in coastal counties is very localized.
Chachalaca	Transplanted in Rio Grande Valley counties	more widespread in South Texas; 187 birds released on 9 sites in 6 counties (1981)	locally common in heavy brush in South Texas	Brush control and intensive farming have reduced its range.

SOURCE: Don Wilson et al., Texas Parks and Wildlife Department, Wildlife Division, November 19, 1982.

officially on December 9, 1935, at College Station, where Walter P. Taylor, biologist with the Biological Survey, and an assistant, Valgene Lehmann, established a facility to educate students at Texas A&M College in wildlife management. The unit's research thrust included the improvement of habitat for quail and Attwater's prairie chickens and the monitoring of the distribution, numbers, and status of the state's mammals and birds. Before it was discontinued in 1954, the unit trained many biologists who worked in the Texas Parks and Wildlife Department.

A similar wildlife unit opened in Arizona in 1951 (a fisheries unit followed in 1964), and biologists have investigated waterfowl, the impact of logging on fish populations, and the ecology and distribution of the grey squirrel, bobcat, and collared peccary. An Oklahoma unit that is part of Oklahoma State University at Stillwater was established in 1948. Recent research there includes the evaluation of wildlife habitat from ERTS satellite imagery, the manipulation of habitat for game mammals and birds, and the ecology of fish species in man-made lakes. New Mexico does not participate in the Cooperative Research Unit program.[59]

The Lone Star State is a principal beneficiary of a federal fish hatchery program, which also dates back to the 1930s, because Texans have constructed many large reservoirs for flood control and water delivery. Texas and Oklahoma are among nine states that contain more than 50 percent of the nation's reservoir surface area. Texas has also benefited from another federal program, the Farm Pond Program. The number of farm ponds in the United States increased from an estimated twenty thousand in 1934 to over two million by 1965.

The Fishery Division in the Texas Parks and Wildlife Department has conducted surveys and research aimed at stocking the growing number of deep-water and warm-water impoundments with suitable sport fish in order to support a growing number of anglers, who purchase annually about 1.5 million fishing licenses. In fiscal year 1975, Texans obtained 17.3 million, or 18,364 pounds, of twelve fish species from national hatcheries and received $842,000 in federal apportionments under the Dingell-Johnson program for fish

[59] U.S. Fish and Wildlife Service, *Thirty Years of Cooperative Wildlife Research Units: 1935–65.*

restoration. Texas also received $2.8 million under the grant-in-aid program of the 1964 Commercial Fisheries Act. The state ranked tenth in the nation in this appropriation, which was used to conduct research on the bays and estuaries, particularly experiments in aquaculture, such as raising shrimp, oysters, and three fish species in artificial ponds.[60]

The federal government's involvement with the nation's wildlife resource has expanded constantly in recent decades to encompass legal, fiscal, and scientific aspects of protection and management. Some persons believe, however, that federal structures, including new international regulations aimed at controlling the harvest and trade in flora and fauna, have eroded states' rights. This trend to centralized oversight and control exemplifies to them an inability to address effectively local and specific problems which are best dealt with by regional or state agencies. Other persons argue that federal directives allow for flexibility and reduce the likelihood of local mismanagement by providing efficient, comprehensive, and progressive policies aimed at managing the nation's wild-animal heritage along sound biological lines.

[60] H. S. Swingle, "History of Warmwater Pond Culture in the United States," in *A Century of Fisheries in North America*, ed. Norman G. Benson, pp. 95–105; U.S. Fish and Wildlife Service, Division of National Fish Hatcheries, *Propagation and Distribution of Fishes from National Fish Hatcheries for the Fiscal Year 1975*, p. 52; and U.S. National Oceanic and Atmospheric Administration, National Marine Fisheries Service, *Grant-in-Aid for Fisheries, Program Activities 1977*, p. 20.

CHAPTER 7

Twentieth-Century Losses
and Gains

AFTER World War II, the Game, Fish and Oyster Commission published a comprehensive survey of the principal game animals in nine "game regions" in Texas. The concept of the game region was derived basically from vegetation zones comprising the habitats for native wild animals. Each region had a unique set of management problems.[1]

The 1945 document illuminated basic issues. First, many animals, notably larger mammals, such as bison, antelope, and bighorn sheep, and game birds, such as prairie chickens, turkey, and quail, had been extirpated from wide areas or even entirely from former habitats. Many of them were extinct or existed in greatly reduced numbers. State biologists, therefore, drew up management plans to complement hunting regulations and concentrated on restocking native animals in order to give them a chance to build up populations.

Experts recognized, however, that in many regions their plans for game conservation were limited by a second major problem, namely, the degree, type, and extent of humanly induced environmental change that had taken place through the expansion of settlement and agriculture. Much of the Blackland Prairie, a game region in Central Texas, for example, had become the state's key agricultural sector in growing cotton and grains in little more than half a century. In many counties the friable limestone soils had washed away. Urbanization had increased rapidly in Dallas, McLennan, and

---

[1]Texas Game, Fish and Oyster Commission, *Principal Game Birds and Mammals of Texas: Their Distribution and Management*, pp. 1–14.

Travis counties. Therefore, plans to "bring back whatever types of native game could be expected to adapt to such environmental modification" were limited, especially when the blackland, less than 10 percent of the state's land area, was home for almost one-third of the total population. There was simply no longer a place in the landscape, or in residents' minds, for bison, antelope, or black bear. Habitats for the remaining deer and turkeys were losing out to agriculture, which had spread over 80 percent of the region; squirrels, furbearers, and reportedly bullfrogs were dwindling through the loss of the more restricted riparian habitat. Of the game animals, only doves appear to have benefitted from the introduction and spread of cultivated grains.[2]

In the west, the Rolling Plains and High Plains grassland in the Plains Game Region presented more opportunities for animal restoration, although much of this environment had been planted under wheat, cotton, and other crops. Bison competed with cattle and thus proved undesirable. Many grassland areas, however, could still support antelope and prairie chickens; deer also inhabited the draws and uplands.[3]

Both white-tailed and mule deer have made dramatic comebacks in Texas in the last fifty years. Effective hunting regulations and restocking programs, which have resulted in the transportation and release of thousands of animals, with the increase in browse, have made the white-tailed deer more abundant now than at any time since first white settlement.[4] In the 1920s deer numbers started to increase when several Hill Country owners of large ranches, who regulated hunting on their lands, began to take an active interest in protection. They instructed ranch hands to enforce prohibitions against killing deer, whose browsing on shrubs and brush for food did not conflict with the cattle grazing. The construction of numerous stock ponds, especially in drier places of the Edwards Plateau, and the eradication of wolves and cougars has assisted the revival of whitetails. Also, fire suppression has permitted brush and shrubs,

[2] Ibid., pp. 5–6; "Game Regions of Texas: The Blackland Prairie," *Texas Game and Fish* 10 (1952): 6–8.
[3] Texas Game, Fish and Oyster Commission, *Game Birds and Mammals*, pp. 1–3, 10–12.
[4] Texas Game, Fish and Oyster Commission, *Review of Texas Wild Life and Conservation*, p. 62.

cover and food for deer, to invade grasslands that cattle, sheep, and goats had overgrazed. A common occurrence in the Hill Country of leaving oaks for the acorns they produce, while cutting out juniper, has also increased fall and winter survival rates.

The U.S. Biological Survey discovered that 250 million acres nationwide were better adapted to raising goats, notably angoras, than to cropping or to stocking with cattle, sheep, and horses. Much of this land, however, was suitable for deer, and promoters claimed that these cervids should be "farmed," as they caused "less injury to the forest cover than would result from its browsing by goats."[5] By this 1908 survey, Texas had already become the nation's leading state in mohair production, and Hill Country ranchers tended to prefer conserving white-tailed deer, which could range with cattle, although not if they made heavy inroads into the forage for angora goats. Enforcement of property rights and trespassing laws assisted in deer protection in Central and in South Texas. The southern brushlands, Coastal Prairie, and motte country supplied many animals for transplanting to counties in the eastern pine and post-oak belt where landowners agreed to prohibit hunting.

By the early 1940s the white-tailed deer had recovered so well that overpopulation—visibly stunted animals and periodic die-offs— became evident in the eastern Edwards Plateau, particularly in Mason and Gillespie counties. In December, 1953, the first antlerless deer season was opened for killing does and immature bucks, and over the past thirty years controversy has surrounded the question of reducing deer populations by hunting does. Biologists argue that killing females is sound management; however, many ranchers will not allow sportsmen to kill does on hunting leases. Many hunters prefer the traditional recreational activity of bagging big-antlered bucks.[6]

By the 1950s, the deer population in East Texas has grown substantially through periodic restocking. One biologist noted in 1953 that "hardly a square mile of suitable deer range" from Crockett in Houston County to Hemphill in Sabine County, which were almost

[5] D. E. Lantz, "Deer Farming in the United States," *Farmers' Bulletin* 350 (1908): 14–15.

[6] Bob Ramsey and Eugene Walker, "Take 'Em or Leave 'Em," *Texas Game and Fish* 12 (1954): 4–6, 20–22; Rodney Marburger and Horace Gore, "Deer Facts and the Antlerless Question," *Texas Game and Fish* 21 (1963): 5–7.

one hundred miles apart, lacked deer. The animals had spread southward into the coastal lowlands.[7]

Mule or black-tailed deer also benefited from trapping. In December, 1948, first authorization was given for the capture of mule deer, and in two years more than two hundred animals were transported to former ranges west of the Pecos River. Later on, other animals were released into Palo Duro Canyon and in the Plains areas further north, such as Randall, Oldham, Armstrong, and Briscoe counties.[8]

The program of deer restoration has been highly successful. After being shot out for meat and hides and sold illegally up to the first years of the present century to the point of becoming endangered species, deer populations have climbed back. Similar successes have been made with the pronghorn antelope. Perhaps as many as sixty million antelope in the United States had been whittled down to less than thirty thousand in the 1920s because of commercial hunting, which had delivered large shipments of meat for sale in urban markets after the Civil War. Antelope associated with buffalo. Between 1874 and 1884 the bison and antelope were almost exterminated. By 1925, the Lone Star State was the home for about twenty-four hundred pronghorns in forty-two areas of forty counties; about seven hundred were in the Trans-Pecos.[9] Hunting was prohibited in 1903, but the closed season was difficult to enforce across remote rangelands. This prohibition contributed to antelope survival, and a few ranches in the Trans-Pecos actively protected them. State restocking programs were begun in 1939 which resulted in the transportation of animals from areas in the Trans-Pecos to the upper and lower Plains.

Between 1939 and 1944, state biologists trapped 1,386 pronghorn antelope and released them in sixty-three areas in thirty-four counties. By 1950 the number had risen to 3,237 antelope. The ordinary trap had three compartments: a Texas pen consisting of a

[7] Daniel W. Lay, "More Deer in East Texas," *Texas Game and Fish* 12 (1954): 8, 26.

[8] O. F. Etheridge et al., "Mule Deer on the Move," *Texas Game and Fish* 9 (1951): 8–11.

[9] Charles F. Waterman, *Hunting in America*, p. 185.; Helmut K. Buechner, "Life History, Ecology, and Range Use of the Pronghorn Antelope in Trans-Pecos Texas," *American Midland Naturalist* 43 (1950): 262–63; and *Texas Game and Fish* 4 (1945): 10–14, 23–24.

wire net five feet high enclosing about six acres, a main pen made from two-inch cord net surrounding about four thousand square feet, and a smaller crowding pen where animals were caught, tagged, and loaded onto wagons. Antelope were guided toward the trap by means of an airplane that stampeded them into a three-hundred-foot-wide funnel entrance where ground personnel moved them more slowly into confinement. This funnel-shaped net was developed by the New Mexico Game Commission.[10]

In 1944, the resident Texas population of pronghorns totaled about 9,000 and, as numbers had risen, the first hunt in thirty years was held in the Trans-Pecos. In the fall of 1944, the Texas Game, Fish and Oyster Commission issued 328 permits, from which 297 antelope were killed. Governor Coke R. Stevenson claimed the first official kill on the Kokernot Ranch, near Alpine, on October 2. Twenty-six other ranches participated in the hunt between October 2 and October 11. Biologists carefully monitored activities to ensure the success of the controlled hunt. In 1945, a second hunt was held on ranchlands in seven counties of the Trans-Pecos, and 316 bucks were shot out of 424 permits. Former Governor Dan Moody and Speaker of the House Emmet Morse obtained a buck apiece on the first day's hunt.[11]

Ten years later, 910 pronghorns were hunted in Texas in the first twenty days of October, with a season in the Trans-Pecos and another one in the Panhandle. In the early 1960s, authorities issued the first permits for does, and 428 antelope were taken in the Panhandle from an overall total of about 12,000 of the animals in Texas. Drought took a toll of pronghorns, and a few years later tarbrush poisoned those animals that depended heavily on it for food. Wire fences also caused injuries. Game biologists discovered that forbs comprised the bulk of the pronghorn's diet; one-third was browse, and barely 6 percent was grass, although feeding in winter and spring was directed at grasses. In other words, pronghorns did not exclude cattle or vice versa. Parks and Wildlife Department personnel have continued to conduct aerial surveys of Texas antelopes and to adjust

[10]A. J. Nicholson, "Restoring the Antelope," *Texas Game and Fish* 1 (1943): 5, 17.

[11]Daniel W. Lay, "Antelope Hunt," *Texas Game and Fish* 3 (1944): 4–6; and *Texas Game and Fish* 4 (1945): 10–14, 23–24.

the number of hunting permits to any animal surplus that they judge to be burdensome to western rangelands. [12]

The bighorn or cimmarron sheep which was a native of the rugged mountains of the Trans-Pecos, has not fared as well as deer or antelope, despite research and organized efforts, including transplants to save it from extinction in Texas. Burch Carson, taxidermist and West Texas resident, observed bighorns around Van Horn for more than twenty years, and the Texas Game Commission employed him in the 1940s to study the mammal's life history and distribution. He reconstructed the story of the bighorn's demise in the Trans-Pecos, pointing out that when a silver mine was opened in 1882 ten miles north of Van Horn, hunters made big kills. That left a few dwindling groups of bighorns in the remote uplands of the Beach, Diablo, and Baylor mountains. In the same decade, buffalo hunters crossed the Pecos and shot bighorns for meat, which they shipped by rail to markets in Kansas City and Saint Louis. [13]

J. E. Bean, who came to Culberson County as a boy in 1884 when an estimated one thousand to fifteen hundred bighorns ranged the mountains around Van Horn, recalled the names of the commercial hunters who went out in pairs every fall to shoot bighorn, antelope, and deer, which they reportedly left in the snow until they were loaded onto a wagon and delivered to refrigerated boxcars at the railhead. These pressures from market men, together with diseases contracted from domestic sheep, largely wiped out bighorns in the mountains (Glass, Chisos, Chinati, and so on) further south. When the first closed season was imposed on them in 1903, the species had virtually disappeared. [14]

In the early 1940s, Carson estimated that no more than 150 bighorn sheep remained in the Trans-Pecos, and subsequent efforts to purchase others and to relocate them met with mixed success. In the mid-1950s, bighorns were transported to Texas from the Kofa Game Range in Arizona. Animals were held in the Black Gap Man-

[12] John Thomas, "Fleeting Target," *Texas Game and Fish* 21 (1963): 19, 24; and Tommy L. Hailey and Richard De Arment, "Droughts and Fences Restrict Pronghorns," *Texas Parks and Wildlife* 27 (1969): 6–9.

[13] Burch Carson, "Man the Greatest Enemy of Desert Bighorn Mountain Sheep," *Texas Game, Fish and Oyster Commission Bulletin* 21 (1941): 1–23.

[14] Ibid., p. 7.

agement Area east of Big Bend National Park and released periodically into suitable habitat.[15] Unfortunately, cougar predation has
been heavy on lambs born in confined areas, and additional animals
were imported from Mexico in 1977 to try to increase the size of
the Texas herd. Efforts to increase lamb survival rates appear most
promising in Culberson County, where there is less of a cougar
menace.

The aoudad or barbary sheep, from the arid, dissected country
of North Africa, an environment similar to the bighorn's, has fared
much better than the native sheep after a number were turned
loose into Palo Duro Canyon, Armstrong County, in February, 1957.
Prior releases of deer and turkey in Palo Duro dating back to the
1940s had not done especially well. However, the thirty-one exotic
aoudad sheep, which originated near Pichacho, New Mexico, flourished in the canyon, and state authorities granted forty-two permits
(from which nine animals were killed) for a three-day hunt in December, 1963. The exotic aoudad has increased in the dry, rough,
and barren lands of Palo Duro Canyon. In 1966 the population was
estimated at four hundred to five hundred sheep, and eight years
later it had increased to over one thousand. Experts judge that
aoudads and bighorns cannot survive together, as they inhabit iden-
tical environments; evidence suggests that the hardy aoudad feeds
off the same plants as does the mule deer, which occurs in the same
range.[16]

Exotic Game

Over a span of about 150 years, more than seven hundred species
of foreign birds have been carried into the United States, mostly
for ornamental purposes; many of them were also considered to be
potential game animals. Fortunately, few of the birds survived for

[15] Daniel W. Lay, "Big Plans for the Big Horn," *Texas Game and Fish* 3 (1945):
23; William S. Jennings, "The Texas Bighorn," *Texas Game and Fish* 14 (1956): 9,
25; Tom D. Moore, "Immigrant on Trial," *Texas Game and Fish* 16 (1958): 16–19;
and Tommy Hailey, "Big Hopes for Bighorns," *Texas Game and Fish* 22 (1964): 4–
5.

[16] A. S. Jackson, "Hunter's Challenge," *Texas Game and Fish* 14 (1958): 12–13,
14, 24–25; Jim Thomas, "Rewards on the Rimrock," *Texas Game and Fish* 22 (1964):
10–12, 29; William B. Davis, "The Mammals of Texas," *Texas Parks and Wildlife
Bulletin* 41 (1974 rev.): 263–64.

The numbers of so-called "Texotics," or alien animals, have increased enormously, to include these ostriches in confinement near Kerrville.

This bull elk on a ranch between Marathon and Alpine in 1942 exemplifies North American animals that, like the bighorn sheep, have been reintroduced or restocked in Texas. (*Courtesy Smithers Collection, Humanities Research Center, University of Texas*)

very long; however, several species, notably pheasants and partridges, established breeding populations and have become commonly accepted additions to the nation's avifauna.

Ring-necked pheasants, chukar and Hungarian partridges,
guinea fowl, and several exotic mammals made early appearances
in Texas, notably on the King Ranch. Game management on this
nine-hundred-thousand-acre ranch, which sprawls over seven
counties in South Texas, grew after 1945; however, both exotic and
native animals were planted in various places as early as 1900. Lesser
prairie chickens, California quail, ring-necked pheasants, chukar
partridges, and Japanese fallow deer were set loose, but they disappeared. In the early 1970s most of more than four thousand nilgai
antelope, native to the Indian subcontinent, were located in Ken-
edy County where the Norias Division of the King Ranch received
about twelve animals in 1929 and 1930.[17]

What appears to have been a localized, piecemeal approach of
keeping a few new animals around a ranch as attractions or as interesting, unusual gifts has developed into a full-fledged effort to raise
mammals and birds for sale as brood stock or for recreational hunting. By the early 1960s, seven species of exotic ungulates, or hoofed
mammals, had become well established and were being progressively dispersed in Texas. By the end of the decade, exotics totaled
twenty-seven thousand, and numbers continued to rise as the state's
Wildlife Department gathered better and more complete data on
them. More and more ranchers have chosen to keep these novel,
often beautiful animals for private hunting and to determine whether
then can adapt to a new environment.[18]

A 1971 census turned up thirty-five species numbering about
forty-five thousand animals—mostly exotic artiodactyls, that is, even-
toed hoofed mammals such as sheep, goats, antelope, and deer—
on private lands in Texas. The mouflon-barbados sheep was the most
numerous with over sixteen thousand individuals. The axis deer
came second, numbering about eleven thousand animals; it was fol-

[17] Corpus Christi *Caller-Times*, *100 Years of Ranching: King Ranch, 1853–
1953*, p. 111; John C. Phillips, "Wild Birds Introduced or Transplanted in North
America," *U.S. Department of Agriculture Technical Bulletin* 16 (1928): 63; and
Texas Parks and Wildlife Department, *Habitat Preference for Exotics, Federal Aid
Project No. W–76–R–15, Job Progress Report No. 18*.

[18] Charles Ramsey, "Texotics," *Texas Parks and Wildlife Bulletin* 49 (1969).

lowed by the blackbuck antelope, the nilgai antelope, the aoudad sheep, and the fallow deer. These species and others existed on 338 ranches comprising 5.5 million acres. The Edwards Plateau remains the principal location for the majority of these six most common exotic animals.[19]

Biologists and range specialists express considerable concern about the impact that exotics are likely to make on native plants and animals. Consequently, several states, like California, which has received sizable shipments of foreign animals, have established strict regulations governing introduction and release practices. Elsewhere, authorities have expressed fewer concerns. New Mexico researchers have generated important data on several drought-adapted African antelopes and favor the release of these big game animals in selected localities where they pose no threat to native species.[20]

Opponents of foreign animal importations point out that the track record for several of these ostensibly useful foreign mammals and birds in North America is a poor one. Once populations build up, they may become pestiferous, not beneficial; the English or house sparrow, the European starling, the nutria, and the "German" carp are testaments to inexact research or unfulfilled expectations. A compromise suggests that a new species must be kept under the tightest security until a precise and complete biological and behavioral profile of it has been drawn up and that there should be no compunction to eliminate it. This opinion rests on several premises: first, an exotic species tends to create conflicts in land use in places already inhabited by domestic stock and native game, and second, a foreign animal may disrupt the life cycles of native species or it may displace them and disturb the structure and equilibrium of preexisting biological systems.

Disease and health considerations are important, too. A foreign animal must survive a sixty-day quarantine in its native land before shipment, then a thirty-day stay at the federal receiving station in New Jersey before authorities release it to U.S. residents. Federal regulations do not permit alien animals to be sold privately,

[19] Texas Parks and Wildlife Department, *Habitat Preferences of Exotics*, Job Progress Report No. 18 (1972).
[20] Frank C. Craighead and Raymond F. Dasman, "Exotic Big Game on Public Lands."

but only to licensed and accredited zoos. Private owners may purchase the offspring of these animals. In 1968, the issue of quarantines and diseases was addressed in a symposium on exotic animals at Texas A&M University. Veterinarian Richard L. Parker admitted: "Many of the animals which might be introduced from other continents might act either as asymptomatic carriers of disease, or be in the incubation period of disease, or carry parasite vectors of various diseases."[21] Obviously, these risks are compounded when federal regulations are violated.

Further criticism stresses the need to devote scarce manpower and resources to conserving an American biota for North America, not accelerating the worldwide trend toward biotic simplification and uniformity through the transport and release of fauna in areas where these novel organisms make potentially aggressive competitors with more specialized endemics. We have tended to introduce and spread useful, hardy, opportunistic, and prolific animals, which prove difficult or impossible to control where circumstances favor their rapid increase and spread.

Conversely, landowners and ranchers interested in exotics argue that most new deer, antelope, or sheep cause little perturbation in the biotic landscape. These ungulates make available to sportsmen a greater variety of huntable game. They are useful food and trophy items and make attractive additions to Texas, where there is ample space for them. In addition, exotics provide the opportunity to preserve in the American Southwest several species that are endangered in their native lands; ultimately, there may be an opportunity to reintroduce them to their homelands. This happened when a number of blackbuck antelope were transported to Pakistan from Texas, where the animal has proved successful.

Fifty years ago, when the first foreign ungulates were introduced (on the King Ranch in South Texas, for example), the animals were a source of interest and curiosity. Landowners soon realized that money could be made from such big game. Thirty-six ranches stocked exotics for the first time between 1930 and 1953, an additional fifty-four added these animals between 1954 and 1958, and another eighty-eight had released them in pastures in the following

[21] Richard L. Parker, "Quarantine and Health Problems Associated with Introductions of Animals," in *Introduction of Exotic Animals: Ecologic and Socioeconomic Considerations*, p. 21.

five years. There are now at least three hundred ranches in Texas that hold foreign mammals, mostly from India and Africa.[22]

The Exotic Wildlife Association of Texas in Kerrville, Texas, acts as a clearinghouse for the buyers and sellers of these animals and publishes a monthly bulletin with details about the availability of different species and their prices. One of the major holders of exotics is the Y-O Ranch in Mountain Home in the Hill Country. Advertisements from the Y-O, which are indicative of others, offer a "no-kill, no-pay" arrangement by which the ranch furnishes accommodations, a hunting guide, and all the necessary equipment for bagging a trophy. One of the main selling points of the hunting ranch is that it is open for the hunting of foreign animals year-round. Customers from throughout the United States and some foreign countries journey to Texas, especially to the Hill Country, for such a recreational opportunity.

Judging from the cost per carcass, hunting exotics is not cheap. Prices range from $1,000 for blackbuck antelope, fallow deer, and sika deer to $1,250 for axis deer and $1,500 for aoudad sheep, which are among the best known and esteemed of the thirteen big game animals for which no hunting license is required. Additionally, the public is encouraged to view and photograph the thirty or so species of exotics (giraffes; zebras; and large flightless rheas, emus, and ostriches) on a safari-style tour of the ranch's large "African pastures."

A number of exotics fit in nicely with livestock operations and, like native game, require little supervision. People argue that they fill ecological niches which native species do not because of low numbers or changes in land use. When private owners take precautions against the escape of these exotics, there is minimal need to ensure that the introduced animal will not affect the niche of native animals. Only about 130 ranches with exotics, however, reported using "deer-proof" (seven-foot-high) fences to confine their mammals. The most numerous species, such as the mouflon-barbados sheep and blackbuck antelope, are relatively easy to fence in; many others, however, are not.

A biologist who worked with exotics at the state's Kerr Wildlife Management Unit near Hunt, Texas, noted that in central and

[22] Charles Ramsey, "State Views of Governmental and Private Programs of Introductions of Exotic Animals," in ibid., p. 9.

western areas only slightly more than one-third of the ranchers used deer-proof fences, which freshets and storms commonly knock down. At least six nearby counties, including Kerr, Real, Medina, Bandera, and Bexar, had free-ranging herds of exotics, and some of these aliens are known to be breeding. Some exotics may prove very competitive with domestic and endemic fauna in the vegetation they consume, and studies have demonstrated that axis and sika deer "successfully compete with native game and domestic livestock for available forage."[23]

The significance of this fact is specifically pointed out by renowned biologist George G. Simpson:

The presence in one community of two or more kinds of animals with roles similar in some essential way is almost always temporary. Sooner or later one kind takes over the role and the other acquires a different role, emigrates, or becomes extinct. The unbalancing of a community by duplication of roles means that somehow more species are present than could normally evolve or continue to live in the given environment. Such a situation means that some species has invaded the community (and its environment) from elsewhere.[24]

This "invasion" is exactly what the opponents of exotics point to as evidence of mismanagement and poor planning. They fear that if a species with a definite role were to disappear for any reason, there may be a tendency for some other organism from within the community or from outside to take over its role. Hence, one group of animals may replace another.

Ranchers and farmers are reportedly well disposed toward exotics; one biologist, however, has predicted that as increasing pressures are placed on the white-tailed deer and even domestic stock, the realization that these familiar animals are going to be the losers will change people's minds about foreign deer. State authorities have reservations about exotics and are concerned about the buildup of populations, particularly about conflicts with native species. This is not to say that exotics should not be kept in captivity, but that they should be controlled; free-ranging animals are particularly worrisome.[25]

[23]Texas Parks and Wildlife Department, *Habitat Preference of Exotics*, Federal Aid Project No. W–76–R–16, Job Progress Report No. 18.

[24]George Gaylord Simpson, *The Geography of Evolution*.

[25]Texas Parks and Wildlife Department, Job Progress Report No. 18 (1973).

James Teer, who headed the Department of Wildlife and Fisheries Sciences at Texas A&M University and conducted research on alien animals, has stated that in-depth research on the effects of exotics on biological communitites has only been emphasized in the relatively recent past. He acknowledges that free-ranging exotics are more likely to harm the community as a whole. Teer stresses the need to study the animal in its native area in order to determine food and habitat preferences. One of the functions of foundation research at Texas A&M has been to send students to Africa to research the behavior of exotics in their own environments.[26]

In summary, the main motive for introducing foreign game is economic. Some animals, like the axis deer, show promise for meat production; others, such as the eland, can subsist in arid conditions where livestock deteriorate rapidly. Under certain circumstances well-managed, captive herds of exotics show considerable promise for both consumptive and nonconsumptive uses. However, once they escape and disappear into ranges that are already stocked with cattle, sheep, goats, and native deer, they add incremental pressures to heavily grazed pastures and may have a lasting, deleterious impact on native plants and animals.

Predators

State authorities were committed to game animal rehabilitation and concentrated efforts on transplanting and managing native birds and mammals. Local and private interests perceived that exotic big game were potential money-makers and built up numbers of African and Asian ungulates in the state. By contrast, predatory mammals have received short shrift from federal, state, and local agencies, who combined efforts and pooled resources to annihilate pestiferous canids and felines. Most of the early, intensive predator control activities occurred in cattle, sheep, and goat ranges across the Edwards Plateau and Rolling Plains. City and county wolf clubs, ranchers, stockmen, and government hunters waged a war of extermination by setting out poisons and traps, digging into dens and breeding places, and hunting cougars, wolves, and coyotes with dogs.

C. R. Landon was the predatory animal inspector for the Bu-

---

[26]James G. Teer "Commercial Uses of Game Animals on Range Lands of Texas" (Caesar Kleberg Reserach Program in Wildlife Ecology, Texas A&M University, College Station, 1973), mimeographed.

reau of Biological Survey, which expended funds (from 1916) to employ a cadre of hunters to track down and kill livestock predators.
Landon was based in San Angelo and worked for more than forty
years to clear out coyotes, bobcats, wolves, and mountain lions from
many areas where they fed on stock and poultry. In his report for
the fiscal year ending June 30, 1916, Landon noted that eight men
worked full time, at a cost of ten thousand dollars, to catch 953
adult coyotes, 135 adult bobcats, 68 red wolves plus pups, 8 lobo
wolves, and additional skunks, opossums, ring-tails, badgers, raccoons, and foxes. His efforts were spread across twenty-two counties, mostly on the Edwards Plateau, and in six other places where
"the predatory animals were doing much damage a year ago. [O]ur
work has so nearly exterminated them that it is a rare thing to hear
of any loss from this source, now." [27]

In the following year, 1917, Landon's men trapped lobo wolves
in the country between Ozona, Sheffield, and Rankin, east of the
Pecos River. These large doglike carnivores had killed "over 100
calves and yearlings this spring, besides some 50 or 60 goats." A
rancher had offered a local trapper one hundred dollars per month
to work on his range; Landon undertook these duties on behalf of
the U.S. Biological Survey and reported that his men, who were
stationed twenty miles apart, had had little success with the wily
lobos; however, numbers of coyotes and bobcats, so destructive to
sheep and goat operations, had been destroyed. [28]

In the fiscal year ending June 30, 1919, Landon reported that
an average monthly force of twenty-seven men were paid from bureau funds, while another fifteen men were paid with monies from
cooperating bodies. Texas provided $25,000, county funds amounted
to $30,750 (seven of the nine counties had already established a
cooperative agreement with federal authorities), and money from
ten stockmen's clubs totaled $7,890. The hunters bagged 5 cougars,
30 lobo wolves, 212 "red or timber wolves," 2,502 coyotes, 474 bobcats, and an assortment of other carnivores, including 13 "stock-
killing dogs" and 5 house cats. [29]

[27] C. R. Landon to A. K. Fisher, July 31, 1916, U.S. Dept. Agriculture, Bureau of Biological Survey, Division of Wildlife Services, Field Reports, Texas Miscellaneous, F.Y. 1916, Record Group No. 22.
[28] C. R. Landon, "Summarized Narrative of Predatory Animal Control Activities in Texas During July, 1917," Aug. 4, 1917, Record Group 22, p. 1.
[29] C. R. Landon, "Annual Report," F.Y. 1919, July 10, 1919, pp. 1–3.

TABLE 3. Federal and Supervised Cooperative Predator Control Operations in Texas.

	Bears	Bobcats	Coyotes	Wolves	Mountain Lions	Total
July 1, 1915–June 30, 1936	10	16,013 (incl. 22 ocelots)	100,428	10,248	226	126,925
1937	—	1,363	10,922	649	32	12,967
1938	10	1,733 (incl. 23 ocelots)	14,307	974	37	17,061
1939	—	2,258 (incl. 1 ocelot)	15,813	807	22	18,900
1940	—	2,086	14,191	849	18	17,144
1941	—	2,068	12,912	839	24	15,843
1942	—	2,229	12,142	239	27	14,637
1943	1	2,162	13,226	334	19	15,742
1944	—	2,283	14,756	422	1	17,462
1945	—	2,057	16,647	515	1	19,220
1946	—	2,076	24,192	650	14	26,932
1947	—	1,753	21,934	420	13	24,120
1948	—	2,294	26,025	274	12	28,605
1949	1	2,628	29,287	336	36	32,288
1950	—	2,825	27,176	356	18	30,375
1951	—	3,252	26,379	437	17	30,085
1952	—	2,968	18,928	369	22	22,287

Year						
1953	—	2,939	20,655	815	6	24,415
1954	1	2,737	16,890	522	10	20,160
1955	—	2,429	15,894	997	24	19,344
1956	—	2,709	17,148	749	21	20,627
1957	—	3,018	18,663	1,085	14	22,780
1958	—	3,058	15,454	1,091	16	19,619
1959	—	3,436	19,493	1,446	22	24,897
1960	—	4,162	30,980	1,574	17	36,733
1961	—	4,537	29,359	1,553	14	35,463
1962	—	4,710	34,754	1,985	15	41,464
1963	—	3,472	22,886	1,955	17	28,330
1964	—	2,956	22,668	1,609	17	27,250
1965	—	2,478	20,483	—	18	22,979
1966	—	1,788	17,133	—	11	18,932
Totals	23	96,623	701,725	34,099	761	833,087

SOURCE: U.S. Fish and Wildlife Service, Division of Wildlife Services, General Box 22, Record Group 22, National Archives, Washington, D.C.

Predatory animal control in Texas proceeded along cooperative lines for many years. Activities concentrated on coyotes, wolves, and cougars (see Table 3), and the annual kills of these animals appear to have increased from an average of 8,000 through the mid-1930s to 17,500 through the mid-1940s, 25,000 through the mid-1950s, and more than 27,500 through the mid-1960s. Totals peaked in 1939 when 18,900 individuals of the four species were trapped, 471 were poisoned, 660 were denned, and 139 were shot. Control activities increased kills after 1945, when experimentation with the "humane fish and wildlife getter," or cyanide gun, was in full swing. Initial efforts in King County were inconclusive; however, a second test on the King Ranch took 112 coyotes in thirty-six days, although two yearling steers killed themselves, too. Between 1944 and 1948, the "getter" was promoted by a U.S. Fish and Wildlife Service official who supervised the taking of almost 42,000 coyotes and wolves.[30]

Predatory control peaked in the early 1960s when almost 41,500 animals, mostly coyotes, were killed. The Bureau of Sport Fisheries and Wildlife supervised operations against these animals and cooperated with the USDA Agricultural Extension Service, the Texas Predatory Animal Control Association, and activities in about 135 counties, 20 cities, and over 100 local organizations. The objective was to educate the public about animal damage and to operate against birds and mammals that damaged crops and livestock.

Rodent control for prairie dogs, gophers, and jackrabbits complemented operations against predators in Texas. In early years efforts against rodents were made easier by the very dry conditions (in 1917 and 1918), which decimated prairie dogs where the need to control them was regarded as "urgent." In the 1950s, 172,300 acres were treated with over 24,200 pounds of poisoned baits set out for prairie dogs.[31]

An interesting tradition aimed at herbivore control developed on the southern plains around Midland, where residents organized

[30] U.S. Fish and Wildlife Service, Division of Wildlife Services, "Annual Tables 1915–1966," Record Group 22; C. R. Landon, "Predator Control in Texas," *Sheep and Goat Raiser*, August, 1952, pp. 11–15.

[31] L. C. Whitehead, "Annual Reports for Fiscal Years 1924–1935," U.S. Department of Agriculture, Biological Survey," Division of Wildlife Services, Field Reports, Box 20 Record Group 22; and Division of Wildlife Services, General, Box 22, Miscellaneous Charts for Texas, Record Group 22, National Archives.

large drives against the California jackrabbit. A field report for the
fiscal year 1925 noted: "This month we conducted four big rabbit
drives in Midland County, the last one on April 21 being the biggest drive of its kind ever conducted in West Texas, there being
about 800 people in attendance. These drives are more or less social gatherings in this section. A big barbecue is always furnished
by either the rancher or the community participating, and the women
interested furnish pies, cakes and other pastries for the hungry
hunters."[32] County Agent Snider estimated that 12,500 rabbits were
killed on these four drives. It was much cheaper to kill them with
strychnine baits furnished by the Biological Survey. People enjoyed
the excitement of these get-togethers, doubtless as much as they
did in other places in the West. California's Central Valley was famous for its rabbit drives, in which the animals were penned and
clubbed to death.

Predatory canids and felines inevitably lost ground when sub-
jected to these organized campaigns to trap and poison them. Landon reported in 1921 that grey wolves had been largely eradicated
from the rough country along the Pecos from Girvin to the Rio
Grande. A few reports of wolves came from the mountains in
Brewster, Presidio, and Jeff Davis counties, but Landon believed
that "grey wolves are practically extinct in Texas." This judgment
contrasts markedly with Vernon Bailey's 1905 report that the lobo
was "still common over most of the plains and mountain country of
western Texas."[33] Federal official Bailey judged that their numbers
were not decreasing rapidly although ranchers hunted and poisoned them. Bounties of $10 or even $150 were placed on some
wolves; however, hunters were not always honest in claiming bounties or in clearing the animals out. Landon's practice of coordinating
efforts against these big wolves undoubtedly produced quick results. Except for the occasional individual that is said to stray into
the Trans-Pecos from Mexico, this big doglike mammal, weighing
as much as 175 pounds, is extinct in Texas.

Red wolves were harder to extirpate. Landon reported them
"scattered . . . over practically all of their old ranges." These sheep,

[32] U.S. Department of Agriculture, Biological Survey, Division of Wildlife
Services, "Field Reports," F.Y. 1925, p. 13.
[33] Landon, "Annual Report," F.Y. 1920, July 12, 1921, pp. 2–3; Vernon Bailey,
"Biological Survey of Texas," *North American Fauna* 25 (1905): 171.

goat, and poultry killers were difficult to destroy because of the difficulties of coordinating effective campaigns among the smaller landholders in the eastern Edwards Plateau, who kept hounds and therefore disliked exposed poisons and traps or had other objections to the intensive efforts to reduce the predators. In eastern Texas, little or nothing was done against wolves in the timber-producing areas; however, Landon did not believe that red wolves were very numerous, certainly not compared with coyotes, which "infested" stock-rearing areas. Heavy tolls were taken of these smallest of the predatory canids, the coyote, from the Canadian River south to Pecos County, but most efforts were concentrated in sheep and goat counties of the Edwards Plateau. "Coyotes and bob-cats are now comparatively scarce over the sheep and goat raising sections of Texas," said Landon. Coyotes, however, tended to drift into sheep and goat sections in the fall "from the big cattle ranges where they raise in large numbers."[34]

The jaguar, ocelot, mountain lion, and bobcat have declined appreciably in Texas since 1900. Kill records for the jaguar are scarce and for all intents and purposes end after 1900. The animal is presumed unlikely to ever return to the borderlands because of the widespread eradication of brush and timber. Ocelots are confined to the thick brush country in the South Texas Plain and to the cedar breaks of the Edwards Plateau; people rarely see or report them. The mountain lion remains an elusive and hard-pressed carnivore. An estimate from the early 1970s placed resident numbers in the state at between 65 and 135; a revised estimate judges the population at 300–500 animals. They are believed to exist most commonly but in dwindling numbers in the Trans-Pecos and in South Texas.[35]

The mountain lion is listed as "threatened" and the red wolf and Mexican race of the timber wolf are considered "endangered" by the Texas Organization for Endangered Species (TOES), which was formed in April, 1972 to monitor the vanishing biota of the Lone Star State.[36] Predator control, plus other factors such as dis-

[34] Landon, "Annual Report," F.Y. 1920, July 12, 1921, p. 3; Landon, "Annual Report," F.Y. 1925, before July 28, 1925, p. 3.

[35] Dennis N. Russell, "History and Status of the Felids of Texas," in *Proceedings of a Symposium on the Native Cats of North America; Their Status and Management*, ed. S. E. Jorgensen and L. David Mech, pp. 54–59; William Brownlee, Texas Parks and Wildlife Department, personal communication, November 19, 1982.

[36] Texas Organization for Endangered Species, "TOES Watch-List of Endangered, Threatened, and Peripheral Vertebrates of Texas," pp. 13–14.

ease or habitat change, appears as one of the principal reasons for the current status of these species, and the same factor is responsible for the similar predicament of the black bear and black-footed ferret. State officials, groups such as TOES, which has more than four hundred members, and the general public have become increasingly aware of and concerned for the aesthetic and nonutilitarian values of nongame animals and others traditionally judged as pestiferous. This growing interest has broadened commitments to threatened and nongame animal research and management. The idea of preserving and retaining a varied, complex plant and animal assemblage as a national heritage and for future generations has been popularized in the last ten years.

Traditions naturally die hard, so urban dwellers who contribute efforts to save dwindling numbers of eagles, hawks, prairie dogs, and wolves may be pleased to know that they will persist, but these citizens fail to appreciate the difficulties that beset rural folk when such predators or rodents cause economic hardships. Recent efforts to expand regulations governing animal destruction and to encourage interest and research in predatory and nongame animals have met with mixed successes.

Approximately 80 percent of the nation's sheep are raised in western states, where commercial operators argue that predators, principally coyotes, cause most losses. In the mid-1970s, ranchers estimated that 8 percent of all lambs born and more than 2 percent of adult sheep were taken by coyotes. This predation totalled $27 million in direct costs and an additional $10 million in benefits to consumers. Public attitudes toward coyote control do not, in general, reflect the opinions of stockmen. Most adults who participated in a national survey emphasized that farmers should have the right to control livestock predators; however, they emphasized that humaneness, not specificity or cost, was most important, and they preferred nonlethal methods of control to lethal ones. In fact, when lamb losses were considered to be light or moderate, a sizable proportion of the public believed that no controls were needed.[37]

Lately, nongame species have attracted widespread sympathy and interest, and biologists in a number of states have expended time and energy in the management of those species that authori-

[37] Richard G. Stuby, Edwin H. Carpenter, and Louise M. Arthur, "Public Attitudes Toward Coyote Control," *Economics, Statistics, and Cooperatives Service* (U.S. Department of Agriculture) 54 (1979): 1–11.

ties have traditionally overlooked. Funding for Texas' endangered species programs, which is directed at about fourteen mammals, twelve birds, six reptiles, four amphibians, and eleven fishes (many are nongame animals) comes mainly from legislative appropriations, not from P-R tax-assessed monies. Budgetary constraints and staff limitations have lessened the quantity of research on species such as the Lone Star State's endemic breeding parulid, the golden-cheeked warbler, which TOES considers to be an endangered bird because of the destruction of its habitat, specifically the "cedar" (Ashe juniper) and oak association of the eastern Edwards Plateau. A publication dealing with the bird's life history was published by the Texas Parks and Wildlife Department, and data on population and distribution were gathered through P-R appropriations.[38] Pulich estimated that between fifteen thousand and seventeen thousand of the birds remain in thirty-one nesting counties. Land development for sheep and goat pastures, which destroys the thick cover of cedar, together with urbanization continue to whittle down preferred habitat. Pulich concludes: "Unless sufficiently large blocks of habitat acreages are left throughout the breeding range in Texas, the Golden-cheeked Warbler could go the way of other extirpated species. It is hoped this beautiful little bird will not slip into the category of species like the Whooping Crane and Attwater's Prairie Chicken in Texas, which came just short of extinction.[39]

The whooping crane is a national success story for animal rehabilitation; the prairie chicken continues to reside in certain suitable grasslands on the coastal lowland, though federal, not state, authorities supervise a recently established refuge for this bird.

The peregrine falcon and the bald eagle continue to nest successfully in Texas, although breeding numbers are small. Peregrines reflect the plight of similar pesticide-affected carnivores at the top of the food chain in North America; eggshell fragments from one eyrie in 1977 were 25 percent thinner than those of thirty years before. However, at least seven pairs nest in West Texas, so "it is clear that the Chihauhuan Desert is one of the last areas . . . where peregrine falcons . . . continue to breed and produce young."[40] Texas

[38] Warren M. Pulich, *The Golden-Cheeked Warbler*.
[39] Ibid., p. 131.
[40] Chihuahuan Desert Research Institute, "Nesting Peregrines in Texas, 1977," *Contribution* 37 (1977): 1.

Parks and Wildlife Department experts have shown an active interest in Big Bend National Park's nesting peregrines and have supported surveys to ascertain the distribution and reproductive potential of this fleet-winged predator. A 1977 check of 126 cliffs of six mountain ranges turned up eleven falcons; some pairs nest outside of the Rio Grande canyonlands.[41]

Other animals, and recently invertebrates and plants that are also judged to be threatened or endangered, are receiving scrutiny, and an increasing number of studies are being undertaken in Texas and in other states to ascertain the most effective ways of preserving them. This research reflects an important short- term objective— that is, to recognize how every animal is supported by an interrelated web of vegetation, soil, and climate that provides the environment or habitat for life. There is, however, a longer-range and broader perspective: to hold down population losses and to restore them wherever possible to sustainable levels so that the "endangered" label becomes archaic and redundant. Strategies aimed at the prevention of organism extinction reflect a need to convert programs from the traditional "game" versus "nongame" format to ones whose purpose is to husband all species uniformly; such an approach prevents the human ignorance, indifference, or neglect that later require "rescue missions" to "save" a plant or animal *in extremis*.[42]

Whether this more open, nonjudgmental, and ethically sensitive position can be strengthened and accepted by management agencies is doubtful. The move, however, to search for new sources of funding for nongame fish and wildlife in order to parallel the successful programs for game established from taxes on hunting and fishing is a bold endeavor. The increasing number of cooperative agreements between the U.S. Fish and Wildlife Service and state authorities, under the auspices of the recent Endangered Species Act, have resulted in surveys of declining biota and the development of plans and teams of specialists to save them. These are crucial steps toward what natural scientist Aldo Leopold termed a "land

[41] Charles T. Kowaleski and Victor R. Wade, "Texas Peregrine Eyrie Search, 1977," *Contribution* 37 (1977): 31.

[42] Wildlife Management Institute, *Current Investments, Projected Needs, and Potential New Sources of Income for Nongame Fish and Wildlife Programs in The United States*, p. 2.

ethic," whereby we recognize the intrinsic right of life forms to exist. Thus our role changes "from conqueror of the land-community to plain member and citizen of it."[43] Such a position implies respect for our fellows and for the life that supports and surrounds us.

[43] Aldo Leopold, *A Sand County Almanac*, p. 240.

CHAPTER 8

Lone Star Biogeography: Trends and Prospects

THE three geographic regions of Texas presented considerable opportunities for land-hungry settlers and for immigrants who were eager to put down roots. The Coastal Prairies and the piney woods of the eastern section were relatively accessible from other places in the South; these rich alluvial lowlands were regarded as an extension of Louisiana's finest bottomlands, where cotton, sugarcane and indigo grew well. The remote, isolated hill and desert country of the west was much more forbidding. People characterized that land as given to extremes of heat and cold, drought and flood, and possessing little usable timber except that which grew along serpentine rivers and ephemeral creeks. This mountain zone was largely unknown, except to soldiers or to tough, well-armed traders who sometimes complained that effective settlement and exploitation of the region's resources was stymied by its harshness and by its hostile, nomadic Indians.

The middle, Rolling Prairie zone proved to be most attractive and tractable. Two aspects of pioneering accounts of daily life in the piney woods or in the prairie and post-oak belt are important. First, one is struck by the degree to which settlers depended on hunting and trapping for both food and recreation. Second, the reader can quickly find in these writings much excitement, often linked to the image of promoting Texas, about "taming" the landscape by agriculture transformation. The belief in individual initiative and self-reliance created the idea that human agency would bring about a bright and much-improved future as Texas became "civilized."

Both the image and the reality contributed to an active and close involvement with native fauna. In the first case, some animals were preferred and welcomed aspects of the new Texas. They sustained body and soul until their numbers dwindled. They also reflected the natural bounty of this rich region. In the second case, overhunting and unregulated killing became customary, so any warnings about exploiting a resource, even to the point of extinction, were ignored or regarded as unimportant. Texas was a vast storehouse of usable wildlife; it was imperative to tap into this seemingly inexhaustible supply.

Useful fauna such as deer, bears, and antelope were expected to disappear as the even more functional domestic stock of hogs, cattle, mules, and horses were turned loose on their ranges. Beautiful and strange animals had to accommodate to tractable barnyard creatures; if they did not, they paid the penalty for being too specialized or competitive.

Redbirds, Texas "nightingales," flycatchers, and other songsters and smaller birds benefited from the presence of newcomers, who opened up woodlands and forest expanses and thereby provided new habitats for insectivorous and seed-loving species along field edges, in clearings, and beside farm buildings and sheds. Many of these smaller birds would eventually pay the price of living too close to humans, as cats and dogs, rats, and alien opportunists such as sparrows and starlings preyed on adults and young or competed for nesting space. Except for youths who liked to impress peers by hunting these birds, people generally had little hostility and even affection for these brilliantly colored and more confiding animals, and sometimes they set up nesting places for them. However, in recent decades contaminants such as hydrocarbon pesticides and air and water pollutants have reduced the numbers of many insectivores and noninjurious species.

Insects posed serious problems for settlers in humid regions. Newcomers were advised to avoid waterlogged areas because they could contract diseases from the vapors wafting from such wetlands. People were encouraged to move away from the coastal zone, where they encountered these miasmas and where biting flies and mosquitos abounded in warm months. Those who remained set up screens in dwellings or lit smoking coils to ward off the flying bugs. Many decades passed, however, before the coastal lowlands lost the stigma of being disease-ridden and unhealthy.

In general, native animals provided the sustenance for keeping body and soul together, especially when domesticated plants and animals were in short supply. They were also the occasion for establishing and strengthening personal and community bonds as settlers hunted game, "lined" bees, and ran their hounds after "varmits." Outdoorsmen spun long and "tall" yarns about their dogs and the prey that they brought to bay. They discussed the advantages of night lighting, jump shooting, and decoys and blinds. Dinner conversations analyzed the effectiveness of these and other techniques, such as the susceptibilities of certain animals to mounted hunters and the use of different firearms in certain terrain or weather conditions. As the number of Texans increased and as hunting lore was passed down from father to son, settlers decimated populations of preferred wild animals. Consequences of this unregulated offtake were even noticeable in the 1830s around settlements in the Rolling Prairies, the most altered region in Texas. Yet people tended to accept this diminution in native wildlife as the inevitable price for conquering the wilderness.

Part of the reluctance to think about the long-term effects of animal exploitation was based on a trust in the inexhaustibility of fauna in such an enormous area. As native game "withdrew," however, new stock from the Old World began to thrive on the same forage in the same habitats. With the cosseting of familiar domesticates, the image of the garden became more firmly entrenched both in the visible landscape and in the minds of residents; dangerous or unpleasant mammals, birds, and reptiles belonging to the wilderness were vanquished with neither complaint nor remorse.

The Mediterranean character of the Lone Star State received elaboration by the importation and spread of those plants and animals that made the analogy clear and simple. Texas was indeed a new frontier; it was also a potential cradle or hearth of civilization in the finest traditions of Greece and Rome. Its landscapes were to be transformed into verisimilitudes of ancient, classical ones, so that through diligent cultivation of semitropical fruits, through viticulture, and through herding sheep and goats, it was possible to portray Texas as having all the advantages of rural Italy. Several promotional tracts embroidered the idea of Texas as the new Mediterranean by extolling it as North America's "Golden Mean":

a climatically and environmentally favored region whose produce and citizens would respectively feed and lead the nation. Such promotional rhetoric was not confined to commentaries about Texas' resources and unique geographical position, but they served to reinforce and underscore the belief that humanly induced environmental change was intrinsically progressive. Toil and husbandry would fashion a new, improved landscape, not preserve a chaotic one. The metaphors extolling this need for change made the protection and rehabilitation of native fauna the incidental and subsidiary concern of a few dedicated experts or sportsmen who were witnessing a process of simplification in native biota.

There is little wonder, therefore, that the incipient legislation for wildlife proved incomplete and unenforceable. Most native animals, it seems, were expendable, except for native freshwater fishes, which were clearly vulnerable through exploitation and habitat loss. The issue of fish conservation resulted in the first state institution for the conservation of animal resources, namely, the office of Fish Commissioner. Commissioner Joe Dinkins, however, complained about conditions and the lack of enforceable laws to protect fish stocks. The imported carp was a new, reportedly better fish, so instead of upgrading conditions for native species, the Commissioner augmented and "improved" the Texas fishery with this cheap, abundant "brain food."

Annual statements of the state's fisheries officers made it clear that remedies to slow down and stop the degradation of both freshwater and marine resources were overdue, but the public was distracted by the carp experiment. Game animals required similar efforts, and for some species effective measures, which came after 1900 when a division for game was added to the Fish and Oyster Commission, were extremely late. Populations of antelope, turkey, quail, even the prolific white-tailed deer were severely reduced, and numbers of bighorn sheep and Attwater's prairie chicken have never recovered.

Laws that limited or closed hunting and established bag limits and preserves have proven most effective for migratory animals such as doves and waterfowl and for native deer and quail. Federal P-R program funds have been used for making population estimates of key animals, for setting aside management areas, and for developing long-term strategies for conserving native fauna. These hunting revenues made it easier to carry out the capture and transplant programs for deer, turkey, antelope, and other species, and populations of most of them have rebounded in the last forty years.

The problem of exotic wildlife, however, remains unsolved. Half a century of slow but steady increases in the numbers and types of alien mammals have led state biologists and others to study the possible conflicts of African or Asian ungulates with native deer. And there appears to be real cause for concern, especially in the Edwards Plateau, where overgrazing by sheep and goats is endemic and where in certain Hill Country counties sizable numbers of free-ranging exotic deer are present.

Concrete, brick, and ornamental trees, bushes, and shrubs continue to spread over Texas landscapes, and these urban environments present new challenges for organisms. Certain animals and plants have taken advantage of urban and suburban expansion; so, too, have rodents and feral cats and dogs, all of which may have significant impacts on native animals. Stray dogs kill millions of dollars worth of stock (usually cattle and sheep) annually across the United States, and experts consider that in several states they outdo the coyote in killing deer. A 1974 survey discovered that 86 percent of responding state wildlife agencies considered uncontrolled dogs to be a significant problem for wildlife. Officials in New Mexico and Louisiana reported that packs of dogs hunted deer and even threatened humans. A study of the life history of stray dogs in Baltimore, Maryland, revealed that free-ranging animals constituted as much as 50 percent of the entire city's canine population and suggested that these animals procured garbage easily, denned in parks and vacant buildings, and posed dangers to citizens from bites and unwholesome feces. In New York City alone, dog excreta amount to approximately twenty thousand tons per year.[1]

An official of Houston's health department has noted that packs of roaming dogs kill stock and pets around the city's outer limits and has estimated that this rapidly growing metropolitan area is the home for up to half a million dogs, more than 230 of which are picked up

[1] Richard N. Denney, "The Impact of Uncontrolled Dogs on Wildlife and Livestock," *Transactions of the Thirty-ninth North American Wildlife and Natural Resources Conference*, pp. 257–91.

as road casualties every week. Unsupervised animals pose hazards to motor vehicles in addition to human health.[2]

The morphology, aspect, and height of city buildings and the materials from which they are made cause wind speeds, temperature ranges, and precipitation regimes and runoff that are markedly different from the weather features in surrounding rural hinterlands. As a result, urban plant and animal communities often differ significantly from the assemblages of native biota. Changing physical factors have an important bearing on the kinds of organisms that exist and thrive, so plants and animals are markedly affected by new building materials, types, and shapes, plus transportation systems and alterations to the densities of urban features and land use characteristics. For example, the switch from tile to concrete or shingle roofing regulates the number of organisms such as bats, birds, and insects that dwell in buildings. The erection of power lines, utility poles, and high communication towers can kill and injure low-flying, nocturnal bird migrants that collide with them. On occasion, thousands of warblers, vireos, sparrows, and other long-distance migrants have been brought down in a single overcast and rainy fall night. Noise and congestion in downtown areas inhibit the presence of shyer birds and mammals. Garbage dumps and landfills within metropolitan places serve to attract scavenging gulls, crows, cowbirds, and blackbirds; the drainage of wetlands for airports and industrial parks deprives shorebirds of feeding and nesting places.

Urban places provide important opportunities for wildlife enhancement, too. City planners are beginning to pay closer attention to wild animals in metropolitan areas as the public discovers aesthetic and educational benefits, especially for children, from feeding, watching, and studying various mammals and birds. City parks and open spaces provide important habitats for migratory and resident birds. Austin's capitol grounds, for example, are well known to birders for being attractive to warblers in spring. Reservoirs, lakes, and water treatment plants are attractive for waterfowl; many wild animals also find food and refuge in botanical gardens and zoological parks. Simple, inexpensive measures to conserve and even increase biological diversity can be accomplished by reducing the

[2]Martin McBride, Rabies Control Center, City of Houston Health Department, personal communication, March 30, 1978; and David McCary, City of Houston, Solid Waste Department, personal communication, March 24, 1978.

frequency of mowing roadsides or by cutting and pruning vegetation only after the peak breeding season for birds. With imagination and foresight, suburban landscapes can become important reservoirs for useful and attractive animals, not merely pestiferous ones.[3]

Research suggests that modern metropolitan places in Texas and across the nation favor aggressive, adaptable, fecund, and quickly reproducing organisms. Prolific sparrows, starlings, and rock doves habituated to urban living in Europe are common in Texas; so, too, are those swallows and swifts that have taken to nesting in man-made structures such as freeway underpasses, culverts, or house chimneys. Large populations of titmice, chickadees, wrens, and other common and easily recognized garden birds visit feeders and nest boxes in urban and suburban situations. Some of them, like hummingbirds, may develop a dependency on food handouts. It is the "narrow niche specialists" who are most threatened by pressures from human beings and their modern urban and agribusiness landscapes. Currently, habitat change poses the greatest threat to animals such as the ivory-billed woodpecker or golden-cheeked warbler, which have marked preferences for specific vegetation associations. The question remains whether the growing number of these increasingly rare or threatened fauna will disappear from the state's environment or whether concerted efforts for such nongame species will be necessary and successful.

Texas is a transition zone betweeen two major faunal realms—the so-called Nearctic realm covering most of North America and the Neotropical realm encompassing southern Mexico and Central and South America. A faunal realm is a land area with a generally uniform and distinct set of animal orders down to the species level. Smaller biotic provinces usually exist within these large geographic areas and are classified according to topography, climate, and vegetation as well as terrestrial vertebrates, excepting birds. Texas, for instance, has seven biotic provinces, most of which possess elements of three major biotas: the pine and hardwood flora and fauna of the humid eastern American piedmont; Chihuahuan Desert–adapted organisms occupying the Trans-Pecos; and tropical and subtropical plants and animals from Old Mexico's Gulf region, which

[3] Daniel L. Leedy, Robert M. Maestro, and Thomas K. Franklin, *Planning for Wildlife in Cities and Suburbs.*

reach their northern limits on the Rio Grande Plain. Because of all this biotic complexity and the state's intermediate position in regard to environmental conditions between the moist eastern pine and hardwood association and droughty southwestern deserts, the Lone Star State's immense area, totalling almost 270,000 square miles, is the aboriginal home for approximately 545 species of birds, 156 mammals, and more than one hundred snake species. It was and still is a biotically rich, complex, and interesting region.[4]

Overhunting and exploitation set in motion a process of animal diminution and redistribution; however, a century of wildlife legislation has helped to restore, where appropriate, native animals to their former areas. Deforestation, reclamation, cropland expansion, and agricultural intensification have all altered and continue to affect ecological conditions, which are used to define biotic provinces. Habitat change remains the most challenging issue for conservationists. Increasing numbers of scientists and informed persons are willing to address the problems of disappearing species by seeking to understand the critical needs of native animals, particularly certain long-neglected nongame species, in order to establish guidelines that will make wildlife conservation a component in plans for growth and development. Pride in the state's history, an understanding of the biological processes within it, and an increasing sensitivity about the future quality of the Lone Star State's environment have become virtues of the Texan character. It is important to greater numbers of citizens, therefore, to know that the unique and extraordinary place that they call Texas will remain the home for a wide variety of animals upon which colonization and settlement depended.

[4] Karl P. Schmidt, "Faunal Realms, Regions, and Provinces," *Quarterly Review of Biology* 29 (1954): 322–31; and W. Frank Blair, "The Biotic Provinces of Texas," *Texas Journal of Science* 2 (1950): 93–117.

Bibliography

Alexander, Gladys. "Social Life in Texas, 1821–1836." Master's Thesis, East Texas State College, 1942.

Allen, John T. *Early Pioneer Days in Texas*. Dallas: Williamson, 1918.

Almonte, Juan N. "Statistical Report on Texas." Edited and translated by C. E. Castañeda. *Southwestern Historical Quarterly* 28 (1925): 177–222.

"Annual Report of the National Association of Audubon Societies." *Bird-Lore* 8 (1906): 272–73.

Arthur, W. J. "Legislative Sportsmen Will Not Protect Birds." *Farm and Ranch* 22 (1903): 1.

"The Audubon Societies." *Bird-Lore* 9 (1907): 57, 143.

"The Audubon Society." *Forest and Stream* 26 (1886): 41.

[Austin, Stephen F.] "Journal of Stephen F. Austin on His First Trip to Texas, 1821." *Quarterly of the Texas State Historical Association* 7 (1903–04): 286–307.

Bailey, Vernon. "Biological Survey of Texas." *North American Fauna* 25 (1905).

Barker, Eugene C. "A Glimpse of the Texas Fur Trade in 1832." *Southwestern Historical Quarterly* 19 (1916): 279–82.

Bartlett, John Russell. *Personal Narrative of Explorations and Incidents in Texas, New Mexico, California, Sonora and Chihuahua*. 2 vols. Chicago: Rio Grande Press, 1965.

Baur, John E. *Dogs on the Frontier*. San Antonio: Naylor, 1964.

Bennett, Dave. "Guns of the Cattlemen, the Winchester." *Cattleman* 46 (1959): 36–37, 62–64.

Benson, Nettie Lee. "Bishop Marín de Porras and Texas." *Southwestern Historical Quarterly* 51 (1947): 16–40.

Bentley, H. L. "Cattle Ranges of the Southwest: A History of the Exhaustion of the Pasturage and Suggestions for its Restoration." *Farmers' Bulletin* 72 (1898): 5–31.

Berlandier, Jean L. *The Indians of Texas in 1830*. Washington, D.C.: Smithsonian Institution Press, 1969.

———. *Journey to Mexico During the Years 1826 to 1834*. Translated by Sheila M. Ohlendorf. 2 vols. Austin: Texas State Historical Association, 1980.

Black, William L. *A New Industry: Or, Raising the Angora Goat and Mohair for Profit*. Fort Worth: Keystone, 1900.

Blair, W. Frank. "The Biotic Provinces of Texas." *Texas Journal of Science* 2 (1950): 93–117.

Bollaert, William. "Notes on the Coast Region of the Texan Territory: Taken During a Visit in 1842." *Journal of the Royal Geographical Society* 13 (1843): 226–44.

Bonnell, George W. *Topographical Description of Texas*. Waco: Texian Press, 1964.

Bracht, Viktor. *Texas in 1848*. San Antonio: Naylor, 1931.

Brown, Harry J., ed. *Letters from a Texas Sheep Ranch*. Urbana: University of Illinois Press, 1959.

Brownlee, William. Texas Parks and Wildlife Dept. Personal communication, November 19, 1982.

Buckley, Samuel B. *A Preliminary Report of the Texas Geological Survey*. Austin: Walker, 1866.

———. *Second Annual Report of the Geological and Agricultural Survey of Texas*. Houston: Gray, 1876.

Buechner, Helmut K. "Life History, Ecology, and Range Use of the Pronghorn Antelope in Trans-Pecos Texas." *American Midland Naturalist* 43 (1950): 257–354.

Burkhalter, Lois W. *Gideon Lincecum, 1793–1874*. Austin: University of Texas Press, 1965.

Burr, J. G. "A Texas Grizzly Hunt." *Texas Game and Fish* 6 (1948): 4–5, 16.

Butler, Pleasant B. "Sixty-Eight Years in Texas." In *The Trail Drivers of Texas*, edited by J. M. Hunter. 2nd ed. Nashville: Cokesbury Press, 1925.

C. W. S. "Game in Season for January." *Forest and Stream* 1 (1874): 380–81.

Camp, R. D. "Guarding the Great Texas Heronry." *Bird-Lore* 24 (1922): 319–22.

Carpenter, Curtis. "Trained Colonists." *Texas Game and Fish* 17 (1959): 9.

Carson, Burch. "Man, the Greatest Enemy of Desert Bighorn Mountain Sheep." *Texas Game, Fish and Oyster Commission Bulletin* 21 (1941): 1–23.

Carter, W. T., and V. L. Cory. "Soils of the Trans-Pecos Texas and Some of Their Vegetative Relations." *Transactions of the Texas Academy of Science* 15 (1932): 19–32.

Cat Spring Agricultural Society. *Century of Agricultural Progress, 1856–1956*. Austin Co.: Cat Spring Agricultural Society, 1956.

Chihuahuan Desert Research Institute. "Nesting Peregrines in Texas, 1977." *Contribution* 37 (1977): 1–57.

Clopper, Edward N. *An American Family*. Huntington, West Va.: Standard, 1950.

Clopper, J. C. "J. C. Clopper's Journal and Book of Memoranda for 1828."

Quarterly of the Texas State Historical Association 13 (1909–10): 44–80.

Cook, James H. *Fifty Years on the Old Frontier*. New Haven: Yale University Press, 1923.

Cooke, P. St. George, William H.C. Whiting, and Francis X Aubry. *Exploring Southwestern Trails*. Edited by Ralph P. Bieber and Areram B. Bender. Glendale: Clark, 1938.

Cope, Edward D. *On the Zoological Position of Texas*. Washington, D.C.: Government Printing Office, 1880.

Craighead, Frank C., and Raymond F. Dasman. "Exotic Big Game on Public Lands." Washington, D.C.: Bureau of Land Management, 1966. Mimeographed.

Davis, Andrew. "Hunting in the 1830's." *Texas Game and Fish* 9 (1951): 20–21.

Davis, M. B. "Texas." In "Annual Report of the National Association of Audubon Societies for 1908." *Bird-Lore* 10 (1908): 315–17.

[Davis, M. B.] "Report of Capt. M. B. Davis." *Bird-Lore* 13 (1911): 350–51.

Davis, William B. "Texas Cats." *Texas Game and Fish* 3 (1945): 21–22.

———. "The Mammals of Texas." *Texas Parks and Wildlife Department Bulletin* 41 (1974 revised).

"Death of Miss Seixas." *Bird-Lore* 2 (1900): 166.

Deaton, E. L. "An Adventure in West Texas." In *Parade of the Pioneers*. By O. A. Hanscom. Dallas: Tardy, 1935.

Defenders of Wildlife. *A Report on the National Wildlife Refuge System*. Washington, D.C.: Defenders of Wildlife, 1977.

Denney, Richard N. "The Impact of Uncontrolled Dogs on Wildlife and Livestock." *Transactions of the Thirty-ninth North American Wildlife and Natural Resources Conference*, 1974, pp. 257–91.

"Destruction of Birds for Millinery Purposes." *Science* Supplement 7 (1886): 196–97.

Dewees, William B. *Letters from an Early Settler of Texas*. Waco: Texian Press, 1968.

"Directory of State Audubon Societies." *Bird-Lore* 1 (1899): 100, 103; 3 (1904): 114; 6 (1904): 104; 7 (1905): 39.

"Distribution of Members." *Bird-Lore* 24 (1922): 402.

Dobie, J. Frank. *The Longhorns*. New York: Grosset and Dunlap, 1941.

———. *A Vaquero of the Brush Country*. Boston: Little, Brown, 1943.

———. *The Mustangs*. Boston: Little, Brown, 1952.

———. *The Flavor of Texas*. Austin: Jenkins, 1975.

Dodge, Richard I. *The Plains of the Great West*. New York: Putnam's, 1878.

———. *The Hunting Grounds of the Great West*. 2d ed. London: Chatto and Windus, 1878.

Doughty, Robin W. "Ostrich Farming American Style." *Agricultural History* 47 (1973): 133–45.

————. *Feather Fashions and Bird Preservation: A Study in Nature Protection.* Berkeley and Los Angeles: University of California Press, 1975.

————. "The English Sparrow in the American Landscape: A Paradox in Nineteenth-Century Wildlife Conservation." University of Oxford, School of Geography, *Research Paper* 19 (1978).

————. "Wildlife Conservation in Late Nineteenth-Century Texas: The Carp Experiment." *Southwestern Historical Quarterly* 84 (1980): 169–96.

————. "Sea Turtles in Texas: A Forgotten Commerce." *Southwestern Historical Quarterly.* Forthcoming.

Drury, William H. "Rare Species." *Biological Conservation* 6 (1974): 162–69.

Duncan, T. C. "Ostrich Farming in America." In U.S. Department of Agriculture, *Report of the Commissioner for 1888*, pp. 685–702. Washington, D.C.: Government Printing Office, 1889.

Dunn, William E. "Apache Relations in Texas, 1718–1750." *Southwestern Historical Quarterly* 14 (1911): 198–274.

Durham, George J. "Game in Texas." *Texas Almanac for 1868.* Galveston: Richardson, 1868.

————. "Game in Texas." *Texas Almanac for 1869.* Galveston: Richardson, 1869.

Dutcher, William. "Report of the A.O.U. Committee." *The Auk* 20 (1903): 145.

————. "Annual Report of the National Association of Audubon Societies for 1905." *Bird-Lore* 7 (1905): 343.

Duval, John C. *Early Times in Texas.* Introduction by John Q. Anderson. Austin: Steck-Vaughn, 1967.

Edward, David B. *The History of Texas.* Austin: Pemberton Press, 1967.

Ehrenfeld, David W. *Conserving Life on Earth.* New York: Oxford University Press, 1972.

Elliot, D. G. "The 'Game Birds' of the United States." In U.S. Department of Agriculture, *Report of the Commissioner for 1864*, pp. 356–85. Washington, D.C.: Government Printing Office, 1865.

Emmett, Chris. *Texas Camel Tales.* Austin: Steck-Vaughn, 1969.

Environmental Law Institute. *The Evolution of National Wildlife Law.* Washington, D.C.: Government Printing Office, 1977.

Etheridge, O.F., et al. "Mule Deer on the Move." *Texas Game and Fish* 9 (1951): 8–11.

Falconer, Thomas. "Notes of a Journey Through Texas and New Mexico in the Years 1841 and 1842." *Journal of the Royal Geographical Society* 13 (1843): 199–226.

Farwell, M. A. E. "Silk Culture in Texas." *Texas Almanac*, pp. 85–86. Houston: Burke, 1885.

Ferris, George A. "Stock Raising in Texas." *Texas Rural Almanac.* Houston: Hardcastle, 1876.

Fest, Henry. "Parents Were Among Early Colonists." In *The Trail Drivers of Texas*. Edited by J. M. Hunter. 2nd ed. Nashville: Cokesbury Press, 1925.

Field, Joseph E. *Three Years in Texas*. Austin: Steck, 1935.

Flint, Wilson. "Textile Fibers of the Pacific States." In U.S. Department of Agriculture, *Annual Report for 1864*, pp. 484–85. Washington, D.C.: Government Printing Office, 1865.

Foreman, Grant, ed. *Adventure on Red River*. Norman: University of Oklahoma Press, 1937.

Friend, Llerena, ed. *M. K. Kellogg's Texas Journal, 1872*. Austin: University of Texas Press, 1967.

Galveston Bay and Land Co., *An Address to Emigrants*. Boston: Galveston Bay and Land Co., 1835.

Galveston, Harrisburg and San Antonio Railroad Co. *A Description of Western Texas*. Galveston: "News" Steam Book, 1876.

"Game Regions of Texas: The Blackland Prairie." *Texas Game and Fish* 10 (1952): 6–8.

Gammel, H. P. N., ed. *The Laws of Texas, 1822–1897*. 10 vols. Austin: Gammel Book, 1898.

Gard, Wayne. *The Buffalo Hunters*. New York: Hastings House, 1954.

———. *The Great Buffalo Hunt*. New York: Knopf, 1959.

———. *Rawhide Texas*. Norman: University of Oklahoma Press, 1965.

Geiser, Samuel Wood. *Horticulture and Horticulturists in Early Texas*. Dallas: Southern Methodist University Press, 1945.

———. *Naturalists of the Frontier*. 2nd ed., rev. Dallas: Southern Methodist University Press, 1948.

"Goat Gossip." *Texas Stockman* 2 (1882): 4.

Gray, Lewis C. *History of Agriculture in the Southern United States to 1860*. 2 vols. Gloucester: Peter Smith, 1958.

Gray, William F. *From Virginia to Texas, 1835: Diary of Col. Wm. F. Gray*. Houston: Fletcher Young, 1965.

Gregg, Josiah. *The Commerce of the Prairies*. Edited by Milo Milton Quaife. Lincoln: University of Nebraska Press, 1967.

Hailey, Tommy L. "Big Hopes for Bighorns." *Texas Game and Fish* 22 (June, 1964): 4–5.

———. "A Handbook for Pronghorn Antelope Management in Texas," Texas Parks and Wildlife Department, F.A. Report Series 20. Austin: Parks and Wildlife, 1979. Mimeographed.

———, and Richard De Arment. "Droughts and Fences Restrict Pronghorns." *Texas Parks and Wildlife* 27 (1969): 6–9.

Haltom, Richard W. *The History of Nacogdoches County, Texas*. Austin: Jenkins, 1880.

Harris, Dilue. "Reminiscences of Mrs. Dilue Harris, I." *Quarterly of the Texas State Historical Association* 4 (1900): 85–127; 155–89.

———. "Reminiscences of Mrs. Dilue Harris, II." *Quarterly of the Texas State Historical Association* 4 (1901): 155–89.

Haupt, William W. "The Angora Goat." *Texas Stockman and Farmer* 4 (1884): 1.

Hazelwood, J. T. "Early Days in Texas." In *The Trail Drivers of Texas.* Edited by J. M. Hunter. 2nd ed. Nashville: Cokesbury Press, 1925.

Henry, W. S. *Campaign Sketches of the War with Mexico.* New York: Arno, 1973.

"History and Status of Cotton Production . . . " In *Texas Department of Agriculture Yearbook 1909.* Austin: Von Boeckmann-Jones, 1910.

Hogan, William R. *The Texas Republic: A Social and Economic History.* Norman: University of Oklahoma Press, 1946.

Holley, Mary Austin. *Texas.* Austin: Steck, 1935.

Hollon, W. Eugene, and Ruth L. Butler, eds. *William Bollaert's Texas.* Norman: University of Oklahoma Press, 1956.

Houstoun, Matilda Charlotte Fraser. *Texas and the Gulf of Mexico; or Yachting in the New World.* Austin: Steck-Warlick, 1968.

Hubbard, John, et al. *Handbook of Species Endangered in New Mexico.* Sante Fe: New Mexico Department of Game and Fish, 1978.

Huey, William S. *Symposium on Rare and Endangered Wildlife of the Southwestern United States.* Sante Fe: New Mexico Department of Game and Fish, c. 1973.

Hunter, J. M., ed. *The Trail Drivers of Texas.* 2nd ed. Nashville: Cokesbury Press, 1925.

Ikin, Arthur. *Texas: Its History, Topography, Agriculture, Commerce, and General Statistics.* Waco: Texian Press, 1964.

Inglis, Jack M. "A History of Vegetation on the Rio Grand Plain." *Texas Parks and Wildlife Department Bulletin* 45 (1964): 1–122.

Jackson, A. S. "Hunter's Challenge." *Texas Game and Fish* 14 (1958): 12, 14, 24–26.

Jenkins, John Holmes, ed. *Recollections of Early Texas: The Memoirs of John Holland Jenkins.* Austin: University of Texas Press, 1958.

Jennings, William S. "The Texas Bighorn." *Texas Game and Fish* 14 (1956): 9, 25.

Johnson, Elmer H. *The Natural Regions of Texas.* University of Texas Bulletin No. 3113. Austin: University of Texas, 1931.

Johnson, James T. "Hardships of a Cowboy's Life in the Early Days in Texas." In *The Trail Drivers of Texas.* Edited by J. M. Hunter. 2nd ed. Nashville: Cokesbury Press, 1925.

Johnston, Marshall C. "Past and Present Grasslands of Southern Texas and Northeastern Mexico." *Ecology* 44 (1963): 456–66.

Jones, Charles G. "A South Texas Big Game Hunt." *Texas Game and Fish* 4 (1946): 29, 32.

Jones, Paul V. "Antelope Management." *Texas Game and Fish* (1949): 4–5, 18–20, 24–25, 28–29.

Jones, R. L. "Folk Life in Early Texas: The Autobiography of Andrew Davis." *Southwestern Historical Quarterly* 43 (1940): 323–41.

Jordan, Terry G. *German Seed in Texas Soil: Immigrant Farmers in Nineteenth-Century Texas*. Austin: University of Texas Press, 1966.

———. "The Imprint of the Upper and Lower South on Mid–Nineteenth-Century Texas." *Annals of the Association of American Geographers* 57 (1967): 667–90.

———. "Pioneer Evaluation of Vegetation in Frontier Texas." *Southwestern Historical Quarterly* 76 (1973): 233–54.

"Junior Work in the South." *Bird-Lore* 15 (1913): 278.

Kendall, George Wilkins. *Across the Great Southwestern Prairies*. 2 vols. N.p.: Readex Microprint, 1966.

Kennedy, William. *Texas: The Rise, Progress, and Prospects of the Republic of Texas*. 2nd ed. Fort Worth: The Molyneaux Craftsmen, 1925.

Kibbe, I. P. *Report on the Coast Fisheries of Texas*. Austin: Von Boeckmann, 1898.

King, C. Richard, ed. *Victorian Lady on the Texas Frontier: The Journal of Ann Raney Coleman*. Norman: University of Oklahoma Press, 1971.

Kleberg, Rosa. "Some of My Early Experiences in Texas." *Quarterly of the Texas State Historical Association* 1 (1898): 297–302.

Kowaleski, Charles T., and Victor R. Wade. "Texas Peregrine Eyrie Search, 1977." *Chihuahuan Desert Research Institute Contribution* 37 (1977): 31–42.

Krueger, Max. *Pioneer Life in Texas*. N.p.: Krueger, 1925.

Kupper, Winifred. *The Golden Hoof: The Story of Sheep of the Southwest*. New York: Knopf, 1945.

Kuykendall, J. H. "Reminiscences of Early Texans." *Quarterly of the Texas State Historical Association* 7 (1903–1904): 29–64.

Lammons, Frank B. "Operation Camel . . . " *Southwestern Historical Quarterly* 61 (1957): 20–50.

Landon, Cedric R. Reports for Fiscal Years 1916 through 1925. U.S. Department of Agriculture, Biological Survey, Division of Wildlife Services, Field Reports: Texas Miscellaneous. Record Group 22. Washington, D.C.: National Archives.

———. "Predator Control in Texas." *Sheep and Goat Raiser*, August, 1952, pp. 11–15.

"Lands, Crops, Stock," *Southern Cultivator* 26 (1868): 68–70.

Lantz, D. E. "Deer Farming in the United States." *Farmers' Bulletin* 330 (1908): 5–20.

[Lawrence, A. B.] *Texas in 1840, or, The Emigrant's Guide to the New Republic*. New York: Arno Press, 1973.

Lay, Daniel W. "Antelope Hunt." *Texas Game and Fish* 3 (1944): 4–6.

———. "Big Plans for the Big Horn." *Texas Game and Fish* 3 (1945): 23.

———. "More Deer in East Texas." *Texas Game and Fish* 12 (1954): 8, 26.

Leedy, Daniel, L., Robert M. Maestro, and Thomas M. Franklin. *Planning for Wildlife in Cities and Suburbs*. Washington, D.C.: Government Printing Office, 1978.

Lehmann, Valgene W. *Forgotten Legions: Sheep in the Rio Grande Plain of Texas*. El Paso: Texas Western Press, 1969.

Leopold, Aldo. *A Sand County Almanac*. New York: Ballantine, 1966.

Lesley, Lewis B. "The Purchase and Importation of Camels . . . " *Southwestern Historical Quarterly* 33 (1929): 18–33.

Lincecum, Gideon. "Native or Indigenous Texas Grasses." *Texas Almanac of 1861*. Galveston: Robertson, 1861.

————. "The Indigenous Texian Grasses." *Texas Almanac of 1868*. Galveston: Robertson, 1868.

————. "Journal of Lincecum's Travels in Texas, 1835." Edited by A. L. Bradford and T. N. Campbell. *Southwestern Historical Quarterly* 53 (1949): 180–201.

Linn, John J. *Reminiscences of Fifty Years in Texas*. New York: Sadlier, 1883.

Loughmiller, Campbell, and Lyon Loughmiller, eds. *Big Thicket Legacy*. Austin: University of Texas Press, 1977.

Lund, Thomas A. *American Wildlife Law*. Berkeley and Los Angeles: University of California Press, 1980.

Lundy, Benjamin. *The Life, Travels and Opinions of Benjamin Lundy, Including His Journeys to Texas and Mexico*. New York: Negro Universities Press, 1969.

McBride, Martin. Rabies Control Center, City of Houston Health Department. Personal communication, March 30, 1978.

McCary, David. Solid Waste Department, City of Houston. Personal Communication, March 24, 1978.

McDonald, Marshall. "Report of Distribution of Carp, 1881–82." In U.S. Commission of Fish and Fisheries. *Report of the Commissioner for 1881*, p. 1125. Washington, D.C.: Government Printing Office, 1884.

McDowell, Catherine W., ed. *Now You Hear My Horn: The Journal of James Wilson Nichols, 1820–1887*. Austin: University of Texas Press, 1967.

M'Gary, D. L. "Central Texas." *Texas Rural Register and Immigrants Handbook*. Houston: Hardcastle, 1875.

McNair, Forest W. *Forest McNair of Texas*. San Antonio: Naylor, 1956.

Marburger, Rodney, and Horace Gore. "Deer Facts and the Antlerless Question." *Texas Game and Fish* 21 (1963): 5–7.

Marcy, Randolph B. *Exploration of the Red River of Louisiana in the Year 1852*. Washington, D.C.: Nicholson, 1854.

————. *The Prairie Traveller: A Hand-Book for Overland Expeditions*. New York: Harper, 1859.

————. *Thirty Years of Army Life on the Border*. Philadelphia: Lippincott, 1963.

Maury, Lieutenant. "Great Commercial Advantages of the Gulf of Mexico." *De Bow's Review* 7 (1849): 510–23.

Mearns, Edgar A. *Mammals of the Mexican Boundary of the United States*. U.S. National Museum Bulletin 56. Washington, D.C.: Government Printing Office, 1907.

Mechanical and Blood Stock Association of Texas. *Report of the Texas State Fair*. Houston: Gray, 1871.

Meinig, Donald W. *Imperial Texas: An Interpretive Essay in Cultural Geography*. Austin: University of Texas Press, 1969.

Mitchell, George F. "Home-Grown Tea." *Farmers' Bulletin* 301 (1907): 1–16.

Moore, Euroda. "Recollections of Indianola." In *Indianola Scrap Book*, pp. 94–132. Port Lavaca: Calhoun Co. Historical Survey Committee, 1974.

Moore, Tom D. "Immigrant on Trial." *Texas Game and Fish* 16 (1958): 16–19.

Muir, Andrew F., ed. *Texas in 1837, an Anonymous, Contemporary Narrative*. Austin: University of Texas Press, 1958.

Munson, Thomas Volney. *Foundations of American Grape Culture*. Denison: Munson, 1909.

Murphy, Robert. *Wild Sanctuaries*. New York: Dutton, 1968.

National Wildlife Refuge Study Task Force. *Recommendations on the Management of the National Wildlife Refuge System*. Washington, D.C.: Government Printing Office, 1978.

Nevin, David. *The Texans*. New York: Time-Life, 1975.

"New Audubon Reservation." *Bird-Lore* 23 (1921): 276–77.

Nicholson, A. J. "Restoring the Antelope." *Texas Game and Fish* 1 (1943): 5, 17.

"Notes and News." *The Auk* 3 (1886): 145.

"Notes and News." *The Auk* 13 (1896): 98.

"Notes and News." *The Auk* 22 (1905): 111.

Nunnely, Sam H. "Associated with Frank James." in *The Trail Drivers of Texas*. Edited by J. M. Hunter. 2nd ed. Nashville: Cokesbury Press, 1925.

Oberholser, Harry C. *The Bird Life of Texas*. Edited by Edgar B. Kincaid, Jr. 2 vols. Austin: University of Texas Press, 1974.

Oldys, Henry. "The Game Market of To-day." In *Yearbook of the U.S. Department of Agriculture, 1910*, pp. 243–54. Washington, D.C.: Government Printing Office, 1911.

Olmsted, Frederick Law. *Cotton Kingdom*. New York: Knopf, 1970.

——. *A Journey Through Texas, Or, A Saddle-Trip on the Southwestern Frontier*. Austin: University of Texas Press, 1978.

Onderdonk, Gilbert. "Olive Culture in Texas." *Texas Almanac for 1881*, p. 145.

——. "Orange Culture in South Texas." *Texas Department of Agriculture Bulletin* 8 (1909): 251–53.

——. "Pomological Possibilities of Texas." *Texas Department of Agriculture Bulletin* 9 (1909): 5–55.

100 Years of Ranching: King Ranch, 1853–1953. Corpus Christi: *Caller Times*, 1953.

Osigian, Vartan K. "Address." *Texas Department of Agriculture Bulletin* 54 (1917): 81–86.

Pacific Railroad Company. *Texas Statistics and Information.* 8th ed. St. Louis: Pacific Railroad Co., 1893.

Palmer, Theodore S. "Legislation for the Protection of Birds." In U.S. Department of Agriculture, Bureau of Biological Survey, *Bulletin* 12 (1902, rev. ed.).

————. "Chronology and Index of the More Important Events in American Game Protection, 1776–1911." In U.S. Department of Agriculture, Bureau of Biological Survey, *Bulletin* 41 (1912).

Parker, Nancy B., ed. "Mirabeau B. Lamar's Texas Journal." *Southwestern Historical Quarterly* 84 (1980): 197–220.

Parker, Richard L. "Quarantine and Health Problems Associated with Introductions of Animals." In *Introduction of Exotic Animals: Ecologic and Socioeconomic Considerations*, pp. 21–22. College Station: Caesar Kleberg Research Program, 1968.

Pearson, T. Gilbert. "The Report of the Secretary." *Bird-Lore* 14 (1912): 383–92.

————. "Least Tern." *Bird-Lore* 20 (1918): 380–83.

————. "A Reddish Egret Colony in Texas." *Bird-Lore* 20 (1918): 384–85.

————. "Exploring for New Bird Colonies." *Bird-Lore* 22 (1920): 255–62, 321–27.

————. "Herons of the United States." *Bird-Lore* 24 (1922): 306–14.

Phillips, John C. "Wild Birds Introduced or Transplanted in North America." *U.S. Department of Agriculture Technical Bulletin* 16 (1928).

Porce, R. H. "Pruning and Training Peach Orchards." *Texas Agriculture Experiment Station Bulletin* 58 (1900): 27–42.

Pratt, Willis W., ed. *Galveston Island: Or, A Few Months Off the Coast of Texas, The Journal of Francis C. Sheridan, 1839–1840.* Austin: University of Texas Press, 1954.

"Productions for Texas." *Texas Almanac for 1869.* Galveston: Richardson, 1869.

"Pronghorn." *Texas Game and Fish* 4 (1945): 10–14, 23–24.

Pulich, Warren M. *The Golden-Cheeked Warbler: A Bioecological Study.* Austin: Texas Parks and Wildlife Department, 1976.

Quaife, Milo M., ed. *The Southwestern Expedition of Zebulon Pike.* Chicago: Lakeside Press, 1925.

Ragan, W. H. "Our Cultivated Fruits—Native and Introduced." In U.S. Department of Agriculture, *Report of the Commissioner for 1888*, pp. 577–95. Washington, D.C.: Government Printing Office, 1889.

Ramsey, Bob, and Eugene Walker. "Take 'Em or Leave 'Em." *Texas Game and Fish* 12 (1954): 4–6, 20–22.

Ramsey, Charles W. "State Views of Governmental and Private Programs of Introductions of Exotic Animals." In *Introduction of Exotic Animals: Ecological and Socioeconomic Considerations*, pp. 9–10. College Station: Caesar Kleberg Research Program, 1968.

————. *Texotics*. Texas Parks and Wildlife Department Bulletin 49 Austin: Texas Parks and Wildlife Department, 1969.

Rankin, Melinda. *Texas in 1850*. Waco: Texian Press, 1966.

Reid, John C. *Reid's Tramp*. Austin: Steck, 1935.

"Report of the National Association." *Bird-Lore* 26 (1924): 497.

"Report of the President." *Bird-Lore* 25 (1923): 436–44; 27 (1925): 443–514; 28 (1926); 30 (1928); 31 (1929): 447–520; 32 (1930): 473, 550.

"Report of States Societies, and of Bird Clubs." *Bird-Lore* 17 (1915): 510.

Revoil, Benedict H. *The Hunter and the Trapper in North America; or Romantic Adventures in Field and Forest*. London: Nelson, 1874.

Rickard, J. A. "Hazards of Ranching on the South Plains." *Southwestern Historical Quarterly* 37 (1934): 313–19.

Rister, C. C. "The Significance of the Destruction of the Buffalo in the Southwest." *Southwestern Historical Quarterly* 33 (1929): 34–49.

————. "Harmful Practices of Indian Traders of the Southwest, 1865–1876." *New Mexico Historical Review* 5 (1931): 231–48.

Robertson, James A. "Preliminary Notes on . . . Plants and Animals to . . . Colonies Overseas." *James Sprunt Historical Studies* 19 (1927): 7–21.

Roemer, Ferdinand. *Texas: With Particular Reference to German Immigration and the Physical Appearance of the Country*. San Antonio: Standard, 1935.

Russell, Dennis N. "History and Status of the Felids of Texas." In *Proceedings of a Symposium on the Native Cats of North America; Their Status and Management*. Edited by S. E. Jorgensen and L. David Mech, pp. 54–59. Fort Snelling: Twin Cities Bureau of Sport Fisheries and Wildlife, 1971.

Russell, C. P. *Guns on the Early Frontier*. Berkeley and Los Angeles: University of California Press, 1957.

Sanchez, Jose M. "A Trip to Texas in 1828." Translated by Carlos E. Castañeda. *Southwestern Historical Quarterly* 29 (1926): 249–88.

Sandoz, Mari. Review of *The Buffalo Hunters*, by Wayne Gard. Southwestern Historical Quarterly 58 (1955): 454–56.

Santleben, August. *A Texas Pioneer*. New York: Neale, 1910.

Schmidt. Karl P. "Faunal Realms, Regions, and Provinces." *Quarterly Review of Biology* 29 (1954): 322–31.

"Second Meeting of the American Ornithologists' Union." *The Auk* 1 (1884): 369–70.

Sennett, George B. "Notes on the Ornithology of the Lower Rio Grande of Texas." *U.S. Geological Survey Bulletin* 4 (1878): 1–66.

"Silk Culture in Texas." *Texas Almanac*, p. 88. Houston: Burke, 1881.

Simmons, George F. *Birds of the Austin Region*. Austin: University of Texas Press, 1925.

Simpson, George Gaylord. *The Geography of Evolution*. New York: Chilton, 1965.

Singley, J. A. "Contributions to the Natural History of Texas." *Fourth Annual Report of the Geological Survey of Texas*. Austin: Jones, 1893.

Siringo, Charles A. *A Texas Cowboy*. New York: Sloane, 1950.

Smiley, Charles W. "Some Results of Carp Culture in the United States." In U.S. Commission of Fish and Fisheries, *Report of the Commissioner for 1884*. Washington, D.C.: Government Printing Office, 1885.

Smith, C. B., and C. F. Longworthy. "Culture and Uses of Olives." *Farmers' Bulletin* 122 (1900): 11–18.

Smith, Hugh M. "Statistics of the Fisheries of the United States." *Bulletin of the U.S. Fish Commission* 13 (1893): 389–417.

Smith, Jared G. "Grazing Problems in the Southwest, and How to Meet Them." U.S. Department of Agriculture, Division of Agrostology, *Bulletin* 16 (1899): 7–47.

Smithwick, Noah. *The Evolution of a State: Recollections of Old Texas Days*. Austin: Steck, 1968.

Solms-Braunfels, Prince Carl of. *Texas, 1844–1845*. Translated from German. Houston: Anson Jones, 1936.

Southern Pacific Railroad, Sunset Route. *A Few Expressions from Various Audubon Societies Regarding the Action Taken on the Preservation of Bird Life*. N.p.: Southern Pacific, 1905.

Spratt, John S. *The Road to Spindletop: Economic Change in Texas, 1875–1901*. Austin: University of Texas Press, 1970.

Starr, Kevin. *Americans and the California Dream, 1850–1915*. New York: Oxford University Press, 1973.

Stevenson, Charles H. "Report on the Coast Fisheries of Texas." In U.S. Commission of Fish and Fisheries, *Report of the Commissioner for 1889 to 1891*, pp. 373–420. Washington, D.C.: Government Printing Office, 1893.

———. "The Preservation of Fishery Products for Food." *Bulletin of the U.S. Fish Commission* 18 (1898): 335–563.

Stiff, Edward. *The Texas Emigrant: Being a Narration of the Adventures of the Author in Texas*. Waco: Texian Press, 1968.

Stockwell, W. A. "The Magnolia Fig." *Texas Department of Agriculture Bulletin* 8 (1909): 253–54.

Stone, Witmer. "Report of the A.O.U. Committee on Protection of North American Birds." *The Auk* 16 (1899): 55–74.

———. "Report of the Committee on Bird Protection." *The Auk* 18 (1901): 68–76.

"The Storm of August 20, 1886." In *Indianola Scrap Book*. Port Lavaca: Calhoun Co. Historical Survey Committee, 1974.

Stuby, Richard G., Edwin H. Carpenter, and Louise M. Arthur. "Public Attitudes Toward Coyote Control." *Economics, Statistics and Cooperatives Service* (U.S. Department of Agriculture) 54 (1979): 1–11.

Swingle, H. S. "History of Warmwater Pond Culture in the United States." In *A Century of Fisheries in North America*. Edited by Norman G. Benson, pp. 95–105. Washington, D.C.: American Fisheries Society, 1970.

Teer, James G. "Commercial Uses of Game Animals on Rangelands of Texas." Caesar Kleberg Research Program in Wildlife Ecology, Texas A&M University, College Sation, 1973. Mimeographed.

Terborgh, John. "Preservation of Natural Diversity: The Problem of Extinction Prone Species." *BioScience* 24 (1974): 715–22.

"Texas." *Texas Almanac for 1878*. Houston: Burke, 1878.

Texas, Fish Commissioner. *First Report of the Texas Fish Commissioner for the Year 1880*. Austin: Von Boeckman, 1880.

Texas, Game, Fish and Oyster Commission. *Principal Game Birds and Mammals of Texas: Their Distribution and Management*. Austin: Von Boeckmann–Jones, 1945.

———. *Review of Texas Wild Life and Conservation*. Austin: Game, Fish and Oyster Commission, 1929.

Texas, Legislative Council, *Wildlife Management in Texas*. No. 53–4. Austin: Legislative Council, 1954.

Texas, Parks and Wildlife Department, Wildlife Division. *Habitat Preferences of Exotics*. Federal Aid Project No. W–76–R–15, Job No. 18. Austin: Texas Parks and Wildlife Department, 1972.

———. *Habitat Preference of Exotics*. Federal Aid Project No. W–76–R–16, Job No. 18. Austin: Texas Parks and Wildlife Department, 1972.

———. *Wildlife Operational Plan, 1978–79*. Austin: Texas Parks and Wildlife Commission, 1977. Mimeographed.

Texas, Thirtieth Legislature, Regular Session. *General Laws of the State of Texas*. Austin: Von Boeckmann–Jones, 1907.

Texas, Twenty-eighth Legislature, Regular Session. *General Laws of the State of Texas*. Austin: Von Boeckmann–Jones, 1904.

Texas Almanac, 1970–1971. Dallas, Belo, 1969.

Texas Field and National Guardsman 13 (1911): 217–18.

Texas Organization for Endangered Species. "TOES Watch-List of Endangered, Threatened, and Peripheral Vertebrates in Texas." Austin: TOES, 1979. Mimeographed.

Tharp, Benjamin Carroll. *The Vegetation of Texas*. Houston: Anson Jones, 1939.

Thomas, Jim. "Rewards on the Rimrock." *Texas Game and Fish* 22 (1964): 10–12, 29.

Thomas, John. "Fleeting Target." *Texas Game and Fish* 21 (1963): 19, 24.

Towne, Charles W. *Shepherd's Empire*. Norman: University of Oklahoma Press, 1945.

Townsend, Charles H. "Statistics of the Fisheries of the Gulf States." In U.S. Commission of Fish and Fisheries. *Report of the Commissioner for 1899*. Washington, D.C.: Government Printing Office, 1900.

United States, Bureau of the Census. *Thirteenth Census of the United States*. Vol. 5. Washington, D.C.: Government Printing Office, 1912.

United States, Bureau of the Census. *Fisheries of the United States, 1908*. Special Reports. Washington, D.C.: Government Printing Office, 1911.

United States, Bureau of Land Management. *Public Land Statistics, 1976.* Washington, D.C.: Government Printing Office, 1977.

United States [Census Office]. *The Seventh Census of the United States: 1850.* Washington, D.C.: Armstrong, 1853.

United States, Census Office. *Agriculture of the United States in 1860: Compiled from the Original Returns of the Eighth Census.* Washington, D.C.: Government Printing Office, 1864.

———. *The Statistics of the Wealth and Industry of the United States.* Vol. 3. Washington, D.C.: Government Printing Office, 1872.

———. *Report on the Productions of Agriculture as Returned at the Tenth Census (June 1, 1880).* Vol. 3. Washington, D.C.: Government Printing Office, 1883.

———. *Report on the Statistics of Agriculture in the United States at the Eleventh Census: 1890.* Washington, D.C.: Government Printing Office, 1895.

———. *Report on the Population of the United States at the Eleventh Census.* Part 1. Washington, D.C.: Government Printing Office, 1897.

United States, Fish and Wildlife Service. *Thirty Years of Cooperative Wildlife Research Units: 1935–65.* Resource Publication 6. Washington, D.C.: Government Printing Office, 1965.

———. *Issuance of Annual Regulations Permitting the Sport Hunting of Migratory Birds.* Washington, D.C.: Fish and Wildlife Service, 1975.

———. *35 Years of Shared Wildlife Management.* Washington, D.C.: Government Printing Office, 1975.

———. *Federal Aid in Fish and Wildlife Restoration, 1976.* Washington, D.C.: Wildlife Management Institute, 1977.

———. "Draft Environmental Impact Statement: Federal Aid in Fish and Wildlife Restoration Programs." Washington, D.C.: Fish and Wildlife Service, 1978. Mimeographed.

———. Division of National Fish Hatcheries. *Propagation and Distribution of Fishes from National Fish Hatcheries for the Fiscal Year 1975.* Washington, D.C.: Fish and Wildlife Service, 1975.

———. Division of Wildlife Services. "Annual Tables 1915–1966." Record Group 22, General, Box 22. Washington, D.C.: National Archives.

United States, National Oceanic and Atmospheric Administration, National Marine Fisheries Service. *Grant-in-Aid for Fisheries, Program Activities 1977.* Washington, D.C.: Department of Commerce, 1977.

United States, Patent Office. *Report of the Commissioner for 1853.* Washington, D.C.: Tucker, 1854.

———. *Report of the Commissioner of Patents for 1887.* Washington, D.C.: Harris, 1858.

Van Deman, H. E. "Report of the Pomologist." In U.S. Department of Agriculture, *Report of the Commissioner for 1887*, pp. 627–52. Washington, D.C.: Government Printing Office, 1888.

Vessels, Jay. "King of the Market Hunters." *Texas Game and Fish* 10 (1952): 12–14.

A Visit to Texas; Being the Journal of a Traveller Through Those Parts Most Interesting to American Settlers. Austin: Steck, 1952.

Von Hinueber, Caroline. "Life of German Pioneers in Early Texas." *Quarterly of the Texas State Historical Association* 2 (1898–99): 227–32.

Von Humboldt, Alexander. *Political Essay on the Kingdom of New Spain.* London: Longman, 1821.

Wallis, Jonnie Lockhart. *Sixty Years on the Brazos: The Life and Letters of Dr. John Washington Lockhart.* Los Angeles: Wallis, 1930.

Waterman, Charles F. *Hunting in America.* New York: Holt, Rinehart and Winston, 1973.

Weber, David J., ed. *Albert Pike: Prose Sketches and Poems.* Albuquerque: Calvin Horn, 1967.

Wentworth, Edward. *America's Sheep Trails.* Ames: Iowa State University Press, 1948.

Wetzel, Nat. "Cunning Wiles of the Hunter and the Hunted." *Texas Game and Fish* 11 (1953): 8–9, 29–30.

Whitcomb, Robert F. "'Island Biogeography" and 'Habitat Islands' of Eastern Forest." *American Birds* 31 (1977): 3–5.

Whitehead, L. C., "Annual Reports for Fiscal Years 1924–1935." U.S. Department of Agriculture, Biological Survey, Division of Wildlife Services, Field Reports (Rodent Control Section), Record Group 22. Washington, D.C.: National Archives.

Wilden, Frank [Captain Flack]. *A Hunter's Experiences in the Southern States of America.* London: Longmans, Green, 1866.

———. *The Texas Ranger.* London: Darton, 1866.

———. *The Texas Rifle-Hunter.* London: Maxwell, 1886.

———. *The Prairie Hunter: A Book of Adventures.* London: Maxwell, n.d.

Wildlife Management Institute. *Current Investments, Projected Needs, and Potential New Sources of Income for Nongame Fish and Wildlife Programs in the United States.* Washington, D.C.: Wildlife Management Institute, 1975.

Williams. Oscar W. *Historic Review of Animal Life in Pecos County.* Fort Stockton: The "Pioneer," 1908.

———. *Pecos County Panther Hunt Around Livingston Mesa.* Fort Stockton: The "Pioneer", 1941.

Wilson, W. J. "W. J. Wilson's Narrative." In *The Trail Drivers of Texas.* Edited by J. M. Hunter. 2nd ed. Nashville: Cokesbury Press, 1925.

Zimmerman, David R. "Endangered Bird Species: Habitat Manipulation Methods." *Science* 192 (1976): 876–79.

Zuber, William Physick. *My Eighty Years in Texas.* Edited by Janis Boyle Mayfield. Austin: University of Texas Press, 1971.

Index